OSCEs
for
MEDICAL
UNDERGRADUATES

VOLUME 2

Ramanathan Visvanathan BM FRCS
Consultant Surgeon, Bronglais General Hospital, Aberystwyth
(Surgical Tutor, Royal College of Surgeons of England)
Lately Honorary Senior Lecturer in Surgery
and Assistant Director to the Professorial Surgical Unit
Medical College and Hospital of St Bartholomew, London

Adam Feather MB MRCP
Lecturer in Clinical Skills,
St Bartholomew's and the Royal London
School of Medicine and Dentistry
Registrar in Medicine of the Elderly,
Newham General Hospital, London

John S P Lumley MS FRCS
Professor of Surgery and Honorary Consultant Surgeon,
Medical College and Hospital of St Bartholomew, London
Member of Council, Royal College of Surgeons of England
Past World President, International College of Surgeons

First published 1999
Reprinted 2000
ISBN: 1 901198 05 7

A catalogue record for this book is available from the British Library.

PasTest Revision Books and Intensive Courses
PasTest has been established in the field of postgraduate medical education since 1972, providing revision books and intensive study courses for doctors preparing for their professional examinations.
Books and courses are available for the following specialties:
MRCP Part 1 and 2, MRCPCH Part 1 and 2, MRCOG, DRCOG, MRCGP, DCH, FRCA, MRCS, PLAB.
For further details contact:

PasTest, Freepost, Knutsford, Cheshire WA16 7BR
Tel: 01565 752000   Fax: 01565 650264
E-mail: enquiries@pastest.co.uk

Text prepared by **BREEZE LIMITED**, Manchester.
Printed and bound by **HOBBS THE PRINTERS**, Totton, Hampshire.

CONTENTS

PREFACE

Followers of recent literature on the assessment of undergraduate medical training could be excused for thinking that traditional methods were incomplete, if not arbitrary, and that potentially harmful doctors were being let loose on an unsuspecting public. This opinion is based on the unmeasurable nature of 'gut feeling' in the marking of an essay and assessing clinical competence. The application of objective measurement in qualifying examinations does add credibility to their outcome.

Every examination must be fair and favour the well-prepared, i.e. valid and reliable. We have discussed the relative merits of essays, SAQs and MCQs elsewhere, this book, (and its companion volume), is directed at the use of OSCEs in medicine. It provides a means of assessing practical procedures and communication skills, as well as knowledge and attitudes in most aspects of training.

The book is aimed at students preparing for their exit examination and will provide experience in this now widely-used examination technique. The book will also help those setting OSCE questions, providing a template onto which they can develop their own themes. OSCEs can assess history, examination, investigation and treatment of disease, together with practical techniques. OSCE stations can also obtain information on attitudes, interpersonal skills and ethical opinions. Some of these stations require the use of standard patients, manikin and videos. Although these media are not all reproduceable in a text book, advice is given on the way to deal with the likely questions, techniques and style of stations that may be encountered. It indicates what the examiner is looking for and how marks are being allocated for the approach to a patient and empathy with their problem. A correct diagnosis is not necessarily the key to obtaining a satisfactory mark: always remember to read the instructions very carefully.

The book follows a systems approach and each chapter includes questions from each type of OSCE station. Space is left for the student to respond to each question. Answers and additional advice are given in a separate section, allowing the students to assess their performance and identify areas needing further attention. In keeping with other books in the series, a revision checklist is given, and mock examinations are laid out: the latter can be undertaken within a prescribed time schedule and used for self-assessment.

INTRODUCTION

Traditional methods of assessing knowledge and clinical skills have been based on the essay and MCQ, for written tests, and the long cases, short cases and the viva for practical aspects. These forms of assessment have been extensively challenged as to their ability to test and rank students. The essay has come under the greatest criticism but the long and short cases have also been questioned as to their objectivity and reliability. Marking a viva can be very subjective and it provides a very patchy assessment of the curriculum.

Objective structured clinical examinations (OSCEs) have been designed to provide a broader coverage of knowledge and skills in a quantifiable, valid and reliable form. They aim to assess interpretive skills, as well as factual recall; they include task-orientated items and they can examine a candidate's powers of decision making and their behavioural attitude in simulated professional practice. The overall effect is to provide a more valid assessment of candidates for their subsequent clinical practice.

The OSCE comprises a number of stations, through which a group of students rotate. The number of students in the examination usually matches the number of stations, so that by the end of the examination, each student has visited every station. There may be more stations than candidates without disturbing the organisation of the examination. Usually the time allowed for each station is the same throughout but it can be increased by inserting rest or preparatory stations before a longer question. Rest stations may also be used to provide natural breaks and to increase the number of candidates being examined at any one time.

The time at a station is usually at least three minutes, five minutes being common; 24 stations are available for a two hour examination. For an examination to be statistically reliable there must be a minimum of 17–20 stations. Formative assessments may use a few selected stations (e.g. 5–10). The design of OSCE questions is usually only limited by the ingenuity of the examiners. However, questions should examine a specific part of the curriculum, rather than just an ability to respond to the style of the examination. Students should be exposed to all proposed designs of question format before the final examination.

Each station of an OSCE should assess a discrete skill. This may be a basic test of practical ability or knowledge, or involve a higher level of thinking. It is wise to have a range of difficulty to help discriminate within a group. A number of questions are included to assess core knowledge: all students are expected to pass these stations. The clinical skills of diagnosis and treatment can be divided up into:

- taking a history
- performing an examination
- requesting appropriate investigations
- making the diagnosis
- assessing the severity of the disease
- prescribing treatment.

The latter should incorporate all aspects of care, including medicine, surgery, nursing and other medical and paramedical disciplines.

The history may be taken from a standardised patient (SP), or presented as a written scenario or a video. SPs may be simulated or actual patients. In the former, a well individual is trained to simulate a patient's illness in a standard way, portraying a patient's problems. Some training is usually required for actual patients, to ensure that the main points are brought out on request and that a history can be covered fully within the time allowed for that station. Simulated patients are usually actors, although sometimes students may act as SPs. In so doing students learn the evaluation process by direct observation and listening to presentations. These stations are usually manned by an examiner who is watching and listening, not only to the style of questioning, but also to student/patient interrelationships, their conversational skills, interpersonal skills, behaviour, attitude and psychomotor assessment. SPs are often asked to give their marks on the student encounter. Written scenarios can form the basis of subsequent questions, along the line of structured answer questions. They can test factual knowledge, understanding and cognitive skills but assess clinical competencies to a variable extent. Well-trained actors can become skilled historians and very persuasive patients, such as when replicating a psychiatric disturbance, although the latter are often more effectively covered with video sequences.

Examination of a patient in a manned station is a very valuable form of assessment. However, it also presents a great problem to the examiner, since very few conditions can be repeatedly examined for two hours at a time, and the number of conditions that can be easily replicated is limited, particularly if there are a number of groups of students being examined simultaneously or consecutively. Fit models can be used for the demonstration of a normal examination and normal anatomy or, alternatively, manikins can be available to assess specific examination techniques such as rectal and vaginal assessment.

A text book has difficulty in reproducing a history and examination, in view of their practical nature and the requirement of simulated patients, videos and models. This book does, however, consider the likely SPs, historical scenarios and types of models and manikins, and the examination techniques that are encountered in OSCEs. Investigations and their interpretation can easily be presented in OSCE form, and candidates can expect charts, and lists of haematological and biochemical results, together with all forms of radiological investigations, with a request to interpret data and radiological abnormalities.

OSCE stations are suitable for most aspects of treatment and prognosis. It is essential to remember that treatment of a 'medical' illness should not be limited to drugs or that of a 'surgical' illness to surgery alone. They should include all forms of available and desirable intervention. This avoids the 'pigeon-holing' of disease entities into conventional specialities which is deprecated in current clinical teaching. Counselling skills and the assessment of ethical factors in clinical practice are readily tested in an OSCE setting as SPs can provide both the background and the patient's attitude to an illness.

The practical application of clinical skills and procedures are also readily assessed, usually with the aid of a manikin which allows such procedures as venous catheterization, cardiopulmonary resuscitation, securing and maintaining an air-way, wound debridement and suturing.

DESIRABLE FEATURES OF OSCEs

OSCEs bring a new dimension to the assessment of medical training. Of particular value is their ability to examine practical and other skills in a unified, measurable and reproducible fashion. This is in keeping with current trends towards performance based assessment throughout health care. OSCEs provide for an effective use of the examination time, examiners' time and commitment. They are effective in assessing knowledge and practical skills and ensure that each student is presented with the same material, thus providing a uniform evaluation with consistent marking of all those involved.

The validity of the response to each question is primarily related to the student's ability: in well constructed questions, very little variation is dependent on the examiner's responses in manned stations. The reliability of OSCEs in differentiating good from bad students and the inter-rater reliability of examiners is good, and becomes increasingly certain as the number of stations devoted to each component part is increased. Both construct and content validity have been well established.

- Construct validity is the ability of the OSCE to differentiate students' ability, or to follow a student's progress before and after a course of instruction.

- Content (criterion-based) validity assesses the value of the station in reaching its specified objective. In all these measures OSCEs have proved effective in student assessment and are accepted by staff and students as a fair and desirable form of assessment.

Well constructed questions are durable and can stand up to repeated use without weakening their value. Like many forms of assessment, effective questions represent the core curriculum material, and once a suitable bank size has been achieved, security of the questions is unnecessary as knowledge of the answers represents a passable understanding of the curriculum. Experiments on presenting a single station at a time to groups of students have not reduced their value in differentiating clinical performance. Assessment can be by the students themselves or by peer review. This modification substantially reduces the necessary space and organisation for an OSCE.

OSCEs can be a useful teaching modality. With the reduced stay of patients in hospitals and increased community-based education, medical schools often have to extend their teaching practice onto a number of sites. All these factors increase the need for uniformity of teaching methods as well as assessment. This can be effectively achieved with the use of OSCEs, and the reduced number of available patients can be addressed by the use of standard patients with good effect. One well-proven example of the use of simulated patients has been in the training and assessment of trauma, linked to the Advanced Trauma Life Support and related programmes. The use of students as SPs has proved an important and enjoyable learning experience, as well as, in some cases, providing financial rewards.

Assessment is a powerful learning tool and should be used as part of the teaching and learning processes but it must be accompanied by adequate feedback in order to benefit individual students. This process should also be used in auditing teaching methods and to stimulate any necessary changes. It is feasible to set up OSCEs in any medical school, provided appropriate staff time is allowed for their introduction. Some schools involve students in the design and development of OSCEs and it can increase their awareness of this form of assessment. The formulation of OSCEs should be closely linked with curriculum development and keyed into the curriculum objectives.

When using OSCEs to evaluate teaching methods, two types of error should be considered.

- Type I errors are those of fact, implying a deficiency of teaching and/or learning, reflecting omissions and ineffective or absent experience.
- Type II errors are defects of understanding, where a student fails to recognise or interpret a clinical situation. This reflects poor concept attainment and an inability to discriminate.

Locating these errors points to the direction that future teaching should follow.

DISADVANTAGES OF OSCEs

As discussed in the previous section, the value of OSCEs in training and assessment has been demonstrated in many fields and many such assessment packages are available. However, medical schools should not become involved in this form of assessment without allowing adequate staff time for their development and OSCEs should not become the only form of assessment.

The preparation of OSCEs requires a good deal of thought and time. The whole staff should be aware of, and preferably involved in, their development and students should have experience prior to any examination so that they can be comfortable with this form of assessment. An OSCE requires a great deal of organisation in collecting material, appropriate patients, laying out stations and making sure staff are available for manned areas. Setting up the examination can be costly on administration and on medical staff and patients, and includes the hidden costs of Faculty time in the development of the exercise.

Analysis of the data and ensuring the validity of the examination requires painstaking activity. The weighting of key questions on essential knowledge has to be resolved before any feedback to staff or students. Standard setting should be based on expected knowledge and the skills required and this relies as much on that much-criticized 'gut feeling' as it does on statistical formulae. Standardised patients, both actual and simulated have to be found and trained and an adequate pool must be available to cover expected needs. When introducing OSCEs, a school has to decide whether it is as an additional assessment or whether it should replace a previous part of the examination. If the latter, it is essential that other important areas are not diluted in the process. OSCEs are not ideal in assessing interpersonal skills: video clips or trained patients can be rather artificial in this respect. For patient examination, OSCEs do not provide a comprehensive evaluation of all aspects of a learning and educational programme and therefore should be part of a multi-component assessment in the final examination, forming a useful means of determining practical skills over a wide area.

In spite of their potential limitations, OSCEs do provide a valuable addition to the clinical exit examination and students and staff should become well acquainted with their format and appreciate their discriminatory properties.

HOW TO USE THIS BOOK

This book contains a series of OSCE questions. The chapters are arranged by organ system, and every chapter follows the same organisation of questions, i.e. history, examination, investigation, treatment, practical techniques and other issues. The second half of the book provides the answers, together with teaching notes and a marking scheme. There is no index but the contents list will direct you to the appropriate organ system.

In the history and counselling stations, you are advised to work with one to two colleagues to act as 'patient' and 'examiner'. The Introduction provides the background required to direct your enquiry or your counselling. Take a history from the 'patient', who will answer your questions using the history provided. The 'examiner' will mark your answers, using the scoring system outlines below, and ensure that the station is concluded in the allotted time.

The clinical examination stations include clinical photographs and test clinical skills which can be practised on appropriate patients on the ward. As the practical skills of examination cannot be assessed by a text book, a check list is included, indicating what the examiner is looking for in your examination of each system. The radiographic questions may be self-assessed by turning to the answer section.

Stations with radiographs or photographs may also carry statements requiring a 'true' or 'false' response. This adds variety to the station format and requires you to assess the answers given with respect to the radiograph or photograph. Similarly, stations with tables depicting clinical scenarios or treatment regimes test your knowledge in rearranging the latter to fit the disease.

At the back of the book, Appendix A explains the marking schedule used for the stations, and Appendix D contains six 21-station OSCE circuits: these provide typical examination scenarios.

By working through each organ system, as denoted by the chapters, you will cover most of the OSCE station scenarios and variations that you can expect to encounter in the undergraduate course.

Scoring your performance

We have chosen not to weight individual questions or items. Good is allocated 3 marks and adequate 2. In the poor/not done column the assessor can differentiate between a reasonable but inadequate mark and poor or not done. This differentiation can direct future study requirements. Each station is allocated the same mark, item scores are added in three column answers. Two of three correct responses or a mean score of 2 is a pass. A 60% correct response rate is required in two column answers. In the mock examinations two-thirds of stations should be passed to pass the examination.

GLOSSARY

A-level	Advanced level General Certificate of Education – School leaving examination, UK
ABGs	Arterial blood gases
ACE inhibitors	Angiotensin converting enzyme
ACTH	Adrenocorticotrophic hormone
ADH	Anti-diuretic hormone
AF	Atrial fibrillation
aGBM	Anti-Glomerular Basement Membrane
Alk Phos	Alkaline phosphatase
ALT	Alanine amino-transferase
ANCA	Anti neutrophil cytoplasmic antibody
Anti dsDNA	Double stranded deoxyribonucleic acid
Anti-Jo	Specific antigen
Anti-La	Specific antigen
Anti-RNP	Ribonucleic protein
Anti-Ro	Specific antigen
Anti-Scl70	Specific antigen
AP	Antero-posterior
APTT	Activated partial thromboplastin time
ASO(T)	Anti streptolysin-O-titre
AST	Aspartate amino-transferase
ATLS	Advanced trauma life support
AV	Arterio-venous
AV	Atrio-ventricular
AXR	Abdominal X-ray
BBB	Bundle branch block
Bd	Bis die – twice daily
BHL	Bilateral hilar lymphadenopathy
BM stix	Blood monitoring
BM	Bone marrow
BMI	Body mass index
BP	Blood pressure
Bpm	Beats per minute
C	Cervical
Ca	Cancer
cAMP	Cyclic AMP
Ca^{2+}	Calcium
CAPD	Chronic ambulatory peritoneal dialysis
cANCA	Cytoplasmic anti-neutrophil cytoplasmic antibody
CAGE questionnaire	**C**ut down **A**nnoyed **G**uilty **E**ye-opener

CD4	A surface antigen principally found on helper-inducer T-lymphocyte
CEA	Carcinoembryonic antigen
CIN I II III	Cervical intraepithelial neoplasia
CK	Creatinine phosphokinase
Cl^-	Chloride
CLL	Chronic lymphocytic leukaemia
CLO	Campylobacter-like organisms
CMV	Cytomegalovirus
CNS	Central nervous system
CO_2	Carbon dioxide
COMT	Catechol O-methyl transferase
CPN	Community psychiatric nurse
Cr	Creatinine
CREST	Crest syndrome – calcinosis; Raynaud's; oesophageal dysmotility; sclerodactyly; telangiectasia
CSF	Cerebro-spinal fluid
CSU	Catheter specimen of urine
CT	Computerised tomography
CVA	Cerebro-vascular accident
CVP	Central venous pressure
CXR	Chest radiograph
DDAVP	Desmopressin, synthetic vasopressin
DIC	Disseminated intravascular coagulopathy
DIP joints	Distal inter-phalangeal joints
DKA	Diabetic keto-acidosis
DNA	Deoxyribonucleic acid
DVT	Deep vein thrombosis
DVLA	Driving vehicle licensing authority
EUA	Examination under anaesthesia
ECG	Electrocardiogram
ESR	Erythrocyte sedimentation rate
FBC	Full blood count
FEV_1	Forced expiratory volume in one second
FFP	Fresh frozen plasma
5-FU	5-fluoro-uracil
5HT	5-hydroxy-tryptamine
fT_4	Free thyroxine
FVC	Forced vital capacity
GCS	Glasgow coma scale

GCSE	General Certificate of Secondary Education
GI	Gastrointestinal
GIT	Gastrointestinal tract
GP	General Practitioner
GPI	General paralysis of the insane
GTN	Glyceryl trinitrate
GU	Genito-urinary
G6PD	Glucose 6-phosphate dehydrogenase
Hb	Haemoglobin
HB Alc	Glycosylated haemoglobin
HBV	Hepatitis B virus
HCV	Hepatitis C virus
HCG	Human chorionic gonadotrophin
HCO_3^-	Bicarbonate
HDL	High density lipoprotein
HIV	Human immunodeficiency virus
HLA	Human leucocyte antigen
HONK	Hyper-osmolar non-ketotic (coma)
HRT	Hormone replacement therapy
HSV	Herpes Simplex virus
IBD	Inflammatory bowel disease
ICP	Intra-cranial pressure
IDDM	Insulin dependent diabetes mellitus
Ig	Immunoglobulin
IgM	Immunoglobulin M
IHD	Ischaemic heart disease
INR	International ratio
IQ	Intelligence quotient
ISMN	Iso-sorbide mono-nitrate
IV	Intravenous
IVU	Intravenous urogram
K^+	Potassium
Kg	Kilogramme
Kpa	Kilopascals
KUB	Kidneys/ureters/bladder
LDL	Low density lipoprotein
LFT	Liver function tests
LH	Luteinising hormone
LHRH	Luteinising hormone releasing hormone
LNMP	Last normal menstrual period
MAOI	Mono-amine oxidase inhibitor
MCH	Mean corpuscular haemoglobin

MCP	Meta-carpophalangeal
MCV	Mean corpuscular volume
Mg^{++}	Magnesium
MI	Myocardial infarction
Mmol	Millimoles
MRI	Magnetic resonance imaging
MSU	Mid stream urine
Na^+	Sodium
NG	Neoplasia (new growth)
NIDDM	Non insulin dependent diabetes mellitus
NSAID	Non steroidal anti-inflammatory drug
O_2	Oxygen
OA	Osteoarthritis
OCP	Oral contraceptive pill
Od	Omni die, once a day
OSCE	Objective structured clinical examination
PA	Postero-anterior
PAN	Polyarteritis nodosa
pANCA	Perinuclear anti-neutrophilic cytoplasmic antibody
PCR	Polymerase chain reaction
PE	Pulmonary embolism
PEFR	Peak expiratory flow rate
pH	Puissance d'Hydrogen = $- \log (H^+)$
Plats	Platelets
PMH	Previous medical history
PND	Paroxysmal nocturnal dyspnoea
PNS	Peripheral nervous system
PO_4^-	Phosphate
PUO	Pyrexia of uncertain origin
Prn	Pro re nata, as required
PSA	Prostatic specific antigen
PVD	Peripheral vascular disease
Qds = qid	Quaque die/quarter in die, four times a day
Retics	Reticulocytes
ROM	Range of movement
RTA	Road traffic accident
RTA (I – IV)	Renal tubular acidosis
SACD	Subacute combined degeneration of the spinal cord
SAH	Subarachnoid haemorrhage
SDH	Subdural haemorrhage

SHBG	Sex hormone binding globulin
SIADH	Syndrome of inappropriate antidiuretic hormone secretion
SLE	Systemic lupus erythematosus
SSRI	Selective serotonin reuptake inhibitors
Substance P	Vasoactive peptide and sensory neurotransmitter found in nerve cells and specialist gut endocrine cells
SVT	Supraventricular tachycardia
SXR	Skull X-ray
TB	Tuberculosis
TBM	Tuberculous meningitis
TFTs	Thyroid function tests
T_3	Tri-iodo thyronine
T_4	Tetra-iodo thyronine (thyroxine)
Tds	Ter die sumendum, to be taken three times a day
T Helper	Thymus (lymphocytes)
TIA	Transient ischaemic attack
TKco	Transfer coefficient
TPA	Tissue plasminogen activator
TPHA	Treponema pallidum haemagglutination assay
TPN	Total parenteral nutrition
TSH	Thyroid stimulating hormone
U&Es	Urea and electrolytes
Ur	Urea
USS	Ultrasound scan
UTI	Urinary tract infection
UV	Ultra violet
VDRL	Venereal disease research laboratory
V/Q scan	Ventilation/perfusion scan
WCC	White cell count

Endocrine disorders often present with multiple, non-specific symptoms and it is, therefore, important to take a precise history. Many are autoimmune in nature and it is important to establish whether patients have a family history of endocrine and autoimmune disease.

General symptoms linked to endocrine disease

- **Malaise**, lethargy and lassitude

- **Weight loss**
  Thyrotoxicosis
  IDDM
  Adrenal malignancy

- **Weight gain**
  Hypothyroidism
  Cushing's (centripetal obesity)

- **Menstrual irregularity**
  Prolactinoma
  Thyroid disease
  Polycystic ovary syndrome
  Ovarian dysfunction
  Hypopituitarism

- **Male impotence**
  Prolactinoma
  Hypopituitarism
  IDDM

- **Proximal muscle weakness/wasting**
  Cushing's
  Thyrotoxicosis
  Acromegaly

- **Sleeping problems**
  Somnolence (hypothyroidism)

- **Loss of libido**
  Hypopituitarism
  Gonadal failure

- **Mood**
  Depression
  Poor concentration (hypothyroidism)

- **Pigmentation**
  Particularly buccal, skin creases and scars (Addison's)

- **Acne and hirsutism**
  Cushing's syndrome
  Polycystic ovary syndrome
  Adrenal malignancy
  Congenital adrenal hyperplasia

Specific symptoms of Endocrine disease

- **Pituitary disease**
  Local symptoms: headache, visual disturbances (classically bitemporal hemianopia)
  Systemic symptoms: classified according to the disorder; functioning and non-functioning pituitary tumours

- **Acromegaly**
  Coarsening and enlargement of facial features
  Overbiting mandible, with increased interdental separation
  Enlargement of hands, feet and head circumference; shoes, gloves and hats do not fit
  Proximal limb girdle weakness
  Symptoms of hypertension and diabetes mellitus
  Visceromegaly: may lead to cardiac failure and hepatosplenomegaly

- **Prolactinoma**
  Galactorrhoea
  Spontaneous expression of milk from the nipples
  Oligo/amenorrhoea
  Female infertility; male impotence; loss of libido in both sexes

- **Cushing's disease**
  Proximal myopathy with centripetal obesity
  Abdominal striae
  Symptoms of hypertension and diabetes mellitus

- **Hypopituitarism**
  Patients may present in a very non-specific manner with symptoms
  of thyroid, gonadal and adrenal insufficiency

DIABETES

- **Diagnostic symptoms**
  Polyuria: passing large volumes of urine
  Polydypsia: increased thirst
  Increased infections: UTIs, candidiasis
  Weight: older NIDDM patients are often overweight
  Younger IDDM patients often lose weight prior to diagnosis
  Patients often complain of non-specific symptoms such as malaise
  and lethargy

- **Complications**
  These should be well defined in the history, particularly in
  established disease.
  Macrovascular: IHD, CVA, PVD
  Microvascular: retinopathy and nephropathy
  Neuropathic: peripheral sensory neuropathy ('stocking and glove'
  distribution)
  Mononeuritis multiplex: these are multiple nerve palsies with no
  apparent anatomical association, e.g. oculomotor, median and
  lateral peroneal palsies
  Autonomic: may present with postural hypotension or male
  impotence
  TIAs and CVAs
  Others: it is important to ask specifically about eye and foot
  problems, particularly visual acuity and foot ulceration.

- **Diabetic control**
  Method of testing: BM stix or urinalysis - frequency and results
  Compliance with diet
  Weight control
  Method of control: diet only, tablets, insulin regime
  Follow up: diabetic liaison nurses, GP, hospital, and frequency

- RF .

- **Risk factors**

  It is essential to address the associated risk factors for diabetic complications.

  Smoking

  Dietary: excess fat and refined sugar must be excluded; dietician review

  Alcohol excess: amongst many other problems, alcohol is high in calories

  Hypertension

  Hyperlipidaemia: diabetes causes hypertriglyceridaemia (as does alcohol excess)

  Obesity: excess fat causes increased insulin resistance.

STATION 1.1

(Answers – page 148)

History

You are a medical student attached to an endocrinology firm. The next patient is a 25-year-old man, who has been referred by his GP with a worsening frontal headache and complaining that his shoes and gloves have become too small for him. Please take a history of the presenting complaint with a view to making a diagnosis.

(10 minute station)

STATION 1.2

History

You are the house officer on a general medical and endocrine firm. The next patient is a 21-year-old woman who has been referred by the gynaecologists with a history of irregular periods. Please take a history of the presenting complaint, including a gynaecological history, with a view to making a diagnosis.

(10 minute station)

STATION 1.3

History

You are the medical student attending endocrine outpatients. The next patient is a 34-year-old woman, who has been referred by her GP for weight gain, striae and bruising. Please take a history of the presenting complaint, with a view to making a diagnosis.

(5 minute station)

STATION 1.4

History

You are the medical student attending endocrine outpatients. The next patient has been referred by the gynaecologists, with irregular periods, hirsutism and obesity. Please take a history of the presenting complaint with a view to making a diagnosis. You should include a full gynaecological history.

(5 minute station)

STATION 1.5

History

You are the medical student attached to a general medical firm. The next patient is a 54-year-old woman, who has been referred to outpatients with a croaky voice and weight gain.

Please take a history of the presenting complaint and any other relevant history, with a view to making a diagnosis.

(5 minute station)

STATION 1.6

History

You are a medical student attending the diabetes clinic. The next patient is a 54-year-old man who has had NIDDM for the last 10 years. Please take a history to establish this gentleman's diabetic control and the complications that may have arisen.

(10 minute station)

STATION 1.7

History

You are the house officer attached to a general medical firm. You have been asked to take a history from a 21-year-old woman with malaise, lethargy and a random blood glucose, taken by her GP, of 35.6 mmol/l. You should concentrate on the presenting complaint and associated relevant history. You should be prepared to discuss the future management of this patient.

(5 minute station)

STATION 1.8

History

You are the house officer on a general medical firm. You have been asked by the registrar to explain the implications, treatment and possible complications of diabetes mellitus to a newly diagnosed 21-year-old female patient.

(5 minute station)

STATION 1.9

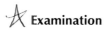

Examination

Examine the swelling in the front of the neck of the 30-year-old woman shown in Fig. 1.9 on page 141 (using a model to demonstrate these skills).

(5 minute station)

STATION 1.10

Examination

Figures 1.10a and 1.10b (see page 141) are women with goitres.

(5 minute station)

1. What are the probable diagnoses in each?
2. State one investigation that would confirm the diagnosis in both patients.
3. State the cause of the abnormality of the eyes in 1.10a and of the swelling on the forehead in 1.10b.
4. State the principles of treatment for each patient.

STATION 1.11

Examination

Figures 1.11a - 1.11e (see page 141) were obtained by fundoscopy. Please answer the relevant questions after examining each fundus.

(10 minute station)

		True	**False**
1.	*(Figure 1.11a)*		
(a)	There is evidence of hypertensive retinopathy	❏	❏
(b)	The macula shows evidence of senile degeneration	❏	❏
(c)	There is a blot haemorrhage in the upper temporal quadrant	❏	❏
(d)	There is evidence of papilloedema	❏	❏
(e)	There are some dot haemorrhages in the lower nasal quadrant	❏	❏

2.	*(Figure 1.11b)*	**True**	**False**
(a)	There is evidence of macular damage	❏	❏
(b)	There is evidence of optic atrophy	❏	❏
(c)	There are soft exudates in the inferior nasal quadrant	❏	❏
(d)	There are hard exudates in the inferior temporal quadrant	❏	❏
(e)	This slide shows evidence of pre-proliferative diabetic retinopathy	❏	❏

3.	*(Figure 1.11c)*	**True**	**False**
(a)	There is a macular 'star' present	❏	❏
(b)	There is a subhyaloid haemorrhage	❏	❏
(c)	There are soft exudates in the inferior nasal quadrant	❏	❏
(d)	There are blot haemorrhages in the upper temporal quadrant	❏	❏
(e)	There is evidence of papilloedema	❏	❏

4.	*(Figure 1.11d)*	**True**	**False**
(a)	The optic disc is normal	❏	❏
(b)	The macula is normal	❏	❏
(c)	There are soft exudates present	❏	❏
(d)	This patient has had previous laser therapy to the retina	❏	❏
(e)	This patient must be treated with insulin	❏	❏

5.	*(Figure 1.11e)*	**True**	**False**
(a)	There is evidence of neovascularisation	❏	❏
(b)	There is evidence of previous laser therapy in the superior and inferior temporal quadrants	❏	❏
(c)	This patient requires urgent ophthalmoscopy review	❏	❏
(d)	There are multiple soft exudates present	❏	❏
(e)	There is evidence of optic atrophy	❏	❏

STATION 1.12
Investigation

Please match the causes of hyponatraemia with the brief histories and diagnoses provided.

(5 minute station)

Patient history

1. 29-year-old man with a long history of steroid use now presents with postural hypotension and pigmented scars

2. 64-year-old woman with a croaky voice, constipation and lethargy

3. 27-year-old man with a six day history of a dry cough, fever and malaise

4. 37-year-old woman drinking 6–7 litres of water per day. Blood glucose = 5.2

5. 69-year-old man with biventricular cardiac failure

Diagnosis

(a) Psychogenic polydypsia

(b) Diuretic use

(c) Addison's disease

(d) Primary hypothyroidism

(e) Atypical pneumonia with SIADH

Answers

1. ( ) c
2. ( ) d
3. ( ) e

4. ( ) a
5. ( )

STATION 1.13

Investigation

The disorders listed below are associated with changes in serum potassium levels. Please list them under the correct headings.

(5 minute station)

Cushing's disease	Frusemide infusion	Acute renal failure
Addison's disease	Conn's syndrome	Lisinopril
Spironolactone	Type IV RTA	Ectopic ACTH secretion
Type I RTA	Fanconi's syndrome	Cardiac failure with secondary hyperaldosteronism

Hypokalaemia
(< 3.5 mmol/l)

Hyperkalaemia
(> 5.5 mol/l)

STATION 1.14

Investigation

Three diabetic patients arrive unconscious in the Accident and Emergency Department.
Please calculate the osmolality and anion gap for each of the three patients and thus the type of diabetic coma each is suffering.
(refer to tables for normal values)

(5 minute station)

Plasma osmolality = 2 [Na^+ + K^+] +Ur +Glucose
Normal range 280 - 295 mosmol/kg

Anion gap = [Na^+ + K^+] - [HCO_3^- + Cl^-]
Normal range 10–18 mmol/l

UTI sepsis > lactic acidosis > hypoglycaemic coma.

Patient A
42-year-old woman
Medication: Metformin 850 mg bd
U+Es: Na^+ 158 K^+ 4.9 HCO_3^- 12 Cl^- 102   Ur 34   Cr 162
      Glucose: 50
      Lactate: 38.7
      Urinalysis: Protein +++ Blood ++ Ketones ++
MSU: Organisms +++

Patient B
26-year-old man
Medication: Mixtard insulin 36 units mane, 20 units nocte
U+Es: Na^+ 145 K^+ 4.0 HCO_3^- 8 Cl^- 106   Ur 14   Cr 44
      Glucose: 45.3
      Lactate: 3.2
      Urinalysis: Protein - trace Blood - nil Ketones +++
CXR: Right lower lobe pneumonia DKA

Patient C
79-year-old man
Medication: Gliclazide 80 mg bd, Metformin 850 mg bd
U+Es: Na$^+$ 155   K$^+$ 4.5   HCO$_3^-$ 25   Cl$^-$ 110   Ur 19.0   Cr 205
       Glucose - 80
       Lactate - 6.0
       Urinalysis - Protein + Blood - nil Ketones ++
ʜₒɴᴋ

STATION 1.15

Investigation

Using the data in the table below, indicate the correct diagnoses for the patients A to E.

(5 minute station)

Normal range: TSH   0.3-3.5 mU/l
Total serum T$_3$ 1.2-3.1 nmol/l
Free serum T$_4$ 13-30 pmol/l

Patient	TSH/mU/l	T$_3$/nmol/l	T$_4$/pmol/l	Diagnosis
A	67.2	0.9	0.5	
B	0.05	8.5	52.3	
C	2.0	1.0	7.0	
D	0.05	39.1	15.5	
E	2.6	2.8	24	

Diagnoses
1. Thyrotoxicosis
2. T$_3$ thyrotoxicosis
3. Primary hypothyroidism
4. Euthyroid
5. Sick euthyroid

STATION 1.16

Investigation

The patients listed below have abnormal bone and/or calcium metabolism. Please rearrange the table to match the histories with the correct data and diagnoses.

(5 minute station)

Patient history	Corrected Ca^{++}	PO$_4^-$	Alkaline phosphatase	Diagnosis
1. 29-year-old Asian woman with proximal limb weakness	(A) 2.32	1.02	3033	(a) Osteoporosis
2. 31-year-old Black woman from Missouri, USA, with lupus pernio	(B) 1.82	1.3	107	(b) Multiple myeloma
3. 73-year-old woman with premature menopause, now presenting with back pain	(C) 3.45	1.02	421	(c) Paget's disease of the bone
4. 71-year-old man with an enlarged skull, deafness and hip and back pain	(D) 2.25	0.76	135	(d) Pseudohypo-parathyroidism
5. 81-year-old man with multiple lytic lesions of the skull and bony pain	(E) 1.65	0.57	678	(e) Sarcoidosis
6. 16-year-old woman with low IQ, short stature and short 4th and 5th metacarpals	(F) 2.98	0.92	104	(f) Osteomalacia

Answers

1. ( ) ( )   4. ( ) ( )
2. ( ) ( )   5. ( ) ( )
3. ( ) ( )   6. ( ) ( )

STATION 1.17

Investigation

Three patients are taking part in a study of polyuria. One has cranial diabetes insipidus, one psychogenic polydypsia and the third is the control. From the water deprivation test results below, match the patients to the correct diagnoses.

(5 minute station)

	Time (hours)	Plasma osmolality (mosmol/kg)	Urine osmolality (mosmol/kg)	Body weight (kg)
Normal Ranges		280–295	350–900	
Patient A	0	290	232	65.7
	4	294	272	63.4
	8	296	300	61.2
After DDAVP		292	596	
Patient B	0	291	550	82.2
	4	289	702	81.6
	8	292	840	81.4
After DDAVP		293	850	
Patient C	0	268	320	72.0
	4	284	424	71.5
	8	290	510	71.1
After DDAVP		291	523	

Answers
Patient A:
Patient B:
Patient C:

STATION 1.18

Investigation

Please state whether the following statements are **True** or **False** with regard to the three radiographs below and opposite.

(5 minute station)

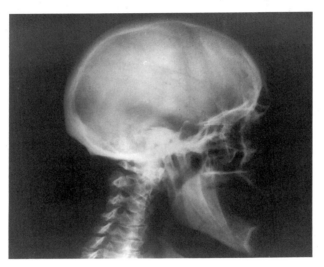

Fig. 1.18a

1. *(Figure 1.18a)*	True	False
(a) This an AP view of the skull	❏	❏
(b) It shows lytic lesions	❏	❏
(c) The bony cortex is normal	❏	❏
(d) The sella is normal	❏	❏
(e) The appearances are consistent with acromegaly	❏	❏

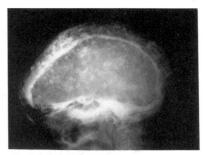

Fig. 1.18c

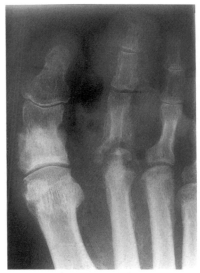

Fig. 1.18b

2.	(Figure 1.18b)	True	False
(a)	This is a lateral X-ray of the foot	❑	❑
(b)	There is calcification of the blood vessels	❑	❑
(c)	The soft tissues are normal	❑	❑
(d)	There is evidence of osteomyelitis	❑	❑
(e)	The changes are suggestive of hyperparathyroidism	❑	❑

3.	(Figure 1.18c)	True	False
(a)	The bony cortex is thickened	❑	❑
(b)	There are multiple lytic lesions	❑	❑
(c)	There is platybasia	❑	❑
(d)	The patient is at increased risk of developing optic atrophy	❑	❑
(e)	The patient is at increased risk of developing an osteosarcoma	❑	❑

STATION 1.19

Investigation

Please indicate whether the statements regarding the radiographs shown below and opposite are **True** or **False**.

(5 minute station)

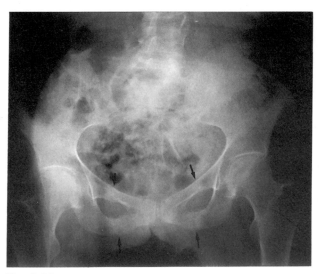

Fig. 1.19a

		True	False
1.	*(Figure 1.19a)*		
(a)	This is a PA X-ray of the pelvis	❏	❏
(b)	The bones are osteopaenic	❏	❏
(c)	There is osteoarthritis of the right hip joint	❏	❏
(d)	The patient's serum calcium will be greater than 3.0 mmol/l	❏	❏
(e)	The alkaline phosphatase will be raised	❏	❏

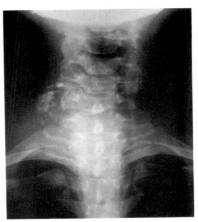

Fig. 1.19b

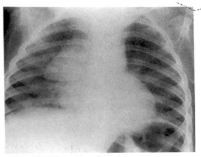

Fig. 1.19c

2. *(Figure 1.19b)*	True	False
(a) This X-ray is a thoracic inlet view	❏	❏
(b) There is evidence of soft tissue swelling and calcification	❏	❏
(c) There is evidence of tracheal deviation	❏	❏
(d) There is a right sided cervical rib	❏	❏
(e) These appearances are consistent with a calcified goitre	❏	❏

3. *(Figure 1.19c)*	True	False
(a) This is an AP chest X-ray	❏	❏
(b) The patient is about six months of age	❏	❏
(c) The lung fields are normal	❏	❏
(d) There is evidence of an aortic aneurysm	❏	❏
(e) This appearance is known as the 'sail' sign	❏	❏

STATION 1.20

Investigation

Please answer the questions regarding the three investigations shown below and opposite.

(5 minute station)

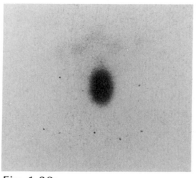

Fig. 1.20a

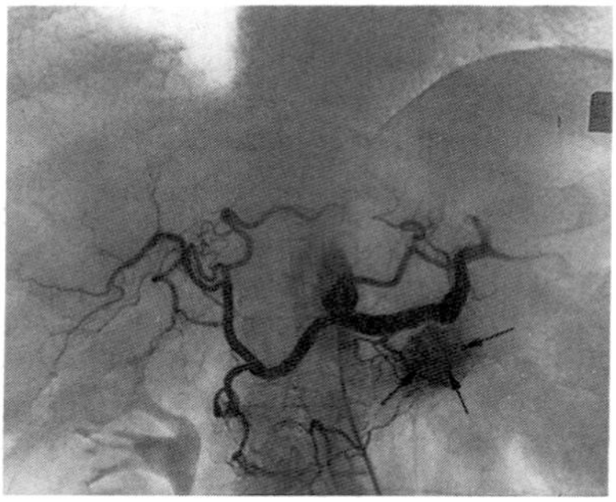

Fig. 1.20b

1.   *(Figure 1.20a)*
(a)   What is this investigation?
(b)   What does it show?

2.   *(Figure 1.20b)*
This patient presented with multiple blackouts and a recorded serum glucose of 2.0 mmol/l

(a)   What is this investigation?
(b)   What do the arrows define?

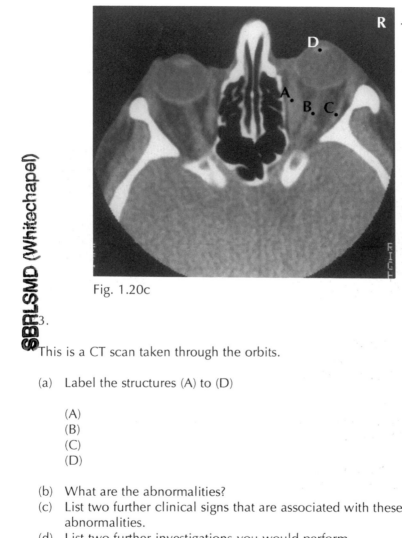

Fig. 1.20c

3.

This is a CT scan taken through the orbits.

(a) Label the structures (A) to (D)

(A)
(B)
(C)
(D)

(b) What are the abnormalities?
(c) List two further clinical signs that are associated with these abnormalities.
(d) List two further investigations you would perform.

STATION 1.21

Investigation

A 37-year-old woman complaining of breathlessness on exertion and orthopnoea, had plain radiology of the thoracic inlet (Figure 1.21).

(5 minute station)

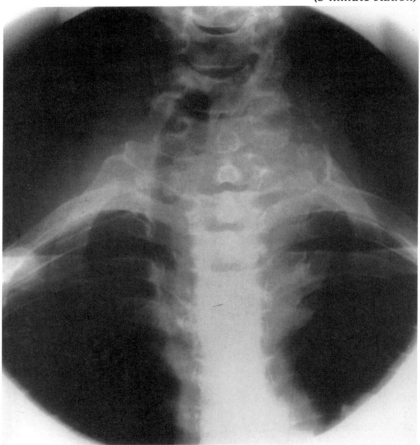

Fig. 1.21

1. What are the radiological findings?
2. What is the probable cause of her symptoms?
3. What radiographs would you request to further evaluate her symptoms?
4. State the definitive measure to relieve her symptoms.

STATION 1.22

Investigation

Please label structures A–G in the MRI scan of the pituitary fossa and surrounding structures (Figure 1.22).

(5 minute station)

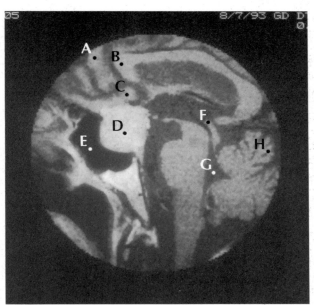

Fig. 1.22

Answers

(A)   (E)

(B)   (F)

(C)   (G)

(D)   (H)

Figure 1.22 and 1.23 reproduced by kind permission of Dr J.P. Monson, Consultant Endocrinologist, St Bartholomew's Hospital, London

STATION 1.23

Investigation

Please label structures A–H in this the CT scan of the abdomen taken at the level of L2 - L3 (Figure 1.23).

(5 minute station)

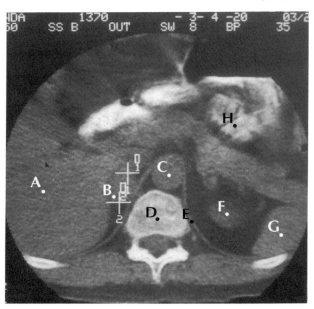

Fig. 1.23

Answers

(A)	(E)
(B)	(F)
(C)	(G)
(D)	(H)

STATION 1.24

Investigation

Figure 1.24 shows the thyroid gland in a 63-year-old euthyroid woman with a palpable nodule in the left lobe.

(5 minute station)

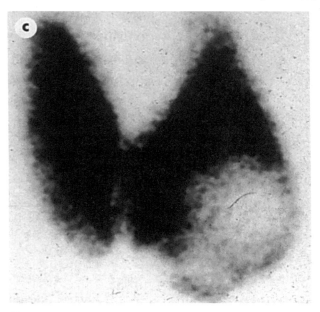

Fig. 1.24

1. State the imaging procedure shown and the agents used to obtain the scan.
2. Identify the site and nature of the abnormality on the scan. State three lesions that may be implicated.
3. What further investigations would be required to arrive at a definitive diagnosis?

Figure 1.24 from Besser GM, Thorner MO, editors: Atlas of Endocrine Imaging, 1993, Mosby Europe Limited Publishers. By permission of Mosby International Ltd.

STATION 1.25

Therapeutics

You are a general practitioner. Your next patient is a 48-year-old woman who believes she has recently started her menopause and has read in several magazines that she should go on hormone replacement therapy. Please discuss the pros and cons of the treatment and establish whether she is a suitable candidate.

(5 minute station)

STATION 1.26

Therapeutics

Please match the diabetic treatments below with their correct side-effects and drug groups.

(5 minute station)

Drug	Drug group	Side-effect
1. Actrapid	(A) Sulphonylurea (t <8 hours)	(a) Flatulence
2. Metformin	(B) α glucosidase inhibitor	(b) Lipoatrophy
3. Tolbutamide	(C) Short acting insulin	(c) Alcohol induced flushing
4. Acarbose	(D) Sulphonylurea (t >24 hours)	(d) Lactic acidosis
5. Chlorpropamide	(E) Biguanide	(e) Hypoglycaemia

Answers

1. ( ) ( )
2. ( ) ( )
3. ( ) ( )

4. ( ) ( )
5. ( ) ( )

STATION 1.27

Therapeutics

> You are a house officer on a diabetes and general medical firm. You have been asked by your registrar to explain to a newly diagnosed 23-year-old diabetic patient how to draw up and inject insulin and to stress the important points of insulin therapy.

> *(10 minute station)*

STATION 1.28

Preparatory

Please read the following prior to attempting the next station.

> Ms James is a 19-year-old nurse who recently underwent trans-sphenoidal surgery for a large pituitary tumour. This has left her panhypopituitary and she must remain on the treatments shown below, until she is seen again in the outpatient department:
> Thyroxine 100 mcg od
> Hydrocortisone 20 mg mane; 10 mg nocte
> Recombinant FSH/LH replacement

You should explain to the patient
(a) The normal function of the pituitary gland hormones
(b) The reason for each of the medications above
(c) The possible problems with the medications.

> *(5 minute station)*

STATION 1.28a

Therapeutics

You are the house officer of the endocrine firm looking after a 19-year-old nurse, who recently underwent hypophysectomy for a large pituitary tumour. You have been requested by the nursing staff on the ward to explain the nature and important points of her hormone replacement to the patient before she goes home.

(5 minute station)

STATION 1.29

History

Please take a history from this 34-year-old woman, who has been referred to the breast clinic with incapacitating breast pain.

(5 minute station)

STATION 1.30

History

Please take a history and address the concerns of this 24-year-old woman seen at the breast clinic, who is anxious over the prospect of developing breast cancer due to a strong family history.

(5 minute station)

STATION 1.31

Examination

Figure 1.31 is that of a 43-year-old woman who has attended the breast clinic for breast asymmetry since puberty. From your observations please state whether the following statements are correct.

(5 minute station)

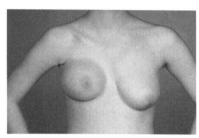

Fig. 1.31

		True	False
1.	The patient has a problem with her self-image.	❑	❑
2.	The right breast:		
(a)	is ptotic	❑	❑
(b)	has developmental abnormality	❑	❑
(c)	is cosmetically disfiguring	❑	❑
(d)	cannot be corrected by breast enlargement	❑	❑
3.	The left breast:		
(a)	has a normal contour	❑	❑
(b)	has had a surgical procedure	❑	❑
(c)	has nipple retraction	❑	❑

STATION 1.32

Examination

Please examine the breasts of the subject (manikin), describing the important features as you proceed.

(5 minute station)

STATION 1.33

Investigation

A 61-year-old woman diagnosed with a recurrent carcinoma of her right breast underwent the staging investigations shown (Figures 1.33a and 1.33b).

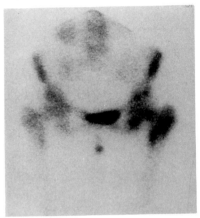

Fig. 1.33a

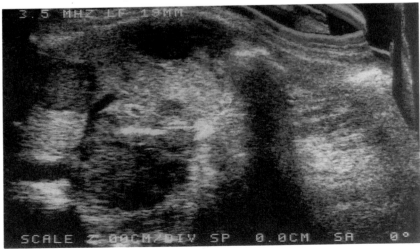

Fig. 1.33b

1.   Please name the imaging procedures in Figures 1.33a and 1.33b and describe the salient features in each.

2.   State your conclusions from your observations.

3.   Comment on how these findings influence the treatment of her breast lesion.

(5 minute station)

STATION 1.34

Investigation

Figures 1.34a and 1.34b are radiological examinations of the right breast in two middle-aged women, taken during a community screening programme.

(5 minute station)

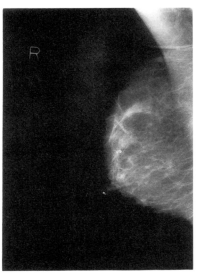

Fig. 1.34a

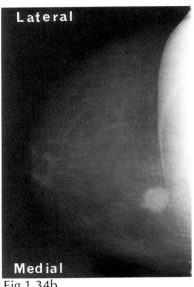

Fig.1.34b

1. What are the radiographs called?
2. Indicate the abnormal findings in any one radiograph.
3. State your radiological diagnosis in each.
4. What other investigation would you perform to confirm the diagnosis?
5. How would you counsel these patients on the need for further assessment?

STATION 1.35

Investigation

Please perform a fine needle aspiration for cytological examination of a breast lump marked on a plastic model.

(5 minute station)

Equipment provided:
Female manikin, syringe and fine needle, microscope slides, specimen bottle containing fixative, spray on fixative for slides, sterile wipes, small adhesive dressing.

STATION 1.36

Treatment

A 40-year-old woman and her partner await the results of the triple assessment of a breast lump which was found to be malignant. Inform the patient (and her partner) of the diagnosis and offer counselling.

(5 minute station)

2: GASTROENTEROLOGY

DIARRHOEA

* **Age of the patient**
  Under 40 - think inflammatory bowel disease, infective, irritable bowel
  Over 40 - think carcinoma

* **Duration of the illness** 'When were you last well?'

* **What does the patient mean by diarrhoea?**
  Increased frequency
  Increased volume of stool

* **Frequency**
  How many times in a 24-hour period is the patient opening their bowels?
  Do they have to get up at night to defaecate?

* **Consistency of the stools**
  Watery/clear/frothy
  Fluid/brown
  Semiformed
  Solid
  Presence or absence of blood
  Presence or absence of mucus
  Steatorrhoea: pale, offensive, porridge-like stools which float in the toilet water and are difficult to flush away

Features associated with diarrhoea

Systemic symptoms: Anaemia pyrexia, arthritis, sacroiliitis, uveitis, erythema nodosum
Nausea and vomiting, dehydration
Abdominal pain: Character, site, radiation, relief, exacerbation
Weight loss, loss of appetite (anorexia)
Recent foreign travel particularly to epi/endemic areas
Family history of inflammatory bowel disease, bowel polyps/cancer

Differential diagnoses of diarrhoea

The main causes of diarrhoea are colitic. Small bowel causes are rare.
- **Colonic causes**
  Inflammatory bowel disease
  Infective colitis
  Bacterial: *E. Coli, Salmonella typhi* and *paratyphi* Campylobacter,
  Shigella, Yersinia, *Vibrio cholerae, Clostridium difficile*
  Viral: Rotavirus, Adenovirus, Astrovirus
  Protozoal: *Giardia lamblia, Entamoeba histolytica,* Cryptosporidium
  (in the immunosuppressed)
  Left sided colonic malignancy
  Ischaemic colitis
  Overflow diarrhoea secondary to constipation

- **Small bowel causes**
  Coeliac disease
  Secretory or high output diarrhoea, e.g. post small bowel resection
  VIPoma
  Terminal ileitis, e.g. TB or Crohn's disease

UPPER GI BLEED

- **History**
  Haematemesis: fresh blood, altered blood or coffee grounds
  Volume of vomitus and amount of blood
  How many episodes/volume of each episode at this presentation
  Passage of melaena
  Previous episodes/causes if known

- **Associated features**
  Epigastric pain – acute/chronic, character, radiation, relief, exacerbation
  Epigastric fullness, weight loss, anorexia
  Dyspepsia
  Features of chronic liver disease

- **Risk factors**
  Use of NSAIDs – duration
  Other medications: steroids, anticoagulants
  Known or previous peptic ulcer disease, varices or hiatus hernia
  Alcohol excess: duration, amount, type of alcohol
  Chronic liver disease
  Familial blood dyscrasia

- **Causes**

In anatomical sequence:

 Oesophageal: oesophagitis, carcinoma, varices, Mallory-Weiss tear, trauma, hiatus hernia

 Gastric: gastritis, peptic ulcer, benign and malignant tumours, e.g. leiomyoma, adenocarcinoma

 Duodenal: duodenitis, peptic ulcer

DYSPHAGIA

- **History**

 Level of the dysphagia: oropharynx; high, mid or lower oesophagus

 Degree of dysphagia: solids, semi-solids, liquids

 Progression: insidious, intermittent onset signifies benign diseases; a rapidly progressive course implies malignancy

 Pain: suggests local inflammatory process or infection, e.g. candidiasis 'Impaction pain' is typical of benign stricturing

 Regurgitation: immediate/delayed

- **Associated features**

 Weight loss, anorexia

 Features of systemic diseases:

  Raynaud's (systemic sclerosis)

  Muscle weakness and wasting (motor neurone disease)

  Ptosis (myasthenia gravis)

 Change in bowel habit

 Coughing/recurrent chest infection – implies aspiration

- **Causes**

 Oropharynx

  Bulbar palsy, e.g. motor neurone disease, myasthenia gravis tonsilitis, pharyngeal pouch

 Oesophageal

  Benign stricture: gastro-oesophageal reflux, corrosives, Barrett's oesophagus

  Malignant stricture: upper oesophagus – squamous carcinoma

           lower oesophagus – adenocarcinoma

 Hiatus hernia

 Infective: candidiasis, CMV, HSV (particularly in HIV disease)

 Chagas' disease (South American trypanosomiasis)

Oesophageal web (Plummer-Vinson or Paterson-Brown-Kelly syndrome)
Extrinsic compression: bronchial carcinoma, left atrial hypertrophy,
retrosternal goitre, mediastinal lymphadenopathy, thymoma

- **Risk factors for oesophageal carcinoma**
  Smoking
  Alcohol excess
  Possible dietary factors (nitrosamines in diet)
  Achalasia of the cardia
  Plummer-Vinson syndrome
  Tylosis

JAUNDICE

- **Causes**
  Pre-hepatic – haemolysis
  Hepatic – cirrhosis, infective hepatitis, drugs
  Obstructive – gallstones, carcinoma of the gall bladder, pancreas,
  ampulla of Vater, pancreatitis, biliary stricture

- **Differentiating questions**

Alcohol consumption	Previous blood transfusions
Travel abroad	Recent contacts
Family history	Sexual contacts
Recreational drug use	Medications
Previous jaundice/cause	Fever/viral prodrome
Weight loss	Dark urine/pale stools – signs
'Food poisoning'	of obstructive disease

- **Differentiating acute and chronic liver disease**
  On examination of jaundiced patients it is important to differentiate
  between acute and acute on chronic liver disease. One must
  therefore look for signs of chronic liver disease.
  Hands: clubbing, leuchonykia, palmar erythema, Dupytren's
  contracture
  Upper limbs: scratch marks, bruising
  Chest: gynaecomastia, loss of male distribution of hair, spider naevi
  Abdomen: hepatosplenomegaly, ascites, caput medusae, gonadal
  atrophy

Confusion, hepatic fetor and flapping tremor are signs of hepatic
encephalopathy.

STATION 2.1   *(Answers – page 196)*

History

> A 24-year-old man presents to the Accident and Emergency Department with a history of bloody diarrhoea.
>
> You are the student on call with the medical team. Please take a history of the presenting complaint with a view to making a diagnosis.

> **(5 minute station)**

STATION 2.2

History

> You are a GP. Your next patient is a 42-year-old woman who has just returned from a foreign holiday with a 10 day history of diarrhoea.
>
> Please take a history of the presenting complaint, explaining to the patient the likely diagnosis and the investigations you wish to carry out.

> **(5 minute station)**

STATION 2.3

History

> You are the medical student attached to a gastroenterology firm. You have been asked to take a history from a 24-year-old woman, who has been referred to the Outpatient Department by her GP with a 3 to 4 month history of 'diarrhoea'.
>
> Please take a history of her presenting complaint with a view to making a diagnosis. (You should be able to give a differential diagnosis at the end of the station.)

> **(5 minute station)**

STATION 2.4

History

You are the medical student attached to the general medical firm on call. You have been asked by the registrar to clerk a 34-year-old woman who has just arrived in the Accident and Emergency Department after vomiting some blood. She is haemodynamically stable.

Please take a history of the presenting complaint and any other relevant history with a view to making a diagnosis.

(5 minute station)

STATION 2.5

History

You are the medical student attached to a gastroenterology firm. You have been asked to take a history from a patient who has been referred to the Outpatient Department with epigastric pain and a proven microcytic anaemia.

Please take a history of the presenting complaint and any other relevant history with a view to making a diagnosis.

(5 minute station)

STATION 2.6

History

Please answer the following questions, which are associated with the history you have just taken from the patient in Station 2.5, indicating whether the statements are **True** or **False**.

(5 minute station)

		True	False
1.	This patient should have an oesphago-gastroduodenoscopy	❑	❑
2.	This patient will have a high plasma ferritin	❑	❑
3.	This patient may have koilonychia	❑	❑
4.	This patient will have a raised MCV	❑	❑
5.	This patient should have a CLO test	❑	❑
6.	This patient may require 'triple therapy'	❑	❑
7.	Triple therapy is given for 3 to 4 weeks	❑	❑
8.	Clarithromycin is commonly used in triple therapy	❑	❑
9.	Cimetidine is a proton pump inhibitor used in triple therapy	❑	❑
10.	This patient will need to be on omeprazole for life	❑	❑

STATION 2.7

History

You are a GP. The next patient is a 47-year-old man who has come to see you with 'swallowing problems'. Please take a history of the presenting complaint and any other relevant history with a view to making the diagnosis.

(5 minute station)

STATION 2.8

History

You are the medical student attached to the medical team on call. You have been asked by the Registrar to take a history from a 33-year-old man who has presented in the Accident and Emergency Department with jaundice.

Please take a history of the presenting complaint and any other relevant history with a view to making a diagnosis.

(5 minute station)

STATION 2.9

History

A 65-year-old woman is referred to the surgical clinic by her GP complaining of abdominal symptoms and an alteration in her bowel habit. Please take a history from this patient.

(5 minute station)

STATION 2.10

History

A 53-year-old man was referred to the surgical clinic complaining of intermittent bleeding per rectum and a fleshy lesion protruding through the anus. Take a history from this patient.

(5 minute station)

STATION 2.11

Examination

Please examine this patient's abdomen (Fig. 2.11 on page 142); describe your actions as you proceed and comment on your findings.

(5 minute station)

STATION 2.12

Examination

Figures 2.12a, 2.12b, 2.12c and 2.12d (see page 142) show abnormalities of the tongue. Please make a diagnosis for each, and match one or more of the following statements to the illustrations.

(5 minute station)

Statements   **Figure(s)**

1. Is frequently a congenital condition   _____
2. Is usually asymptomatic   _____
3. Is caused by overgrowth of filiform papillae _____
4. Is associated with tobacco smoking or chewing _____
5. Is a pre-cancerous condition   _____
6. Is managed by regular oral hygiene   _____

STATION 2.13

Examination

Figures 2.13a and 2.13b (on page 143) are endoscopic views of the distal oesophagus and the gastric antrum respectively.

(5 minute station)

1. Please list the features observed in each
2. (a) State the probable diagnosis in each
   (b) How would you confirm your diagnosis in 2.13b?
3. State an aetiological factor associated with each of these conditions
4. List two symptoms in each that could lead a patient to seek medical advice

STATION 2.14

Examination

Figures 2.14a and 2.14b (on page 143) are colonoscopic findings in the transverse colon and rectum respectively.

(5 minute station)

1. Please list the features observed in each
2. What is the probable diagnosis in each?
3. (a) State the predisposing factor in 2.14a where the patient had been on long-term antibiotic therapy
   (b) State the probable sequelae of leaving 2.14b untreated
4. How would you treat both conditions?

STATION 2.15

History

The following patients are all attending the gastroenterology clinic. Please match the patient histories with the most appropriate diagnosis and full blood count result.

(5 minute station)

Patient history	Full Blood Count	Diagnosis
1. A 23-year-old woman with weight loss, lethargy and steatorrhoea	(A) Hb 9.9 MCV 67 WCC 10.3 Plats 302	(a) Peptic ulcer disease
2. A 32-year-old with chronic liver disease and a raised red cell transketolase	(B) Hb 8.9 MCV 85 WCC 6.5 Plats 221	(b) Pernicious anaemia
3. A 54-year-old man with weight loss and constipation	(C) Hb 11.2 MCV 70 WCC 11.8 Plats 654	(c) Inflammatory bowel disease
4. A 74-year-old woman with known hypothyroidism and a history of collapse	(D) Hb 7.5 MCV 104 WCC 3.9 Plats 64	(d) Coeliac disease
5. A 27-year-old man with epigastric pain and melaena	(E) Hb 9.2 MCV 105 WCC 4.7 Plats 353	(e) Alcoholic liver disease
6. A 29-year-old man with a 2 year history of treated episodic bloody diarrhoea and mucus PR	(F) Hb 3.6 MCV 122 WCC 2.1 Plats 32	(f) Colonic carcinoma

Answers

1. ( ) ( )
2. ( ) ( )
3. ( ) ( )

4. ( ) ( )
5. ( ) ( )
6. ( ) ( )

STATION 2.16

Investigation

The patients below have all presented with weight loss. Please match the patient histories with the most appropriate investigation results and diagnosis.

(5 minute station)

Patient history

1. A 67-year-old man with jaundice, pale stools and anorexia

    t C

2. A 52-year-old woman with palmar erythema, spider naevi and hepatosplenomegaly

    B E

3. A 25-year-old woman with steatorrhoea and general malaise

    A B

4. A 59-year-old man with weight loss, constipation and blood PR

    D A

5. A 43-year-old obese woman with generalised abdominal pain and fever

    C d

Investigations

(A) Albumin 23
    Alk phos 232
    AST 31 Bili 13
    CCa^{++} 1.80
    Amylase 23

(B) Albumin 24
    Alk phos 454
    AST 54 Bili 32
    CCa^{++} 2.42
    Amylase 43

(C) Albumin 35
    Alk phos 321
    AST 93 Bili 124
    CCa^{++} 1.92
    Amylase 1098

(D) Albumin 26
    Alk phos 607
    AST 109 Bili 45
    CCa^{++} 3.05
    Amylase 32

(E) Albumin 21
    Alk phos 644
    AST 245 Bili 308
    CCa^{++} 2.56
    Amylase 204

Diagnosis

(a) Colonic carcinoma with multiple metastases

(b) Coeliac disease

(c) Carcinoma of the head of the pancreas

(d) Acute pancreatitis

(e) Primary biliary cirrhosis

Answers

1. ( ) ( )
2. ( ) ( )
3. ( ) ( )

4. ( ) ( )
5. ( ) ( )

STATION 2.17

Investigation

The following patients have presented to the hepatology clinic with deranged LFTs. Please match the patient histories with the most appropriate diagnosis and disease marker.

(5 minute station)

Patient history	Diagnosis	Marker
1. A 47-year-old man who has known chronic hepatitis B disease now presenting with hepatomegaly and weight loss	(A) Wilson's disease	(a) Raised serum ferritin
2. A 58-year-old woman with recent weight loss and constipation	(B) Primary biliary cirrhosis	(b) Antismooth muscle antibody
3. A 34-year-old man with diabetes, a 'suntan' and jaundice	(C) Colonic carcinoma with metastases	(c) Antimitochondrial antibody
4. A 56-year-old woman with signs of chronic liver disease and periorbital xanthelasma	(D) Hepatoma	(d) Low serum copper and caeruloplasmin
5. A 33-year-old woman with signs of chronic liver disease, jaundice and a cushingoid appearance	(E) Haemochromatosis	(e) Alpha fetoprotein
6. A 39-year-old man with tremor, gait problems and Kayser-Fleischer rings	(F) Autoimmune hepatitis	(f) Markedly raised Carcinoembryonic antigen

Answers

1. ( ) ( )
2. ( ) ( )
3. ( ) ( )

4. ( ) ( )
5. ( ) ( )
6. ( ) ( )

STATION 2.18

Investigation

Please indicate which of the statements regarding the patients a to d are **True** or **False**.

(5 minute station)

Patient	HBs Ag	aHBs Ig	HBc Ag	aHBc IgG	aHBc IgM	HBe Ag	aHBe Ig
a	+	-	-	-	+	+	-
b	-	+	-	-	-	-	-
c	+	-	-	+	-	+	-
d	+	-	-	+	-	-	+

		True	False
1.	Patient (a) has developed immunity to the hepatitis B virus	☐	☑
2.	Patient (a) has evidence of acute viral replication	☑	☐
3.	Patient (a) is a chronic carrier	☐	☑
4.	Patient (b) has chronic active hepatitis	☑	☐
5.	Patient (b) is immune to further infection with hepatitis B	☑	☐
6.	Patient (b) is more susceptible to hepatoma	☑	☐
7.	Patient (c) shows evidence of high risk infectivity	☑	☐
8.	Patient (c) may transmit the virus transplacentally	☑	☐
9.	Patient (c) is at risk of cirrhosis	☑	☐
10.	Patient (d) has chronic active hepatitis	☑	☑
11.	Patient (d) shows evidence of low risk infectivity	☑	☐
12.	Patient (d) may still donate blood	☐	☑

STATION 2.19

Investigation

The following patients have all presented to their General Practitioner with diarrhoea. Please match the patient histories with the most appropriate causative organism and description.

(5 minute station)

Patient history	Organism	Description
1. A 73-year-old woman who ate luncheon meat at her club 24 hours ago. She now has profuse vomiting and diarrhoea and is hypotensive. Several other diners have been admitted to hospital	(A) *Clostridium difficile*	(a) Coccidian oocysts in faeces
2. A 22-year-old man who presents 24 hours after eating a reheated, luke-warm Chinese take-away	(B) *Entamoeba histolytica*	(b) Flagellate protozoan
3. A 61-year-old man who has been on oral cefuroxime for 10 days for a UTI	(C) Cryptosporidium	(c) Motile trophozoite
4. A 31-year-old man who has just returned from Russia with a 5 day history of watery diarrhoea	(D) *Bacillus cereus*	(d) Gram negative lactose fermenting rod
5. A 27-year-old woman who is HIV positive presenting with 2 weeks of profuse watery diarrhoea	(E) *Escherichia coli*	(e) Gram positive spore forming aerobe
6. A 32-year-old woman returns to England after teaching for a year in South East Asia. She is feeling listless and tired, with a six week history of episodic watery diarrhoea, containing flecks of blood and mucus.	(F) *Giardia lamblia*	(f) Gram positive anaerobic motile rod

Answers

1. ( ) ( )
2. ( ) ( )
3. ( ) ( )

4. ( ) ( )
5. ( ) ( )
6. ( ) ( )

STATION 2.20

Investigation

These plain abdominal radiographs (Figures 2.20a and 2.20b) are those of a 47-year-old man with a six day history of colicky abdominal pain and vomiting.

(5 minute station)

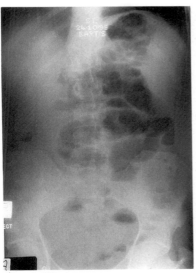
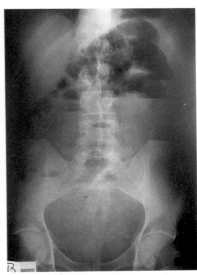

Fig. 2.20a   Fig. 2.20b

1. How were these two radiographs taken?
2. List the salient features of each
3. State your radiological diagnosis
4. List your definitive management

STATION 2.21

Investigation

A 33-year-old man suffering from AIDS developed abdominal cramps and constipation over two weeks. The result of a radiological investigation is shown (Figure 2.21).

(5 minute station)

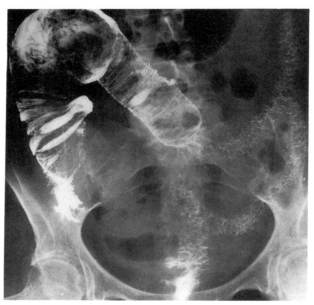

Fig. 2.21

1. Please name the investigation performed
2. How would you perform this investigation?
3. State the positive findings and your diagnosis
4. How would you treat this condition?

STATION 2.22

Investigation

The radiographs below and overleaf are taken from patients presenting with abdominal pain. Please indicate whether the statements are **True** or **False**.

(5 minute station)

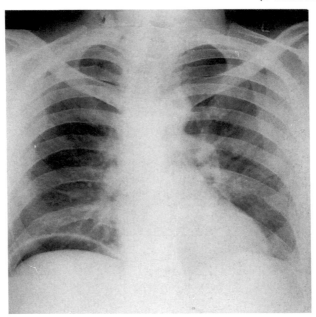

Fig. 2.22a

		True	False
1.	*(Figure 2.22a)*		
(a)	This is an erect CXR	❏	❏
(b)	The appearances are normal post ERCP	❏	❏
(c)	The appearances are normal 2 days post laparoscopy	❏	❏
(d)	There is evidence of a perforated viscus	❏	❏
(e)	The patient should be treated initially by 'drip and suck'	❏	❏

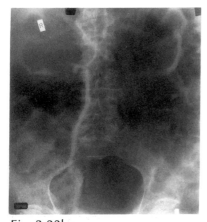

Fig. 2.22b

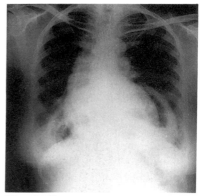

Fig. 2.22c

2.	*(Figure 2.22b)*	True	False
(a)	This is a supine AXR	❏	❏
(b)	There is evidence of small bowel obstruction	❏	❏
(c)	There are multiple fluid levels	❏	❏
(d)	The caecum is loaded with faecal residue	❏	❏
(e)	A common cause of this appearance is adhesions	❏	❏

3.	*(Figure 2.22c)*	True	False
(a)	There is evidence of cardiomegaly	❏	❏
(b)	There is evidence of free air in the peritoneum	❏	❏
(c)	The LFTs will be normal in this case	❏	❏
(d)	There may be a microcytosis on the blood film	❏	❏
(e)	The features are consistent with gallstone ileus	❏	❏

STATION 2.23

Investigation

The three patients below and overleaf have all presented with dysphagia. Please indicate whether the statements are **True** or **False**.

(5 minute station)

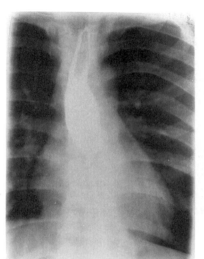

Fig. 2.23b

Fig. 2.23a

		True	False
1.	*(Figure 2.23a)*		
(a)	This is a barium meal	❑	❑
(b)	It shows a benign oesophageal stricture	❑	❑
(c)	There is evidence of presbyoesophagus	❑	❑
(d)	Impact pain is a common presenting symptom	❑	❑
(e)	A common cause of this appearance is reflux oesophagitis	❑	❑

		True	False
2.	*(Figure 2.23b)*		
(a)	This is a single contrast barium swallow	❑	❑
(b)	The oesophageal lumen is within normal limits	❑	❑
(c)	The appearances are caused by Barrett's oesophagus	❑	❑
(d)	The condition shown is linked to cigarette smoking	❑	❑
(e)	Patients are at increased risk of adeno-carcinoma of the oesophagus	❑	❑

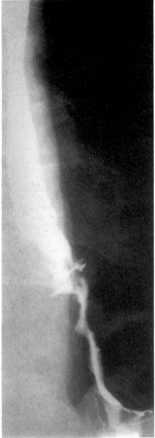

Fig. 2.23c

3. *(Figure 2.23c)*   **True**   **False**
(a) This is a barium follow-through study   ❏   ❏
(b) It shows severe peptic ulceration   ❏   ❏
(c) The disorder shown is common in Iran   ❏   ❏
(d) The condition may be cured by bismuth
    colloid   ❏   ❏
(e) YAG laser can be used to treat this condition ❏   ❏

STATION 2.24

Investigation

The three patients below and overleaf have all presented with a microcytic anaemia and weight loss. Please indicate whether the statements are **True** or **False**.

(5 minute station)

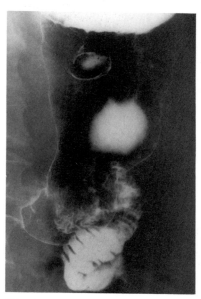

Fig. 2.24a

		True	False
1.	*(Figure 2.24a)*		
(a)	This is a barium meal and follow-through study	❏	❏
(b)	There is evidence of gastric atrophy	❏	❏
(c)	There is a benign ulcer in the pylorus of the stomach	❏	❏
(d)	There are numerous jejunal and duodenal diverticulae	❏	❏
(e)	This disorder is associated with *Campylobacter jejuni*	❏	❏

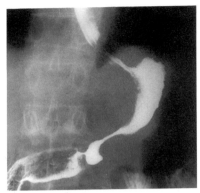

Fig. 2.24c

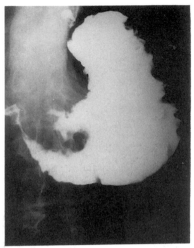

Fig. 2.24b

2. (Figure 2.24b)	True	False
(a) This is a barium follow-through study	❑	❑
(b) There is evidence of pyloric stenosis	❑	❑
(c) There is a large ulcer on the lesser curvature	❑	❑
(d) The disorder shown may be cured by triple therapy	❑	❑
(e) The disorder shown is associated with pernicious anaemia	❑	❑

3. (Figure 2.24c)	True	False
(a) This is a barium meal and follow-through study	❑	❑
(b) There is evidence of a duodenal ulceration	❑	❑
(c) The oesophagus is normal	❑	❑
(d) The stomach is abnormal	❑	❑
(e) The condition shown is referred to as linitis plastica	❑	❑

STATION 2.25

Investigation

The three patients below and overleaf have all presented with bleeding per rectum. Please indicate whether the statements are **True** or **False**.

(5 minute station)

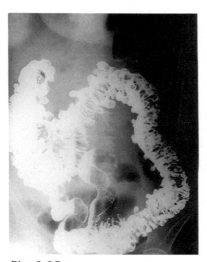

Fig. 2.25a

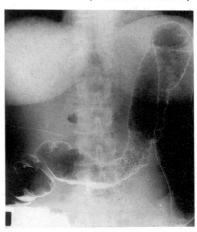

Fig. 2.25b

		True	False
1.	*(Figure 2.25a)*		
(a)	This is a barium enema	❏	❏
(b)	There has been poor bowel preparation	❏	❏
(c)	This is a decubitus view	❏	❏
(d)	The disorder shown is more common in black Africans	❏	❏
(e)	This disorder is a complication of inflammatory bowel disease	❏	❏

2. *(Figure 2.25b)* **True** **False**
(a) This is a single contrast barium study ❏ ❏
(b) The loss of haustral pattern in the
descending colon is termed 'lead piping' ❏ ❏
(c) There is evidence of diverticulae ❏ ❏
(d) The disorder shown is more common in
women ❏ ❏
(e) The patient is at increased risk of colonic
carcinoma ❏ ❏

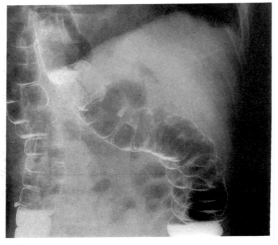

Fig. 2.25c

3. *(Figure 2.25c)* **True** **False**
(a) This is a double contrast study ❏ ❏
(b) It shows a benign stricture of the
transverse colon ❏ ❏
(c) The stricture is sited in the descending
limb of the transverse colon ❏ ❏
(d) This stricture is almost certainly related to
IBD ❏ ❏
(e) This patient is probably in their 6th to 7th
decade ❏ ❏

STATION 2.26

Please label the CT scan of the abdomen shown below.

(5 minute station)

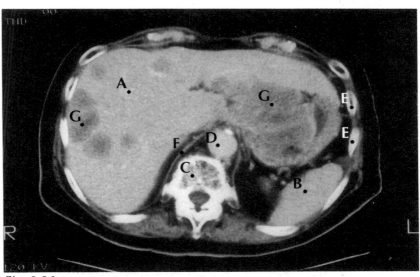

Fig. 2.26

(A)   (E)

(B)   (F)

(C)   (G)

(D)

STATION 2.27

Investigation

Please answer the questions regarding the investigations shown below.

(5 minute station)

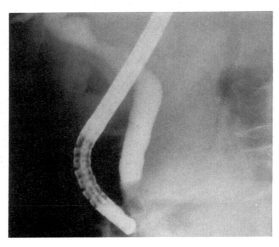

Fig. 2.27a

1.
(a) What is this investigation?
(b) Describe the abnormalities

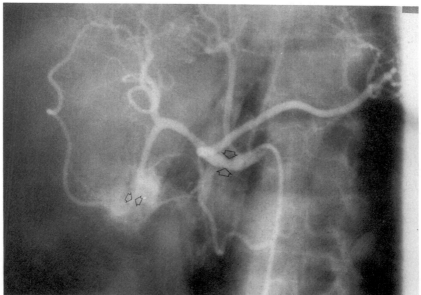

Fig. 2.27b

2.
(a) What is this investigation?
(b) What are the structures labelled by the arrows?

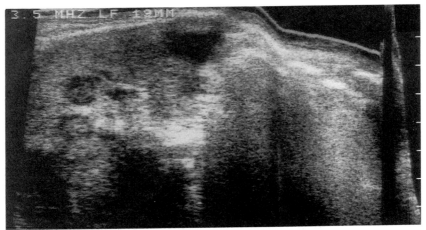

Fig. 2.27c

3.
This investigation is of the liver

(a) What is this investigation?
(b) List three abdominal indications for it?

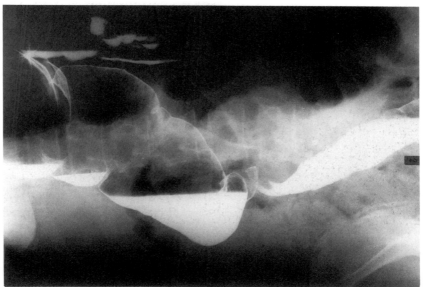

Fig. 2.27d

4.
(a) What is this investigation?
(b) What is the major abnormality?

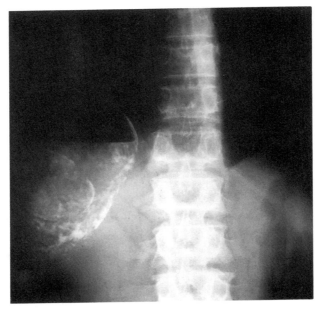

Fig. 2.27e

5.
(a) What is this investigation?
(b) What is the major abnormality?
(c) List three differential causes

STATION 2.28

Therapeutics

A 23-year-old woman returns to outpatients for the results of her biopsies taken recently at OGD. The biopsy report is shown below.

'Areas of chronic inflammatory changes consistent with benign duodenal ulceration. *Helicobacter pylori* is also identified within this section.'

From the patient's details and the selection of drugs listed opposite please write out a prescription for this patient.

(5 minute station)

Gastroenterology

Mrs Helen Myers   Hospital Number 013645   DOB 13/7/75
24 Gardenia Road
Cravenbrook
Middleton, M34 2NT

Drugs:

Ranitidine 300 mg nocte	Lansoprazole 30 mg bd
Metronidazole 400 mg bd	Clarithromycin 250 mg or 500 mg bd
Flucloxacillin 500 mg qds	Amoxycillin 750 mg tds or 1g bd
Cimetidine 800 mg nocte	Omeprazole 20 mg bd
Misoprostol 400 mg bd	Tetracycline 250 mg qds
Ranitidine-bismuth citrate 400 mg bd	

Hospital number   [ ] [ ] [ ] [ ] [ ] [ ]
Mr/Mrs/Ms Surname ....
Forename   ....
Address   ....
                    ....
DOB   [ ] [ ] / [ ] [ ] / [ ] [ ]

Doctor's Signature ....

Print Name   ....

Date   [ ] [ ] / [ ] [ ] / [ ] [ ]

STATION 2.29

Therapeutics

You are the house officer on a gastroenterology firm. You have been asked by the pharmacy to check a prescription for a TPN bag which has been ordered for one of your patients. The constituents of the bag and some of the patient's details are shown below.

(10 minute station)

Mr L.B. is a 27-year-old man who was admitted 9 days ago after suffering a severe head injury in an RTA. He also suffered multiple fractures of the lower limbs. Since admission he has been electively paralysed and ventilated on the intensive care unit. He has had TPN running for three days and has a post-traumatic small gut ileus. Today he has a temperature of 38.5 °C. He is at present haemodynamically stable.
He has a triple lumen central venous line in situ, an indwelling urinary catheter and a pelvic external fixator.
Height = 1.80m   Weight = 80kg

His most recent investigations are:
FBC: Hb 10.5, WCC 14.6, Platelets 355
U+Es: Na^+ 139, K^+ 2.6, Bicarbonate 21, Urea 21, Creatinine 399
Glucose 17.5
Calcium 1.90, Albumin 24, Phosphate 1.0
Magnesium 0.61
CXR: Several rib fractures
CT head scan: generalised cerebral oedema and contusions.

TPN constituents
Na^+: 80 mmol
K^+: 80 mmol
Protein: 14g
Kcals: 2,650 (fat 1000 Kcals; carbohydrate 1300 Kcals;
protein 350 Kcals)
Calcium: 10 mmol
Phosphate: 20 mmol
Magnesium: 7.5 mmol
Volume: 2.5 litres

Please indicate whether the following statements are **True** or **False**

		True	False
1.	This patient is likely to be in an anabolic state	❑	❑
2.	He has normal renal function	❑	❑
3.	His corrected calcium is within normal limits	❑	❑
4.	He does not require more than 40 mmol K^+ per day	❑	❑
5.	He could have his insulin added to the TPN bag	❑	❑
6.	He should not have a very high protein concentration in his TPN	❑	❑
7.	His BMI is indicative of malnutrition	❑	❑
8.	He can have all his fluid requirements given by TPN	❑	❑
9.	Sepsis will not affect his TPN requirements	❑	❑
10.	The TPN can be given through his central venous line	❑	❑

STATION 2.30

Procedures

The instruments (A) to (F) shown in figure 2.30 on page 143 are all used in gastroenterological procedures. Please indicate whether the statements below are **True** or **False**

(5 minute station)

		True	False
1.	Instrument A is used to look directly into the oesophagus	❏	❏
2.	Colonic biopsies may be taken through Instrument A	❏	❏
3.	Instrument A should only be inserted with local anaesthetic	❏	❏
4.	Instrument B has become obselete because of the use of endoscopy	❏	❏
5.	A tennis ball is often attached to one end of instrument B to stop the patient swallowing it	❏	❏
6.	Instrument B is used to stop oesophagogastric variceal bleeding	❏	❏
7.	Instrument C is principally used to view the rectum	❏	❏
8.	Instrument C should always be used before using instrument A	❏	❏
9.	Instrument C is used for vaginal examination	❏	❏
10.	Instrument D is used with the patient lying in the left lateral position	❏	❏
11.	The patient should have a check FBC and clotting screen prior to the use of instrument D	❏	❏
12.	Instrument D is only used with a general anaesthetic	❏	❏
13.	Instrument E cannot be used to diagnose coeliac disease	❏	❏
14.	Instrument E can cause a pneumomediastinum	❏	❏
15.	Instrument E is used in ERCP	❏	❏
16.	One indication to use instrument F is in a patient with a stroke	❏	❏
17.	Instrument F is radio-opaque	❏	❏
18.	Instrument F may be used for parenteral feeding	❏	❏

- **Dysuria**
  Pain on passing urine; often described as a burning or stinging sensation

- **Strangury**
  Sudden painful cessation of micturition usually caused by vesical or urethral calculi.

- **Frequency**
  Is the number of times the bladder is emptied during the Day and Night $\left(\dfrac{D}{N} \right)$ Nocturia is the passing of urine at night

- **Haematuria**
  May be blood mixed with the urine or frank blood. It is also important to define whether it is painful or painless. Painless haematuria should always be regarded as 'sinister' till proven otherwise

- **Incontinence**
  May be stress or urge; it is often a feature of infection if of acute onset

- **Prostatism**
  Symptoms of prostatic enlargement include hesitancy, frequency, poor urinary stream and terminal dribbling

- **Abdominal pain**
  Suprapubic - implies cystitis: loin pain - sharp, severe or spasmodic implies renal colic: dull, non-specific pain may occur due to renal cyst or tumour enlargement

- **Polyuria**
  Passing large volumes of urine; may be associated with polydipsia (increased thirst and fluid intake), it is a sign of diabetes mellitus or diabetes insipidus

- **Cloudy/offensive urine**
  This is a sign of stagnation of the urine within the renal tract and often indicates infection. Patients on CAPD commonly present with 'cloudy' dialysate bags and abdominal pain when they are suffering with peritonitis secondary to their dialysis

Associated features
Vaginal and penile discharge: other features of sexually transmitted diseases should be sought, and a full sexual history taken. This should include all recent sexual contacts

Fever/rigors: pyelonephritis is a common cause of rigors, shaking episodes secondary to fever. Renal cell carcinoma may present as a low grade fever and is a differential of a PUO

Uraemia: confusion leading to coma; nausea and vomiting; pruritus, hiccups and pericarditis

Peripheral oedema: is a sign of fluid overload and may be associated with ascites and symptoms of cardiac failure

Systemic features of malignancy: weight loss, anorexia, malaise and fever

Systemic features of hypertension: headaches and visual disturbance

STATION 3.1

(Answers – page 234)

History

You are a GP. The next patient is an 18-year-old woman who is presenting with her fifth UTI in the past year.

Please take a history of her urinary problems with a view to referring her to renal outpatients.

(5 minute station)

STATION 3.2

History

You are a medical student attached to a surgical firm.

Please take a history from this 24-year-old patient with a view to making a diagnosis. You should be prepared to discuss the patient's management.

(5 minute station)

STATION 3.3

History

You are a medical house officer. You have been asked by your registrar to obtain a history from the wife of a confused patient who he is examining.

Please take a history of the presenting complaint. You should be prepared to discuss the management options.

(5 minute station)

STATION 3.4

History

A 53-year-old man presents to urology outpatients with haematuria. You are the medical student attached to the firm.

Please take a history of the presenting complaint with a view to making a diagnosis. You should be prepared to discuss the management of the patient.

(5 minute station)

STATION 3.5

History

You are the medical student attached to a general medical firm.

Please take a history of the presenting complaint from the next patient who is a 37-year-old woman with systemic lupus erythematosus.

(5 minute station)

STATION 3.6

History

A 59-year-old woman sees you, her GP, with a complaint of urinary incontinence.

Please take a history of the present complaint, and any other relevant factors, with a view to making a diagnosis.

(5 minute station)

STATION 3.7

Examination

Figures 3.7a–e (see page 144) depict five scrotal conditions, listed in Table 3.7a. The typical history, symptoms, signs and the treatment of each condition are arranged in a haphazard manner.

(5 minute station)

Table 3.7a

Condition	History	Symptoms	Signs	Treatment
1 Testicular torsion	1a History of trauma	1b Painless scrotal swelling	1c Swollen, red and tender scrotum with high transverse lie of testis	1d Repair of testicular injury
2 Varicocele	2a Enlarged testis	2b Painless testicular swelling	2c Swollen, red and tender with ecchymotic scrotum	2d Orchidectomy
3 Haematocele	3a Intermittent scrotal pain	3b Sharp onset of scrotal pain followed by swelling and redness	3c Cystic, non-tender scrotal swelling that trans-illuminates	3d Ligation of spermatic vein
4 Testicular tumour	4a Sub-fertility	4b Scrotal pain and swelling	4c Visible, palpable dilated veins above testis	4d Excision or inversion of sac
5 Vaginal hydrocele	5a Slow enlargement of scrotum	5b Scrotal discomfort, viz. following exertion	5c Loss of testicular sensation	5d Urgent surgical relief of torsion and orchidopexy of both testes

A.   Label each illustration with the appropriate diagnosis.

1.	Testicular torsion	Fig.
2.	Varicocele	Fig.
3.	Haematocele	Fig.
4.	Testicular tumour	Fig.
5.	Vaginal hydrocele	Fig.

B.   Identify the appropriate clinical presentation and treatment for each condition in Table 3.7a by rearranging the columns in your answer.

Clinical condition (diagnosis)	History	Symptoms	Signs	Treatment
1. Testicular torsion				
2. Varicocele				
3. Haematocele				
4. Testicular tumour				
5. Vaginal hydrocele				

STATION 3.8

Investigation

The following haematology results were obtained from patients in the renal outpatient department.

Please indicate whether the following statements are **True** or **False**.

(5 minute station)

Patient	Symptoms	Blood Results
(i) 21-year-old woman	Haematuria and recurrent UTIs	FBC - Hb 17.6, Hct 0.57, WCC 9.2, Platelets 398
(ii) 55-year-old man	Long-standing hypertension and diabetes mellitus	FBC - Hb 6.9, MCV 82, MCH 32, WCC 6.4, Platelets 288
(iii) 61-year-old man	Painless haematuria	FBC - Hb 8.1, MCV 70, WCC 13.9, Platelets 539
(iv) 52-year-old woman	Bony pain	Blood film - plasma cells, ESR 132

		True	False
1.	Patient (i) has polycythaemia	☑	☐
2.	Patient (i) may have adult polycystic kidney disease	☑	☐
3.	Patient (i) will have low plasma erythropoietin level	☐	☑
4.	Patient (ii) has a hyperchromic, macrocytic anaemia	☐	☑
5.	Patient (ii) probably has a chronic renal disorder	☑	☐
6.	Patient (ii) will have a low plasma ferritin	☐	☑
7.	Patient (iii) has a microcytic anaemia	☑	☐
8.	Patient (iii) has results most consistent with a renal abscess	☐	☑
9.	The results of patient (iii) are consistent with active bleeding	☑	☐

	True	False
10. Patient (iv) should have urine sent for Bence-Jones protein analysis	☑	❏
11. Patient (iv) would be expected to have hypocalcaemia	❏	☑
12. Patient (iv) may have systemic lupus erythematosus	❏	❏

STATION 3.9

Investigation

The following biochemistry results were obtained from patients on a general medical ward.

Please indicate whether the subsequent statements are **True** or **False.**

(5 minute station)

Biochemistry results

i. U+Es - Na^+ 149, K^+ 4.2, Bicarbonate 22, Urea 23.2, Creatinine 202, Glucose 8.6

ii. U+Es - Na^+ 121, K^+ 2.6, HCO_3^- 18,   Urea 1.6,   Creatinine 34,   Glucose 40

iii. U+Es - Na^+136, K^+ 4.3, HCO_3^- 15,   Urea 33.6, Creatinine 563, Glucose 21.1,
    HbA1c 13.9%

iv. U+Es - Na^+ 127, K^+ 7.2, HCO_3^- 21,   Urea 22.1, Creatinine 687, CCa^{2+} 2.4

v. U+Es - Na^+ 131, K^+ 6.4, Bicarbonate 20, Urea 19.5, Creatinine 512, PSA 109

		True	False
1.	The results of patient (i) are consistent with an obstructive nephropathy	❏	❏
2.	Patient (i) may have had an acute GI bleed	❏	❏
3.	Patient (ii) is dehydrated	❏	❏
4.	Patient (ii) has diabetic nephropathy	❏	❏
5.	Patient (iii) has results consistent with chronic renal failure	❏	❏
6.	Patient (iii) may have the Kimmelstiel-Wilson lesion	❏	❏
7.	Patient (iv) will probably require treatment with dialysis	❏	❏
8.	Patient (iv) has results suggestive of multiple myeloma	❏	❏
9.	Patient (v) has pre-renal failure	❏	❏
10.	Patient (v) should have a bone scan as part of his management	❏	❏

STATION 3.10

Investigation

The following urine sample results have been reported in the microbiology laboratory.

Please match the specimens with the histories.

(5 minute station)

Urine sample results

1. MSU – E. coli >105, WCC 750,
    Resistant – amoxycillin, trimethoprim;
    Sensitive – gentamycin, nalidixic acid

2. EMU – AAFBs grown after 6 weeks

3. Urgent microscopy – No organisms,
    WCC 100, red cell casts identified

4. MSU – No organisms seen, WCC >1000

5. CSU – Pseudomonas >105, WCC <1
    Sensitive – gentamycin, ciprofloxacin

Patient history

A. 29-year-old Asian woman
    with night sweats and rigors

B. 74-year-old man with
    indwelling catheter

C. 25-year-old man with a
    history of renal stone and
    acute severe loin pains

D. 33-year-old man with
    deranged U+Es and ankle
    oedema

E. 25-year-old pregnant woman

Answers

Urine sample results

1.
2.
3.
4.
5.

Patient

(　)
(　)
(　)
(　)
(　)

STATION 3.11

Investigation

Please match the brief patient history with the diagnosis and the correct immune marker.

(5 minute station)

Patient history	Diagnosis	Immune marker
1. 23-year-old woman with a malar rash and features of a nephrotic syndrome	(A) Systemic sclerosis	(a) HBV
2. 61-year-old man with severe hypertension and micro-aneurysms on renal angiography	(B) Goodpasture's disease	(b) Anti- ds DNA antibodies
3. 51-year-old woman with dysphagia, telangiectasia and calcinosis	(C) Wegener's granulomatosis	(c) aGBM antibodies
4. 29-year-old man with a 3-week history of 'flu, now presenting with a nephrotic syndrome and haemoptysis	(D) Polyarteritis nodosa	(d) cANCA
5. 38-year-old man with a dry cough, nasal discharge and haematuria	(E) Systemic lupus erythematosus	(e) Anti-Scl 70 antibody

Answers

1. (E) (b)
2. (D) (a)
3. (A) (e)

4. (B) (c)
5. (C) (d)

STATION 3.12

Investigation

Please indicate whether the following statements are **True** or **False**.

(5 minute station)

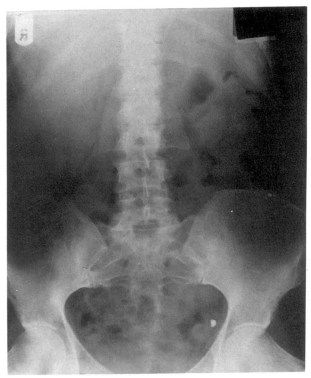

Fig. 3.12a

		True	False
1.	*(Figure 3.12a)*		
(a)	This is a supine AXR	❑	❑
(b)	There is a right renal stone	❑	❑
(c)	The kidneys are enlarged	❑	❑
(d)	There is renal calcification	❑	❑
(e)	The bones are osteopaenic	❑	❑

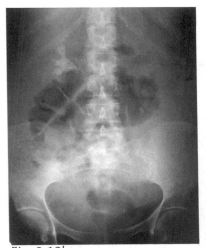

Fig. 3.12b

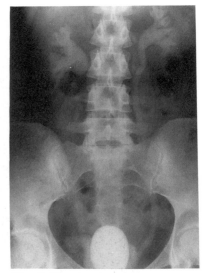

Fig. 3.12c

2.	*(Figure 3.12b)*	**True**	**False**
(a)	Both renal outlines are clearly seen	❑	❑
(b)	There is left sided renal calcification	❑	❑
(c)	There is bladder calcification	❑	❑
(d)	The bowel gas pattern is within normal limits	❑	❑
(e)	The appearances of the right kidney are associated with proteus infection	❑	❑

3.	*(Figure 3.12c)*	**True**	**False**
(a)	This is an IVU	❑	❑
(b)	There is a wedge fracture of L3	❑	❑
(c)	There is poor excretion of contrast on the left	❑	❑
(d)	The sacroiliac joints are normal	❑	❑
(e)	There is a foreign body in the bladder	❑	❑

STATION 3.13

Investigation

Figure 3.13 is a plain radiograph of a 49-year-old man who complained of long-standing backache, previously diagnosed and treated as musculo-skeletal pain.

(5 minute station)

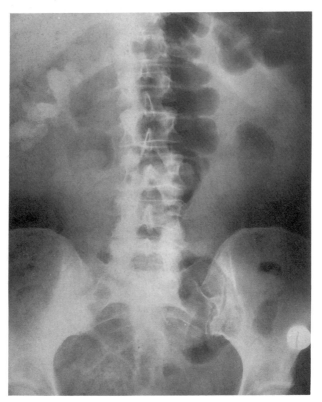

Fig. 3.13

1. State the abnormal finding(s)
2. List the complications of this condition
3. How would you treat this condition?

STATION 3.14

Investigation

Figure 3.14 is a plain X-ray of an 18-year-old Asian youth with a history of recurrent urinary tract infection.

(5 minute station)

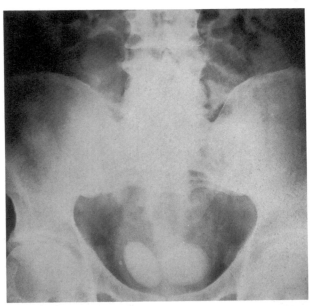

Fig. 3.14

1. State your diagnosis
2. List two aetiological factors that predispose to this condition
3. How would you treat this condition?

STATION 3.15

Investigation

Figure 3.15 is a radiograph of a 38-year-old woman complaining of left-sided loin pain radiating to the groin.

(5 minute station)

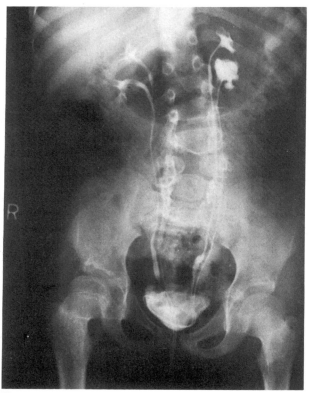

Fig. 3.15

1. Name the investigation
2. State the abnormality
3. Give another means of demonstrating this abnormality
4. State the likely cause of this lady's symptoms

STATION 3.16

Investigation

A 28-year-old man complained of intermittent right loin pain for five months. He underwent a radiological investigation (Figure 3.16).

(5 minute station)

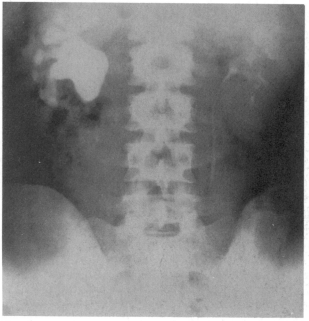

Fig. 3.16

1. Please name the investigation
2. Comment on the positive findings and state your diagnosis
3. How would you treat this condition?
4. What would be the sequelae of this lesion, left untreated?

STATION 3.17

Investigation

Please answer the questions below regarding the three investigations shown.

(5 minute station)

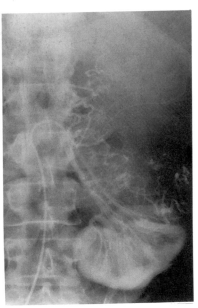

Fig. 3.17ai

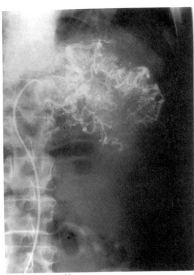

Fig. 3.17aii

1. *(Figures 3.17ai and 3.17aii)*
(a) What is this investigation?
(b) List three indications for it
(c) List two important questions you should ask the patient prior to starting the investigation

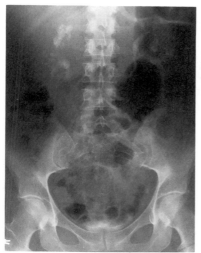

Fig. 3.17b

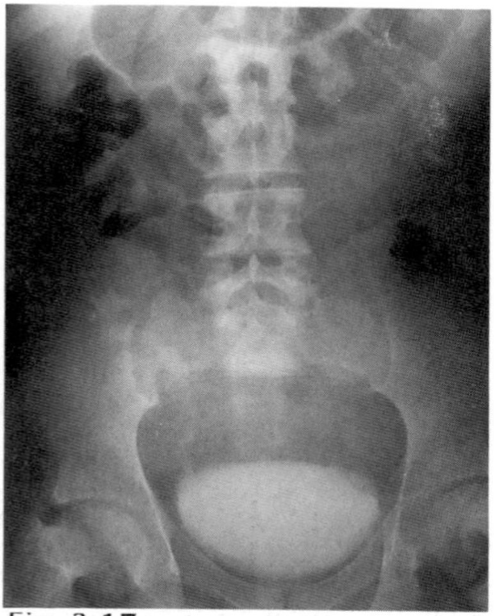

Fig. 3.17c

2.   *(Figure 3.17b)*
(a)   What is this investigation?
(b)   What is the abnormality?
(c)   List three causes of this abnormality

3.   *(Figure 3.17c)*
(a)   What is this investigation?
(b)   What are the abnormalities?
(c)   What is the likeliest explanation?

STATION 3.18

Investigation

Shown below are five different IVU films (a) to (e). ((a) is a normal IVU for comparison). Using the table, please indicate the abnormalities shown and whether they are unilateral (and the side) or bilateral. In each case you should try to give one cause or diagnosis for the abnormality.

(5 minute station)

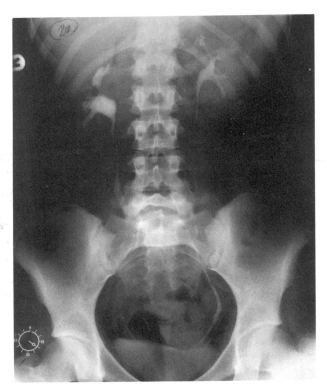

Fig. 3.18a

IVU	Unilateral abnormality Right/Left	Bilateral abnormality	Description of abnormality	Cause or diagnosis
3.18b				
3.18c				
3.18d				
3.18e				

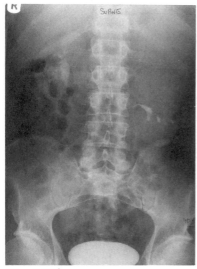

Fig. 3.18b

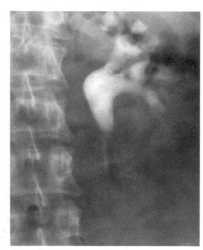

Fig. 3.18c

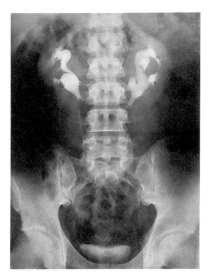

Fig. 3.18d

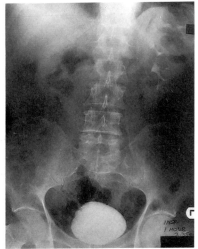

Fig. 3.18e

STATION 3.19

Investigation

Please label this CT scan of the abdomen.

(5 minute station)

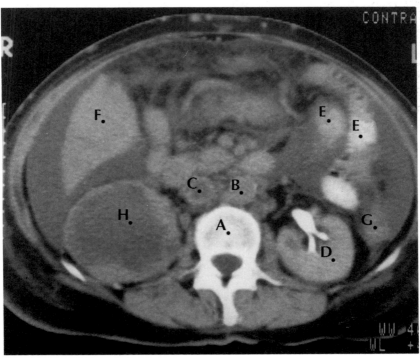

Fig. 3.19

Answers

(A)   (E)

(B)   (F)

(C)   (G)

(D)   (H)

STATION 3.20

Investigation

Figure 3.20a shows the normal recording obtained from an investigation of the urinary tract.

(5 minute station)

Fig. 3.20a

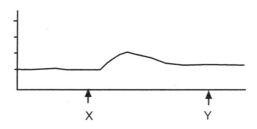

Fig. 3.20b

1. Name the investigation
2. List three pathological states requiring this investigation
3. Please label the axes in figures 3.20a and 3.20b
4. In figure 3.20b state what happens at points X and Y.

STATION 3.21

Therapeutics

You will need a copy of the British National Formulary (BNF) to answer this station.

You are the house officer in general medical outpatients. The next patient is a 69-year-old NIDDM with known IHD and mild renal impairment. She tells you that she has been non-specifically unwell recently with nausea, dizziness on standing and a cough.

(10 minute station)

U+Es 2 months ago: Na^+ 132, K^+ 4.5, HCO_3^- 20, Ur 11.7, Cr 245
U+Es Yesterday: Na^+ 127, K^+ 3.1, HCO_3^- 18, Ur 23.2, Cr 468

Medications -   Gliclazide 160 mg bd
Acarbose 50 mg bd
Enalapril 10 mg bd
Diclofenac 50 mg tds
Aspirin 150 mg bd
Bumetanide 3 mg od
Omeprazole 20 mg nocte
Amoxycillin 500 mg tds (started by her GP 5 days ago)
GTN spray 1–2 puffs prn

Using the BNF provided and your own knowledge, answer the following questions.

1. Which of the medications could be worsening her renal function?
2. List two drugs that may affect her diabetic control
3. List three of her drugs that may directly be causing the nausea
4. List four drugs that may be contributing to her dizziness on standing
5. List five investigations that you would request after her admission

STATION 3.22

Therapeutics

The medications listed below are all used in renal tract disease. Please match the medication with the correct patient history and the relevant clinical information.

(5 minute station)

Patient history	Drug action	Medication
1. 73-year-old man with BPH	(A) ACE inhibitor	(a) Epoetin alpha
2. 29-year-old woman with CRF and a normochromic, normocytic anaemia	(B) Antiandrogen	(b) Allopurinol
3. 69-year-old man with prostatic carcinoma	(C) Anticholinergic	(c) Finasteride
4. 81-year-old woman with urinary incontinence. Post micturition residual <100mls	(D) 5α reductase inhibitor	(d) Quinapril
5. 32-year-old man with IDDM and diabetic nephropathy	(E) Xanthine oxidase inhibitor	(e) Cyproterone
6. 55-year-old man with lymphoma and hyperuricaemia	(F) Replacement for human erythropoietin	(f) Oxybutynin

Answers

1. ( ) ( )
2. ( ) ( )
3. ( ) ( )

4. ( ) ( )
5. ( ) ( )
6. ( ) ( )

STATION 3.23

Procedure

Please catheterize this patient (manikin) who is in urinary retention.

(5 minute station)

Equipment provided (figure 3.23, page 145):
Catheterization model, catheter trolley containing antiseptic cleansing fluid, sterile drapes, Foley size 12 urethral catheter, lubricant, forceps, catheter bag with tubing, sterile gloves, 10 ml syringe with 10 ml ampule of normal saline.

STATION 3.24

Procedure

Figure 3.24 (see page 145) shows the components of an appliance laid out for a surgical procedure.

(5 minute station)

1. Name items A, B and C
2. Name the procedure the appliance is used for
3. State the clinical diagnosis that requires this procedure
4. Name an important clinical prerequisite prior to performing this procedure

STATION 3.25

History/Consent

A married couple attend the Urology Clinic with a request for a vasectomy. In order to complete the consent form for the procedure, take a relevant history from the couple.

(5 minute station)

4: OBSTETRICS AND GYNAECOLOGY

INTRODUCTION

Obstetric History

- **Previous pregnancies**
  Number
  Successful deliveries
  Miscarriages
  Abortions – spontaneous and planned terminations.
  A full term pregnancy is regarded as 40 weeks, with the duration of the pregnancy written as a division of this, e.g. a pregnancy of 22 weeks and 3 days is written $\dfrac{22^{+3}}{40}$

- **Number of children and ages**
  Gravidity, G, describes the number of times a woman has been pregnant.
  Parity, P, describes the number of pregnancies that have proceeded after 28 weeks (x) and those that terminated before (y) i.e. P=x+y. A woman who has had 2 terminations, 2 miscarriages before 28 weeks and 1 full term delivery, and who is now expecting her second child is described as G6, P1 + 4.

- **Antenatal problems**
  Hypertension
  Diabetes
  Heart disease
  Polyhydramnios
  Intrauterine death
  Family history/previous history of multiple pregnancies

- **Method of delivery**
  Normal vaginal delivery
  Forceps/vacuum extraction
  Caesarean section

- **Birth weight**

- **Perinatal problems**
  Mother and baby
  Congenital abnormalities

Antenatal/postnatal haemorrhage
Last normal menstrual cycle/period (LNMP)
Last sexual intercourse
Fertility treatment
Methods of contraception/planning of pregnancy

- **Symptoms of early pregnancy**
  Amenorrhoea
  Breast engorgement
  Nausea and vomiting (hyperemesis gravidarum)
  Associated urinary symptoms

  Feelings of patient and partner about pregnancy

Gynaecological History

Menarche: age of onset of menstruation, usually between 10 and 16 years old.

Normal menstrual cycle, expressed as: Duration of menstrual bleeding
                                                                    Duration from start of one
                                                                    normal menstruation to the
                                                                    start of the next

e.g. 3-4
        24-26

Dysmenorrhoea: painful periods.

Menorrhagia: heavy menstrual bleeding defined by the number of days of bleeding, number of towels and tampons used, volume of blood and clots passed.

Polymenorrhagia: frequent heavy bleeding.

Oligomenorrhoea: infrequent menstruation.

Amenorrhoea: absence of menstruation; this may be primary or secondary. Primary applies to girls who have passed pubescent age and have not menstruated. Secondary applies to female patients who have experienced menstruation which has subsequently stopped.

Causes of amenorrhoea
Hypothalamic: Kallman's syndrome (isolated LHRH deficiency).
Pituitary: prolactinoma; large pituitary tumours causing loss of pituitary function, or those interfering with the pituitary stalk causing hyperprolactinaemia.
Ovarian: benign and malignant tumours, polycystic ovary syndrome.
Vaginal: imperforate hymen, vaginal stenosis.
General: anorexia nervosa, severe illness, testicular feminization, thyroid dysfunction, endurance athletes e.g. marathon and triathletes.

Intermenstrual bleeding: may be secondary to infection, cervical polyp or carcinoma.

Post coital bleeding: causes include cervical erosion/infection, trauma and malignancy.

Vaginal discharge: types; physiological, infective, erosive or neoplastic. Nature and duration. Association with menstrual cycle or intercourse.

Vaginal bleeding: types; physiological, erosive, neoplastic. Menstrual abnormalities. Post-coital.

Cervical smear: last smear date, result, family history of cervical carcinoma.

Premenstrual syndrome (PMS): this is a cyclical pattern of symptoms experienced by a woman prior to menstruation. Common symptoms include bloating, breast tenderness, irritability, labile mood, fluid retention and headache.

Sexual history: includes number of partners and sexual contacts, contraceptive method, terminations of pregnancies (abortions), sexually transmissable diseases/pelvic inflammatory disease.

Dyspareunia: pain on sexual intercourse; may be superficial, due to local infection or atrophic vaginitis, or deep, due to pelvic inflammatory disease or endometriosis.

Menopause: this is when a woman stops menstruating. There is often a period around this time when a woman will have infrequent periods and suffer with symptoms of increasing oestrogen deficiency. This is known as the climacteric. Symptoms include hot flushes, palpitations and atrophic vaginitis. Symptoms of oestrogen deficiency are improved by hormone replacement therapy, which also reduces the risks of developing atherosclerotic disease and osteoporosis.

Post menopausal bleeding: this must be regarded as carcinoma of the uterus or cervix until proven otherwise.

Examination

• **Gynaecological**
Abdominal palpation for pelvic masses or tenderness
Bimanual pelvic examination
Speculum examination should precede digital examination if there is a history of vaginal discharge or bleeding

• **Obstetric**
Fundal height after first trimester should correspond to the period of amenorrhoea
Determine foetal position at near term and auscultate for foetal heart rate
Vaginal examination when indicated to be done by obstetrician; it should be avoided in the first trimester.

STATION 4.1 *(Answers – page 264)*

History

A 27-year-old woman sees you, her GP, on her first antenatal visit. Please take her history.

(5 minute station)

STATION 4.2

History

A 29-year-old woman seeks an urgent consultation with you, her GP. She is worried that she may be pregnant. Please take a history.

(5 minute station)

STATION 4.3

History

The same patient as in Station 4.2 is found to have a positive pregnancy test. Please counsel her on her pregnancy, and elicit her underlying concerns.

(5 minute station)

STATION 4.4

Preparatory

Please read through the following information before attempting the next station.

(5 minute station)

You are the house officer attached to an obstetric and gynaecology firm. The next patient is a 24-year-old primigravida who is returning to the antenatal clinic one week after an oral glucose tolerance test, the results of which are shown below:

Glucose tolerance test
Ms. Phoebe Oxley DOB 13.01.74
Unit no. 098456

0 mins – 6.8 mmol/l
30 mins – 10.9 mmol/l
120 mins – 15.5 mmol/l

STATION 4.4a

History

The 24-year-old primigravida is attending the antenatal clinic today for the results of her glucose tolerance test.

Please explain the results, implications and management to the patient.

(5 minute station)

STATION 4.5

Preparatory

Please read through the following information before attempting the next station.

(5 minute station)

You are a medical student attached to a general practitioner. The next patient is 34 weeks pregnant and is under shared care between the hospital and the GP. She has been under weekly review because her blood pressure has been raised, as shown below. The practice nurse has measured her blood pressure and performed a urinalysis, the results of which are shown.

Please explain the results to the patient, the implications to the mother and child, and the course of management you would advise.

CWD = consistent with dates; NAD = no abnormality detected

Date	Week	Fundal Height	BP	Urinalysis
12.4	32^{+4}	CWD	155/87	NAD
17.4	33^{+2}	CWD	162/78	NAD
22.4 (today)	34^{+2}	CWD	187/98	Protein/++

STATION 4.5a

History

The patient is 34 weeks pregnant and has been under weekly review because her blood pressure has been quite high.

Please explain the results of today's blood pressure and urinalysis to her, the implications to her and her baby and the management you think should be followed.

(5 minute station)

STATION 4.6

History

You are the medical student attached to an antenatal clinic. The next patient is a 24-year-old primigravida who had a routine ultrasound at 20 weeks gestation which showed a low lying placenta. She had a repeat scan at 34 weeks gestation, yesterday, which shows the placenta lying anteriorly in the lower segment and covering the os.

Please explain the ultrasound findings to her and the future management.

(5 minute station)

STATION 4.7

History

A 20-year-old primigravida wishes to be informed and reassured on pain relief during her prospective labour and childbirth. How would you, a doctor at the antenatal clinic, enquire after her concerns and counsel her?

(5 minute station)

STATION 4.8

History

A 25-year-old woman and her partner arrange to see you, a member of their obstetric team, following the stillbirth of their first child. Please answer their questions and discuss future pregnancies.

(10 minute station)

They ask the following questions:

1. Why did it happen?
2. Were there any mistakes in my care that led to this?
3. Will it happen again?
4. When can we try for a baby again?
5. Would I be monitored more closely and admitted sooner, when I am pregnant again?

Please attempt to answer these questions in a compassionate and professional manner.

STATION 4.9

Examination

Examine this patient (manikin) attending the antenatal clinic in her 36th week of pregnancy. (A vaginal examination is to be deferred until the onset of labour.)

(5 minute station)

Equipment provided:
A 'pregnant' manikin, sphygmomanometer, foetal stethoscope.

STATION 4.10

Investigation

Figures 4.10a, b and c are foetal cardiotocographs (CTGs) taken as labour progressed in a 27-year-old primigravida. Comment on each of the tracings and the underlying factors producing the changes.

(5 minute station)

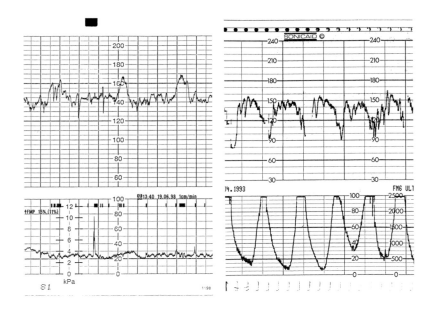

Fig. 4.10a   Fig. 4.10b

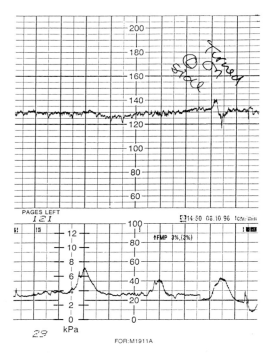

Fig. 4.10c

STATION 4.11

Examination

Please complete the following Apgar score table of the newborn infant.

(5 minute station)

Apgar Score Table

	0	1	2
Colour			
Heart rate			
Respiratory effort			
Muscle tone movement			
Reflex response			

STATION 4.12

Examination

Please perform a clinical examination of the newborn baby (represented by a manikin) to detect any abnormalities that may have been missed soon after birth.

(5 minute station)

STATION 4.13

Treatment

Please demonstrate on the model, using the equipment provided, the resuscitation procedure in a neonate born in an asphyxiated condition.

(10 minute station)

Materials provided:
 Manikin for neonatal cardio-respiratory resuscitation
 Resuscitation (tilt) trolley
 Piped 100% oxygen and suction source, face mask, ambu-bag and tubing
 Oro-pharyngeal intubation set
 Heart rate monitor
 Sodium bicarbonate ampule, with 2 ml syringe, venous IV catheter set
 Mechanical ventilator
 Blankets, heating pad

STATION 4.14

History

You are a medical student attached to a gynaecology outpatient clinic. The next patient is a 19-year-old student, who has been referred by her GP for amenorrhoea.

Please take a history of the presenting complaint and any further relevant history with a view to making a diagnosis.

(5 minute station)

STATION 4.15

History

A married couple in their thirties have come to see you, their GP, with difficulty in starting a family. Please take a history from the wife with a view to assessing their infertility problems.

(5 minute station)

You may assume she is alone on this visit; you should be prepared to discuss management options.

STATION 4.16

History

A 33-year-old woman is referred to the gynaecology clinic by her GP for sterilisation. Please take a history in order to assess her request.

(5 minute station)

STATION 4.17

History

A 27-year-old, single woman consults you, her GP, with severe period pains. Please take a history of the presenting complaint with a view to making a diagnosis.

(5 minute station)

STATION 4.18

History

A 45-year-old woman consults you, her GP, with a history of dysfunctional uterine bleeding. Please take a history of the presenting complaint and relevant medical history with a view to making a diagnosis.

(5 minute station)

STATION 4.19

A 27-year-old woman is referred to the gynaecology clinic complaining of a vaginal discharge which, despite the GP's reassurance, continues to trouble the patient. Please take an appropriate history, with a view to making a diagnosis.

(5 minute station)

STATION 4.20

History

Please read the following information before attempting the next station.

You are a medical student attached to a general practitioner's surgery. The next patient is a 34-year-old woman who has returned to see the GP for the results of a cervical smear which she has had recently, and was reported:

'Dyskaryotic squamous cells with enlarged nuclei consistent with a diagnosis of CIN III. A colposcopy and biopsy is advised.'

Please explain the cervical smear report to the patient, address the concerns she expresses and the management involved.

(5 minute station)

STATION 4.21

History

A 58-year-old woman consults you, her GP, complaining of a dragging sensation in her lower abdomen. Please take a history with a view to making a diagnosis.

(5 minute station)

STATION 4.22

Examination

Please carry out a vaginal examination on the pelvic manikin, explaining your actions to the observer as you proceed. You are not required to perform a smear test or pass a speculum.

(5 minute station)

STATION 4.23

Examination

1. Please name the instruments labelled A and B in Figure 4.23 (see page 146).
2. State the use of each instrument.
3. State 2 common but different lesions that can be identified by using each instrument.

(5 minute station)

STATION 4.24

Examination

Please perform a cervical smear on the pelvic manikin, using the appliances provided in Figure 4.24 (see page 146). You should explain your actions to the observer as you proceed.

(5 minute station)

STATION 4.25

Investigation

A 31-year-old woman complains of vaginal irritation and discharge. She was found to be infected by organisms as shown in Figures 4.25a and 4.25b.

(5 minute station)

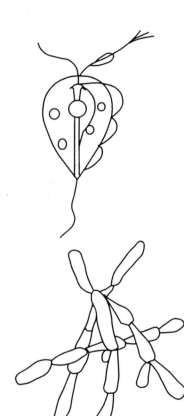

Fig. 4.25a

Fig. 4.25b

1. Name the organisms shown in Figures 4.25a and 4.25b.
2. How would you arrive at an immediate diagnosis?
3. State your treatment measures for Figures 4.25a and 4.25b.
4. What factors predispose to infection with these pathogens.

STATION 4.26

Investigation

Figure 4.26a shows the endometrial changes during the menstrual cycle of a healthy 38-year-old woman not on hormonal therapy. Figure 4.26b shows the concentrations of progesterone, luteinizing hormone, oestradiol and follicle stimulating hormone on the Y axis and the duration of the menstrual cycle on the X axis.

Please complete the last three graphs in Figure 4.26b.

(5 minute station)

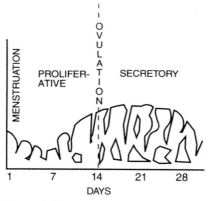

Fig. 4.26a

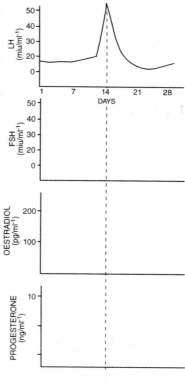

Fig. 4.26b

1. Draw in the curves showing the fluctuations of these hormones during the menstrual cycle.
2. At what point on the graphs would ovulation occur?
3. Indicate the proliferative, secretory and menstrual phases on the graphs.

STATION 4.27

Investigation

Figure 4.27 was obtained as part of the investigation of a 33-year-old woman at the infertility clinic.

(5 minute station)

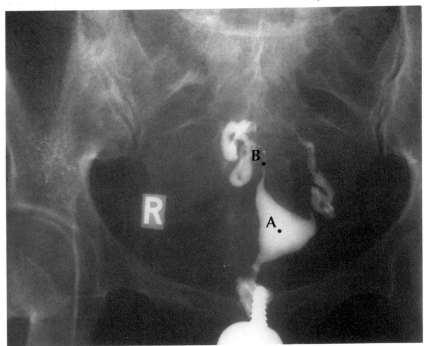

Fig. 4.27

1. Name the investigation performed.
2. State a clinical condition requiring this investigation.
3. Identify the structures labelled A and B.
4. How is this investigation performed?

STATION 4.28

Investigation

A 33-year-old woman was found to have human chorionic gonadotrophin (HCG) levels in excess of 100,000 IU/l in her urine following a miscarriage at 20 weeks. Figure 4.28 is her chest radiograph.

(5 minute station)

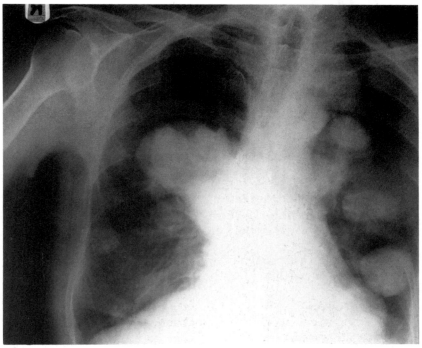

Fig. 4.28

1. State three causes of elevated urinary HCG levels during or following a pregnancy.
2. State the positive finding on the radiograph and your diagnosis.
3. How would you treat this patient?

RHEUMATOLOGY

Arthritis
- Acute arthritis:
  erythema, an increase in temperature, swelling and pain of a joint/joints.
- Chronic arthritis:
  deformity and pain

Arthritis may also present with acute on chronic disease.

- Age of onset: childhood, adolescent, adult

- Patterns: symmetry versus asymmetry, monoarticular versus polyarthropathy

- Small joint involvement
  Proximal interphalangeal joints: rheumatoid arthritis, psoriatic arthropathy
  Distal interphalangeal joints: osteoarthritis, gout, psoriasis

- Large joint involvement: osteoarthritis

- Sacro-ileitis: associated with HLA B27diseases, psoriasis, inflammatory bowel disease, ankylosing spondylitis

- Early morning stiffness: characteristic of rheumatoid and ankylosing spondylitis

Multisystem disease
Many arthritides are multisystem diseases and one should ask the patient about specific systems involvement. Many of these systemic diseases present with non-specific symptoms, e.g. malaise, lethargy, fever, myalgia and arthralgia.

- CNS
  Aseptic meningitis
  Hypopituitarism
  Psychiatric symptoms
  Cranial nerve palsies (mononeuritis multiplex)
  Eyes: keratoconjunctivitis, iritis, uveitis, episcleritis

- PNS: mononeuritis multiplex, peripheral neuropathy, spastic paraparesis
- CVS: myocarditis, pericardial effusion, valvular regurgitation, conduction system fibrosis/ECG abnormalities
- RS: pleural effusions, pleuritic pain, fibrosis, pneumonitis
- GIT: dysmotility and dysphagia ; GI bleed secondary to NSAIDs
- Renal: nephrotic syndrome, glomerulonephritis, renal hypertension
- Skin: rashes, e.g. malar rash of SLE; erythema multiforme; psoriasis
  Nail changes: psoriasis; vasculitides
  Raynaud's syndrome: changes of the skin of the digits associated with cold exposure. The digits become painful, cyanosed and then colourless, eventually becoming red.

Activities of daily living
With all arthritides it is important to assess the impact of the arthritis on the patient's everyday functions, particularly mobility, cooking, eating, washing, occupation and handwriting.

DERMATOLOGY

All rashes should be characterised by:
- Site of initial rash
  Peripheral or central
  Flexor or extensor surfaces
- Sites of spread
  Peripheral to central = centripetal
  Central to peripheral = centrifugal
- Erythema
- Macular: flattened lesions
- Papular: raised lesions
- Vesicular vesicles: raised fluid filled lesions
- Blistering: whether tense or shearing
- Scaling
- Plaques
- Pigmentation and depigmentation
- Involvement of:
  Eyes – conjunctivitis
  Mucous membranes – mouth
  Hair/scalp
  Nails
  Genitalia – urethral and vaginal discharge

All pigmented skin lesions should be defined by:

Size: increasing size or previously unrecognised lesions need investigation

Site: sun exposed areas are common sites of melanomas. The palms and soles do not contain melanocytes and are therefore abnormal sites for pigmented lesions. Other sites where pigmented lesions need to be investigated are under the nails, i.e. subungal and the retina.

Surface: ulceration/crusting

Shape: change in margins, rapid enlargement is a sinister sign

Satellite lesions: smaller lesions surrounding the original lesion

Similar distant lesions: skin metastases

Bleeding: spontaneous bleeding from a lesion is sinister

Pruritus: itching of a lesion may be associated with malignant change

Pigmentation: change in the colour of a lesion needs investigation

Lymph nodes: associated lymphadenopathy

Metastases: melanoma commonly metastasise to the brain and the liver

Non-pigmented lesions: amelanotic melanomas may be found in nail beds, palms and soles

Rashes may be manifestations of systemic disease and one should always ask about associated systemic upset.

* Other important factors:
  Drugs/medications
  Allergies – medicines, foods, other environmental factors
  Contacts with similar rash

It is important to take a comprehensive dermatological history, particularly when you do not instantly recognise the rash. If you are able to describe the rash to a dermatologist over the telephone, or a video link, they can often make a diagnosis and give you advice about management.

STATION 5.1 *(Answers – page 306)*

History

You are a medical student attending a rheumatology outpatient clinic. The next patient is a 23-year-old woman who has been referred by her GP with arthritic pains in her hands.

Please take a history of the presenting complaint and any other relevant history with a view to making a diagnosis.

(10 minute station)

STATION 5.2

History

You are a medical student attending a rheumatology outpatient department clinic. The next patient is a 16-year-old schoolboy, who has been referred by his GP with back pain.

Please take a history of the presenting complaint and any other relevant history with a view to making a diagnosis.

(10 minute station)

STATION 5.3

History

You are a medical student attached to a GP practice. The next patient is a 27-year-old woman who has come to see the doctor because of a worsening rash over her cheeks and aching of the joints in her hands.

Please take a history of the presenting complaint, and any other relevant history, with a view to making a diagnosis.

(10 minute station)

STATION 5.4

History

You are a medical student attached to a rheumatology outpatient clinic. The next patient is a 37-year-old woman who has been referred by her GP complaining of painful hands in the cold and increasing difficulties with swallowing.

Please take a history of the presenting complaint and any other relevant history, with a view to making a diagnosis.

(10 minute station)

STATION 5.5

History

You are a medical student attached to a rheumatology outpatient clinic. The next patient is a 25-year-old man, who has been referred by his GP with a hot swollen knee and gritty, sticky eyes.

Please take a history of the presenting complaint, and any other relevant history, with the aim of making a diagnosis.

(5 minute station)

STATION 5.6

History

You are a GP. The next patient is a 65-year-old woman with headaches and shoulder pains. Please take a history of the presenting complaint with a view to making a diagnosis.

(10 minute station)

STATION 5.7

Investigation

A 24-year-old woman is being treated in the rheumatology outpatient clinic for SLE.

Please study the data shown below and then indicate whether the statements are **True** or **False**.

(5 minute station)

FBC: Hb 9.4 , MCV 102, WCC 6.9, Plat 33, retics 5%

U+Es: Na$^+$ 139, K$^+$ 6.8, HCO$_3^-$ 16, Ur 19, Cr 523

Glucose: 4.8

LFTs: Albumin 19, Alk phos 598, AST 235, ALT 310, Bili 28

		True	False
1.	The patient has a macrocytic anaemia	❏	❏
2.	The anaemia is probably due to vitamin B12 deficiency	❏	❏
3.	There is evidence of haemolysis	❏	❏
4.	The patient has a pancytopenia	❏	❏
5.	In SLE the thrombocytopenia is usually due to splenomegaly	❏	❏
6.	The renal function indicates pre-renal impairment	❏	❏
7.	The hyperkalaemia indicates acute on chronic renal failure	❏	❏
8.	A cause of renal failure in this patient is glomerulonephritis	❏	❏
9.	The albumin is consistent with a nephrotic syndrome	❏	❏
10.	This patient has a metabolic alkalosis	❏	❏
11.	The LFTs indicate a predominantly hepatitic jaundice	❏	❏
12.	Gallstones commonly produce the pattern of LFTs shown	❏	❏

	True	False
13. The LFTs may be deranged due to the drug therapy	❏	❏
14. The haemolysis accounts for some of the hyperbilirubinaemia	❏	❏
15. The patient should have a CT scan of the abdomen as a matter of urgency	❏	❏

STATION 5.8

Investigation

Please match the patient histories with the corresponding diagnoses and immune markers.

(5 minute station)

Patient history	Diagnosis	Immune marker
1. A 34-year-old woman with a symmetrical erosive polyarthropathy and subcutaneous nodules	(A) Diffuse cutaneous systemic sclerosis	(a) Anti – Jo
2. A 23-year-old woman with a photosensitive rash and pleurisy	(B) Microscopic polyangiitis	(b) Anti-proteinase 3
3. A 43-year-old man with a cough, haematuria and a nasal discharge	(C) Polymyositis	(c) Anti-DS DNA
4. A 29-year-old man with Raynaud's phenomenon, exertional dyspnoea and renal hypertension	(D) Rheumatoid arthritis	(d) Anti SCL-70
5. A 54-year-old with pain and weakness in pelvic and shoulder girdle muscles	(E) SLE	(e) P-ANCA
6. A 35-year-old woman with purpura, nephrotic syndrome, pleurisy and haemoptysis	(F) Wegener's granulomatosis	(f) IgM against IgG

Answers

1. ( ) ( )
2. ( ) ( )
3. ( ) ( )

4. ( ) ( )
5. ( ) ( )
6. ( ) ( )

STATION 5.9

Please match the patient histories with the corresponding diagnosis and HLA association.

(5 minute station)

Patient history

1. A 32-year-old man with uveitis, oral and genital ulcers, arthralgia and erythema nodosum

2. A 21-year-old woman with an acute arthritis of the right knee, urethritis and conjunctivitis after an acute diarrhoeal illness

3. A 31-year-old woman with a symmetrical polyarthropathy, parotitis, dry eyes and mouth

4. A 45-year-old woman with a symmetrical erosive polyarthropathy, pulmonary fibrosis and mononeuritis multiplex

5. A 38-year-old woman with calcinosis, Raynaud's phenomenon, swollen fingers, telangiectasia and dysphagia

Diagnosis

(A) Sjögren's syndrome

(B) Rheumatoid arthritis

(C) Limited cutaneous systemic sclerosis

(D) Behçet's disease

(E) Reiter's syndrome

HLA association

(a) HLA DR4

(b) HLA B27

(c) HLA DR3

(d) HLA DR1 (DQ5)

(e) HLA B51

Answers

1. ( ) ( )
2. ( ) ( )
3. ( ) ( )

4. ( ) ( )
5. ( ) ( )

STATION 5.10

Investigation

Please match the patient histories with the joint aspirate results and the correct diagnosis.

(5 minute station)

Patient history

1. A 27-year-old woman with acute arthritis of the right knee, severe headache and a purpuric rash

2. A 51-year-old bank manager with an acutely inflamed interphalangeal joint of the left big toe

3. A 39-year-old woman with acutely inflamed right knee and intra-articular calcification on the X-ray

4. A 12-year-old school boy with factor VIII deficiency and a swollen painful left knee

5. A 31-year-old man with an acute swelling of the left knee, conjunctivitis and penile discharge

Diagnosis

(A) Heavily blood-stained fluid

(B) Positively birefringent crystals

(C) Aseptic tap laden with neutrophils

(D) Gram positive intracellular diplococci

(E) Negatively birefringent crystals

HLA association

(a) Gout

(b) Spontaneous haemarthrosis

(c) Meningococcal septic arthritis

(d) Reiter's syndrome

(e) Pyrophosphate arthropathy

Answers

1. ( ) ( )
2. ( ) ( )
3. ( ) ( )

4. ( ) ( )
5. ( ) ( )

STATION 5.11

Investigation

Please indicate whether the statements about the radiographs shown below are **True** or **False**.

(5 minute station)

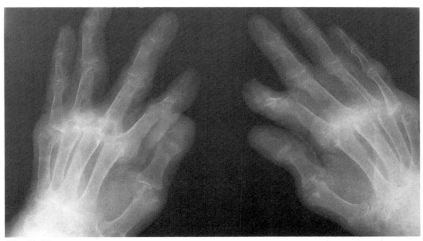

Fig 5.11a

		True	False
1.	*(Figure 5.11a)*		
(a)	The radiograph shows periarticular erosions	❑	❑
(b)	The arthritis is usually asymmetrical	❑	❑
(c)	The MCP joints are unaffected	❑	❑
(d)	The arthropathy principally affects the DIP joints	❑	❑
(e)	These changes may arise in psoriatic arthropathy	❑	❑

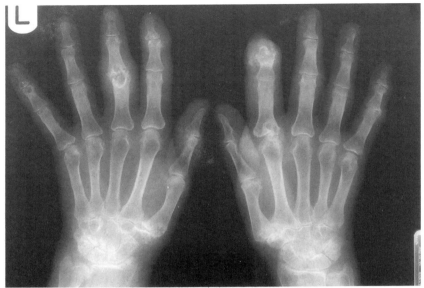

Fig. 5.11b

2. *(Figure 5.11b)*   **True**   **False**
(a) The radiograph shows evidence of
     periarticular sclerosis   ❑   ❑
(b) The arthropathy principally affects the DIP
     joints   ❑   ❑
(c) This arthropathy is associated with intra-
     articular calcification   ❑   ❑
(d) The radiograph shows ulnar deviation of
     the digits   ❑   ❑
(e) The changes are consistent with pyrophosphate
     arthropathy   ❑   ❑

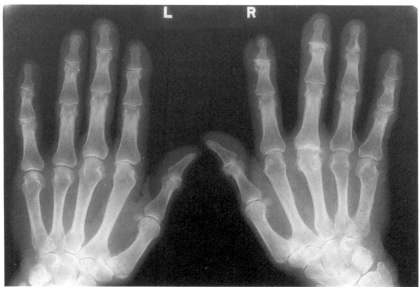

Fig. 5.11c

3.	*(Figure 5.11c)*	True	False
(a)	The radiograph shows evidence of osteopaenia	❏	❏
(b)	The arthropathy shown is associated with periarticular cysts	❏	❏
(c)	The arthropathy principally affects the PIP joints	❏	❏
(d)	There is an association with HLA B27	❏	❏
(e)	The changes are consistent with an erosive arthropathy	❏	❏

STATION 5.12

Investigation

Please indicate whether the statements about each of the radiographs shown below are **True** or **False**.

(5 minute station)

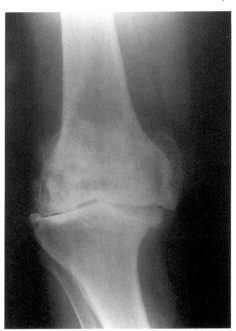

Fig. 5.12a

1. *(Figure 5.12a)*	True	False
(a) There is relative sparing of the patello femoral joint	❏	❏
(b) There are several osteophytes	❏	❏
(c) There is evidence of periarticular sclerosis	❏	❏
(d) This disorder should be treated with immunosuppressants	❏	❏
(e) The changes are consistent with a diagnosis of rheumatoid arthritis	❏	❏

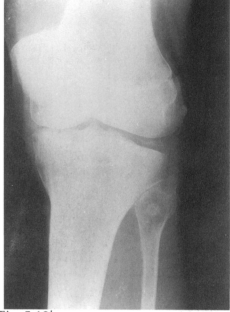

Fig. 5.12b

2.	*(Figure 5.12b)*	True	False
(a)	The changes shown are usually symmetrical	❑	❑
(b)	The crystals within the joint are positively birefringent under polarised light	❑	❑
(c)	There is loss of medial joint space	❑	❑
(d)	There is evidence of periarticular cysts	❑	❑
(e)	One cause of the intra-articular changes seen is hyperparathyroidism	❑	❑

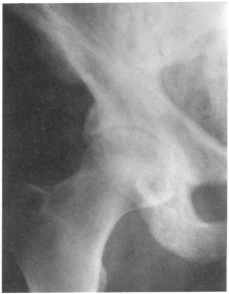

Fig. 5.12c

3. *(Figure 5.12c)*	True	False
(a) The radiograph shows evidence of cortical thinning and osteopenia	❏	❏
(b) The patient will have a normal serum calcium and phosphate	❏	❏
(c) There is evidence of petrusio acetabulum	❏	❏
(d) The patient has evidence of a pathological fracture	❏	❏
(e) The patient is at increased risk of deafness	❏	❏

STATION 5.13

Investigation

Please indicate whether the statements about the radiographs shown below are **True** or **False**.

(5 minute station)

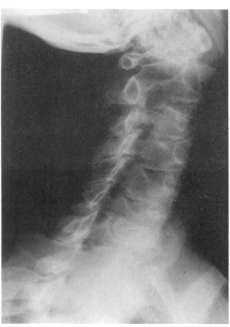

Fig. 5.13a

		True	False
1.	*(Figure 5.13a)*		
(a)	This a lateral radiograph of the cervical spine	❑	❑
(b)	All 7 cervical vertebrae are shown	❑	❑
(c)	There is evidence of osteophyte formation	❑	❑
(d)	The radiograph shows disc space narrowing between C6 and C7	❑	❑
(e)	There is evidence of cervical osteosclerosis	❑	❑

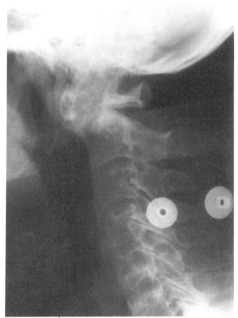

Fig. 5.13b

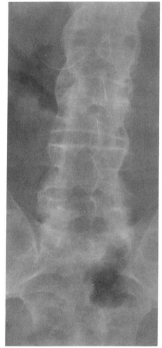

Fig. 5.13c

2.	*(Figure 5.13b)*	True	False
(a)	The radiograph shows evidence of soft tissue injury	❑	❑
(b)	There is loss of height of C3	❑	❑
(c)	The patient is wearing a cervical collar	❑	❑
(d)	The condition shown is a recognised complication of rheumatoid arthritis	❑	❑
(e)	There is a risk of tetraplegia	❑	❑

3.	*(Figure 5.13c)*	True	False
(a)	The radiograph shows ligamentous ossification	❑	❑
(b)	There are syndesmophytes	❑	❑
(c)	The radiograph shows evidence of sacroiliitis and ankylosis	❑	❑
(d)	There are osteophytes	❑	❑
(e)	This disorder is associated with HLA DR4	❑	❑

STATION 5.14

Investigation

Please answer the questions below regarding each of the investigations.

(5 minute station)

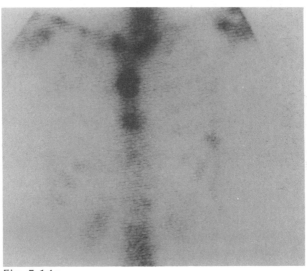

Fig. 5.14a

1. *(Figure 5.14a)*
(a) What is this investigation?
(b) What are the principal abnormalities shown?
(c) What are the treatment options?

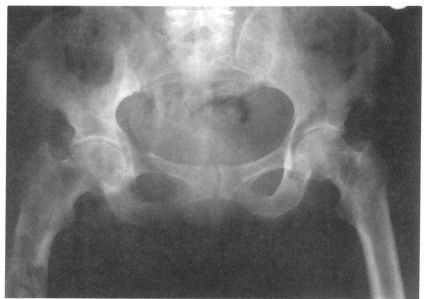

Fig. 5.14b

2.   *(Figure 5.14b)*
(a)   What is this investigation?
(b)   What abnormality does it show?
(c)   List two possible causes

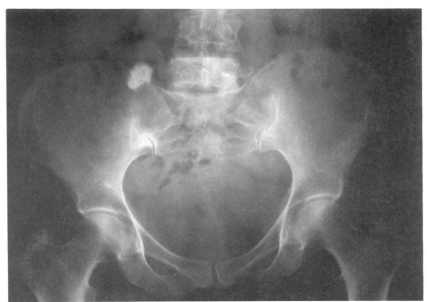

Fig. 5.14c

3. *(Figure 5.14c)*
(a) What is this investigation?
(b) What abnormalities are shown?
(c) List three common causes

STATION 5.15

Therapeutics

All of the patients listed below are attending the rheumatology clinic. Please match the patient histories with the drug therapies and the most commonly associated complication.

(5 minute station)

Patient history	Complication	Drug therapy
1. A 27-year-old woman with systemic sclerosis now presenting with fatigue and bilateral ptosis	(A) Neutrophilia and thrombocytopenia	(a) Allopurinol
2. A 31-year-old man with rheumatoid arthritis presenting with poor urinary output and peripheral oedema	(B) Corneal opacities	(b) Sulphasalazine
3. A 41-year-old man with severe SLE presenting with acute abdominal pain	(C) Peripheral neuropathy	(c) Methotrexate
4. A 37-year-old woman with rheumatoid arthritis, presenting with recurrent infections and spontaneous bruising	(D) Myasthenic syndrome	(d) Hydroxy-chloroquine
5. A 49-year-old man with rheumatoid arthritis and increasing exertional dyspnoea	(E) Nephrotic syndrome	(e) Azathioprine
6. A 61-year-old man with severe gout now presenting with pins and needles in the hands and feet	(F) Acute pancreatitis	(f) Gold
7. A 42-year-old man with primary Sjögren's syndrome and worsening visual acuity	(G) Pulmonary fibrosis	(g) D-penicillamine

Answers

1. ( ) ( )
2. ( ) ( )
3. ( ) ( )
4. ( ) ( )

5. ( ) ( )
6. ( ) ( )
7. ( ) ( )

STATION 5.16

History

You are the medical student attached to a dermatology clinic. The next patient is a 36-year-old woman who presents with the rash shown in figure 5.16 (see page 146). Please take a history of the presenting complaint with a view to making a diagnosis.

(10 minute station)

STATION 5.17

History

You are a GP. The next patient is a 24-year-old woman with a fair complexion and multiple 'freckles'. She would like you to look at one of the freckles on her thigh shown in figure 5.17 (see page 146), which has become unsightly. Please take a history to assess this lesion with a view to referring her to a dermatologist.

(5 minute station)

STATION 5.18

Examination

The patients shown in figures 5.18a–d (see page 146) all have nail disorders. Please indicate whether the statements regarding each picture are **True** or **False**.

(5 minute station)

		True	**False**
1.	*(Figure 5.18a)*		
(a)	The nail has an increased angle	❏	❏
(b)	The nail bed will be 'boggy'	❏	❏
(c)	This disorder may be congenital	❏	❏
(d)	A recognised cause is coeliac disease	❏	❏
(e)	This disorder is associated with acromegaly	❏	❏

		True	**False**
2.	*(Figure 5.18b)*		
(a)	This patient shows longitudinal ridging of the nail	❏	❏
(b)	This disorder is associated with squamous cell carcinoma of the lung	❏	❏
(c)	The nail bed is normal	❏	❏
(d)	This disorder is associated with HLA B27	❏	❏
(e)	This disorder is associated with thyroid disease	❏	❏

		True	**False**
3.	*(Figure 5.18c)*		
(a)	This disorder is caused by a bacterial infection	❏	❏
(b)	There is evidence of nail bed onychogryphosis	❏	❏
(c)	This is an autoimmune disorder	❏	❏
(d)	The disorder shown is associated with carcinoma of the stomach	❏	❏
(e)	The disorder shown is benign	❏	❏

		True	**False**
4.	*(Figure 5.18d)*		
(a)	The nail shows evidence of pitting and ridging	❏	❏
(b)	The nail bed is fluctuant	❏	❏
(c)	The patient may have subcutaneous nodules	❏	❏
(d)	The patient may have plaques over the flexor surfaces of their elbows	❏	❏
(e)	This patient has increased chance of being HLA B27 positive	❏	❏

STATION 5.19

Therapeutics

Preparatory

Please read the information below carefully prior to attempting the next station.

(5 minute station)

You are a house officer attached to a dermatology firm. You have been requested by your registrar to explain PUVA treatment to a patient with poorly controlled psoriasis. You should mention the following:

PUVA consists of 2 elements:

(a) **Psoralen:** taken as a tablet 2 hours prior to therapy. It sensitises the skin to UV radiation and care must be taken after each course of treatment to avoid exposure to sunlight.

(b) **UVA:** this is ultraviolet radiation, similar to that of the sun. It is delivered by a system similar to a sun lamp.

Each course of treatment consists of 2 sessions per week and will run for 2 to 6 weeks depending on the resolution of the rash.

Benefits: relatively free from side-effects; providing patients follow directions given at each session, short and long term side-effects are relatively rare.

Side-effects

Short term: skin sensitivity to sunlight - post treatment sun burn

Long term: (particularly with repeated courses of treatment)

Cataracts - patient must wear protective goggles

Premature ageing of skin

Rarely: increased risk of skin cancers

STATION 5.19a

Therapeutics

You are the house officer attached to a dermatology firm. You have been asked to explain PUVA treatment to a 43-year-old inpatient, who has poorly controlled psoriasis.

(5 minute station)

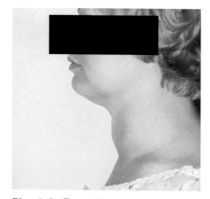

Fig. 1.9 (Page 7)

Fig. 1.10a (Page 8)

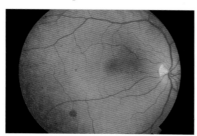

Fig. 1.11a (Page 8)

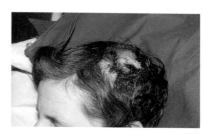

Fig. 1.10b (Page 8)

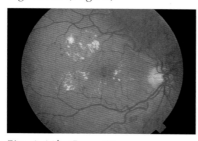

Fig. 1.11b (Page 8)

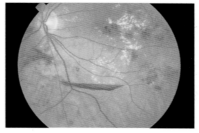

Fig. 1.11c (Page 8)

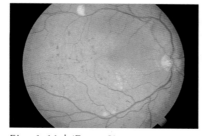

Fig. 1.11d (Page 8)

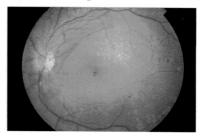

Fig. 1.11e (Page 8)

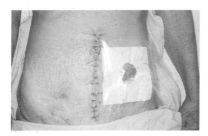

Fig. 2.11 (Page 42)

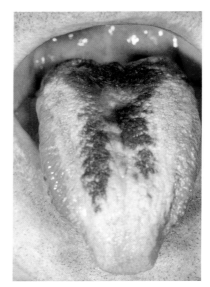

Fig. 2.12a (Page 42)

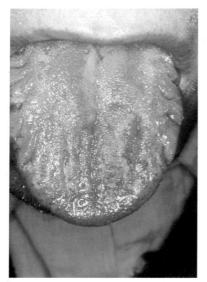

Fig. 2.12b (Page 42)

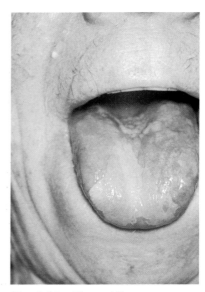

Fig. 2.12c (Page 42)

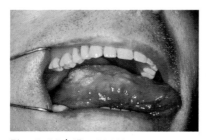

Fig. 2.12d (Page 42)

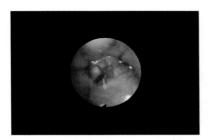

Fig. 2.13a (Page 43)

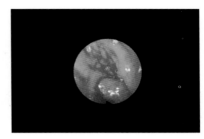

Fig. 2.13b (Page 43)

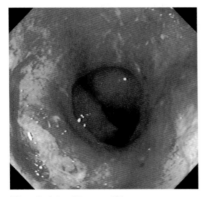

Fig. 2.14a (Page 43)

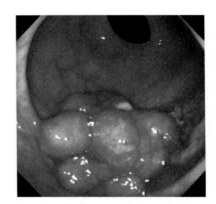

Fig. 2.14b (Page 43)

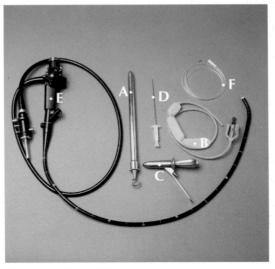

Fig. 2.30 (Page 68)

143

Fig. 3.7a (Page 73)

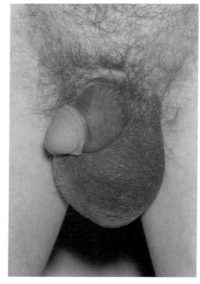

Fig. 3.7b (Page 73)

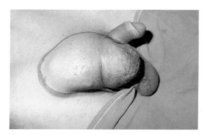

Fig. 3.7c (Page 73)

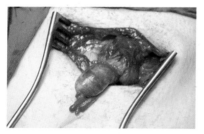

Fig. 3.7d (Page 73)

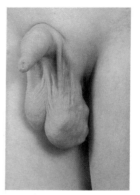

Fig. 3.7e (Page 73)

144

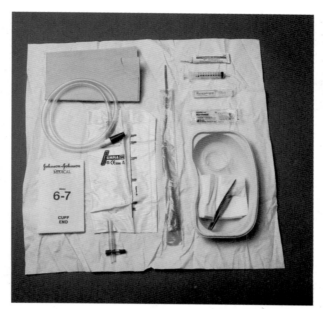

Fig. 3.23 (Page 95)

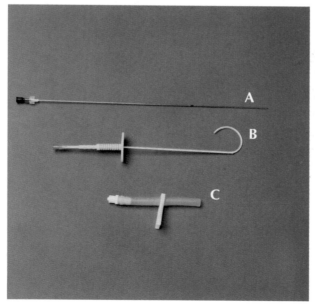

Fig. 3.24 (Page 95)

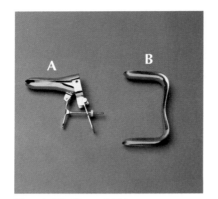

Fig. 4.23 (Page 111)

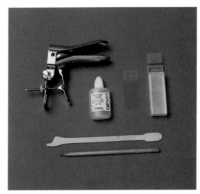

Fig. 4.24 (Page 111)

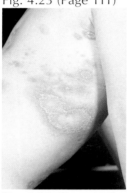

Fig. 5.16 (Page 137)

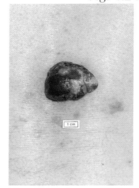

Fig. 5.17 (Page 137)

Fig. 5.18a (Page 137)

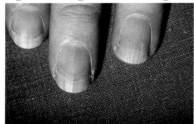

Fig. 5.18b
(Page 138)

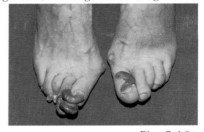

Fig. 5.18c
(Page 138)

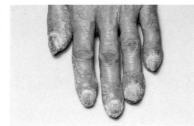

Fig. 5.18d
(Page 138)

146

STATION 1.1

Patient history

I am a 25-year-old engineering student, and I have been unwell for 4 to 5 months. Initially I had a headache in the front of my head, which has slowly worsened, particularly in the mornings. The headache radiates from the front to the top of my head. I do not get nauseated, but along with the headaches I have noticed a loss of peripheral vision which has forced me to give up playing golf and driving a car. In the last month I have had to buy larger shoes and during the recent cold spell, I noticed my gloves were also too small. My girlfriend has commented that "your face seems to be widening" and I have noticed that my teeth don't seem to fit properly inside my mouth. I have not had any other symptoms of note and I am on no regular medicines other than some paracetamol for the headaches. No one in my family has any endocrine or autoimmune diseases.

Assessment

	Good	Adequate	Poor/not done
1. Polite introduction; establishes rapport	❑	❑	❑
2. Establishes the duration of the illness	❑	❑	❑
3. Establishes the presence of local pituitary symptoms:			
Headache: site, radiation, relieving/exacerbating factors	❑	❑	❑
Visual disturbance, in particular loss of peripheral fields	❑	❑	❑
4. Establishes the presence of systemic features of acromegaly:			
Overbiting mandible/enlarged tongue	❑	❑	❑
Change in facial appearance	❑	❑	❑
5. Confirms hands/feet enlargement	❑	❑	❑
Proximal limb weakness	❑	❑	❑
Symptoms of hyperprolactinaemia, e.g. galactorrhoea	❑	❑	❑
Carpal tunnel symptoms	❑	❑	❑
Sweating; skin changes	❑	❑	❑
Symptoms of diabetes mellitus	❑	❑	❑
6. Establishes general features of endocrine disease, e.g. weight changes and sleep problems	❑	❑	❑
7. Excludes family history of endocrine disease	❑	❑	❑
8. Summarises the findings and makes a reasonable attempt at the diagnosis	❑	❑	❑
9. Does all in a fluent, professional manner	❑	❑	❑

Diagnosis

Growth hormone secreting pituitary tumour with local pituitary and systemic features of acromegaly

STATION 1.2

Patient history

I am 21 years old and I have had problems with my periods for the last six months. My periods began when I was 13 and they have generally been regular, lasting 4 to 6 days and coming every 24 to 27 days. My periods have now become increasingly irregular, and now last anything from 1 to 11 days and come every 33 to 45 days. I have never been pregnant and am not using any form of contraception. I have not had sexual intercourse for over a year as my long-term boyfriend is working in the Gulf.

I have recently noticed some milk coming out of my nipples. I have had no headaches or visual problems. I am otherwise generally well, my weight is stable and I am on no medications.

Assessment	Good	Adequate	Poor/not done
1. Polite introduction; establishes rapport	❑	❑	❑
2. Establishes the duration of the present illness	❑	❑	❑
3. Establishes the time of the patient's menarche	❑	❑	❑
4. Establishes her normal menstrual cycle	❑	❑	❑
5. Establishes precise history of menstrual irregularity	❑	❑	❑
6. Establishes obstetric history	❑	❑	❑
7. Establishes method of contraception, if being used	❑	❑	❑
8. Establishes history of associated galactorrhoea	❑	❑	❑
9. Excludes local pituitary symptoms e.g. headache and visual disturbances	❑	❑	❑

	Good	Adequate	Poor/not done
10. Excludes other causes of menstrual problems:			
Pregnancy	❑	❑	❑
Weight loss	❑	❑	❑
Drugs	❑	❑	❑
Stress	❑	❑	❑
Thyroid disease	❑	❑	❑
11. Summarises the findings and makes a reasonable attempt at the diagnosis	❑	❑	❑
12. Does all in a fluent, professional manner	❑	❑	❑

Diagnosis
Prolactinoma – with oligomenorrhoea and galactorrhoea

Comment

Hyperprolactinaemia may be physiological or pathological. Physiological causes include stimulation of the nipples (sexual or suckling), sexual intercourse, pregnancy and stress. Pathological causes incluse micro- and macroadenomas of the pituitary gland, acromegaly, disorders causing interference of the hypothalamic/ pituitary stalk (e.g. suprasellar expansion of a pituitary tumour), polycystic ovary syndrome, hypothyroidism, renal and hepatic failure and idiopathic. Dopaminergic antagonists are a common cause, e.g. metoclopramide and the phenothiazines, as well as other medications e.g. cimetidine and methyl dopa.

Prolactin release is inhibited by dopaminergic control from the hypothalamus. The treatment of pathological causes of hyper-prolactinaemia is, therefore, based on dopamine agonists. Bromocriptine may be given either in tablet or pessary form and is often used as the only treatment in pituitary microadenomas. Bromocriptine has many gastrointestinal side-effects and is being superseded by other dopamine agonists, particularly cabergoline. Lisuride and pergolide are also used.

STATION 1.3

Patient history

I am 34 years old and have previously been fit and well. Over the last 8 to 12 months, I have been unwell with various ailments. Initially I felt lethargic and not myself. Over the next few months I lost weight around the shoulders and hips and it all seemed to collect around my tummy. I have also developed deep purple stripes over my abdomen which are like stretch marks but ten times worse. More recently I have started having problems with hair and spots around my chin. I feel increasingly weak, particularly when standing up from a chair. In the last few weeks I have been permanently thirsty and I am drinking 4 to 5 litres of fluid a day. I have had no headaches or visual disturbances and am otherwise relatively well, with no other specific symptoms. My mother has diabetes and a thyroid problem, as did my grandmother. I am not and never have been on any regular medications.

Assessment

	Good	Adequate	Poor/not done
1. Polite introduction; establishes rapport	❑	❑	❑
2. Establishes the duration of the illness	❑	❑	❑
3. Establishes weight gain, principally around the abdomen	❑	❑	❑
4. Establishes wasting and power loss around the shoulders and hips	❑	❑	❑
5. Confirms the presence of striae, bruising, acne and hirsutism	❑	❑	❑
6. Establishes symptoms of hyperglycaemia	❑	❑	❑
7. Excludes symptoms of local pituitary disease	❑	❑	❑
8. Excludes symptoms of other endocrine disease	❑	❑	❑
9. Establishes family history of endocrine disease	❑	❑	❑
10. Excludes the use of long term steroids	❑	❑	❑
11. Establishes otherwise systemically well	❑	❑	❑
12. Summarises findings and is able to make a reasonable attempt at diagnosis	❑	❑	❑
13. Does all in a fluent, professional manner	❑	❑	❑

Diagnosis
Cushing's disease

STATION 1.4

Patient History

I am 18 years old and over the last year I have been getting increasingly irregular periods. My periods started when I was aged 12 and they were regular, with a cycle of 4 to 5 days every 26 to 28 days until the age of 16 to 17, when I began to put on a lot of weight. In the last year my cycle has become very irregular, lasting 1 to 9 days every 23 to 35 days. I have put on about 15 kilogrammes in the last 18 months and have had a lot of problems with acne and hair growth around the chin and face. I do not have a boyfriend and have had no sexual contact in the last 2 years. I am not on the pill. I am otherwise well and have had no other significant symptoms. I am not on any medications and have no family history of note.

Assessment	Good	Adequate	Poor/not done
1. Polite introduction; establishes rapport	❏	❏	❏
2. Establishes duration of the illness	❏	❏	❏
3. Establishes menarche and normal menstrual cycle	❏	❏	❏
4. Establishes present menstrual cycle	❏	❏	❏
5. Confirms obesity, asks about weight problems	❏	❏	❏
6. Establishes associated history of acne and hirsutism	❏	❏	❏
7. Excludes symptoms of pituitary tumour and hyperprolactinaemia	❏	❏	❏
8. Asks about general symptoms, e.g. loss of libido, sleep	❏	❏	❏
9. Excludes family history of endocrine disease	❏	❏	❏
10. Makes a reasonable attempt at diagnosis	❏	❏	❏
11. Does all in a fluent professional manner	❏	❏	❏

Diagnosis

Polycystic ovary syndrome

Comment

Polycystic ovary syndrome is a common cause of menstrual irregularity, sub-fertility, acne and hirsutism. The principal pathological features are multiple cysts of the ovaries associated with an increase in androgen production by the ovaries and adrenal glands. The initiating mechanism for these processes remains unclear.

The diagnosis is confirmed on ultrasound scan of the ovaries and biochemically by the raised LH:FSH ratio (> 2:1), although the FSH level is often normal or low. Other findings include a raised total androgen level, a low SHBG and hyperprolactinaemia.

It is important to exclude signs of virilization e.g. clitoromegaly, as adrenal carcinoma may present in a similar fashion.

STATION 1.5

Patient history

I am 54 years old and have been fit and well until four months ago. Initially I felt unwell without any specific symptoms, just off colour and tired. More recently I have been unable to concentrate on anything such as watching television or reading the newspaper.

In the last few weeks none of my clothes seem to fit and when I went to the GP, she commented that my weight had increased over 7 kilograms in the last year. I am not eating any more than usual and can't understand how I've put on this amount of weight. I have been constipated recently, which is unusual for me, but I've had no other change in bowel habit. My hair seems very dry and feels terrible.

I have these patches of non-pigmented skin, which my sister and mother both have. My mother also had thyroid gland problems. I am on no medications and am otherwise well.

Assessment	Good	Adequate	Poor/not done
1. Polite introduction; establishes rapport	❏	❏	❏
2. Establishes the duration of the symptoms	❏	❏	❏
3. Establishes nature of 'croaky voice', e.g. complete loss of voice; other speech problems, e.g. dysphasia	❏	❏	❏
4. Excludes stridor and other upper respiratory tract symptoms, e.g. nasal discharge and pharyngitis	❏	❏	❏
5. Quantifies weight gain and dietary habits	❏	❏	❏
6. Establishes other symptoms of hypothyroidism:			
Cold intolerance	❏	❏	❏
Lethargy and malaise	❏	❏	❏
Constipation	❏	❏	❏

	Good	Adequate	Poor/not done
Dry, coarse hair	❑	❑	❑
Poor concentration	❑	❑	❑
7. Establishes history of other autoimmune disease, e.g. pernicious anaemia, vitiligo, diabetes	❑	❑	❑
8. Establishes family history of autoimmune disease	❑	❑	❑
9. Summarises findings and makes a reasonable attempt at the diagnosis	❑	❑	❑
10. Does all in a fluent, professional manner	❑	❑	❑

Diagnosis
Primary hypothyroidism with previous history of vitiligo

Comment

Distinguishing symptoms of thyrotoxicosis
- Heat intolerance
  Patient may feel hot and bothered
  Sweating
- Palpitations; may be a precipitant of atrial fibrillation.
  All patients presenting with atrial fibrillation should have a thyroid function test.
- Diarrhoea
- Weight loss
- Tremor
- Proximal myopathy/weakness

Graves' disease is an autoimmune disease of the thyroid which may present incidentally, with the patient being euthyroid, thyrotoxic or hypothyroid. It is characterised by Graves' eye disease, now termed Graves' orbitopathy, pretibial myxoedema and thyroid acropachy, which is pseudo clubbing of the fingernails, swelling of the distal phalanges and periosteal bone formation.

STATION 1.6

Patient history

I am 54 years old and was diagnosed as having diabetes mellitus 10 years ago when I was admitted with my first myocardial infarction. Subsequently I had a further MI, eight years ago, but have been well since. I test my blood with BM stix on one day in each week at 7 am and then two hours after each meal. The readings usually show 4–7, with occasional 7–11. I stick to the diabetic diet quite strictly and take Gliclazide tablets 80 mg BD. I also take Atenolol 50 mg OD and aspirin 75 mg once a day. Over the last eight years my weight has remained steady at 78 kg, after losing 16 kg in the 18 months after my initial MI. I stopped smoking after my second MI. I previously smoked 20 cigarettes per day. My lipids are normal. I do have the occasional beer but no more than 4 to 5 pints per week. I am otherwise well and have had no eye or foot problems. I have not had any recent angina and have had no other vascular or neurological symptoms. As far as I know my kidneys are working well.

Assessment   **Good Adequate Poor/not done**

		Good	Adequate	Poor/not done
1.	Polite introduction; establishes rapport	❑	❑	❑
2.	Establishes method, frequency and results of testing	❑	❑	❑
3.	Establishes method of control and compliance	❑	❑	❑
4.	Establishes weight control and dietary compliance	❑	❑	❑
5.	Specifically asks about the following complications: *Macrovascular disease:*			
	IHD, CVA, PVD	❑	❑	❑
	Microvascular disease:			
	Retinopathy, nephropathy	❑	❑	❑
	Neuropathic disease:			
	Sensory neuropathy	❑	❑	❑
	Visual problems	❑	❑	❑
	Foot problems	❑	❑	❑
6.	Establishes/excludes associated risk factors, e.g. cigarettes, alcohol excess and hypercholesterolaemia	❑	❑	❑
7.	Establishes frequency and method of follow up at outpatients and GP clinics	❑	❑	❑
8.	Summarises the case in a reasonable manner with the correct deductions	❑	❑	❑
9.	Does all in a fluent, professional manner	❑	❑	❑

STATION 1.7

Patient history

I am 21 years old and work in a factory. Previously I have been well but over the last three to four months I have become increasingly lethargic and have suffered recurrent vaginal candida infections. I have noticed I have been drinking 4 to 5 bottles of diet coke a day and am forever going to pass water. In the last three weeks I have lost about 5 kg in weight and it was this that finally prompted me to go to the local doctor. My grandmother and an uncle on my mother's side both had diabetes and an aunt had thyroid problems. I smoke 20 cigarettes per day and drink between 20 to 30 units of alcohol in the form of vodka and lemonade, mainly at weekends. I don't eat a lot of sweet things and my weight is steady at 61kg. I am 1.65m. I do not do any regular exercise.

Assessment	Good	Adequate	Poor/not done
1. Polite introduction; establishes rapport	❏	❏	❏
2. Establishes the duration of the presenting illness	❏	❏	❏
3. Establishes history of polyuria and polydypsia	❏	❏	❏
4. Establishes history of recurrent vaginal candidiasis	❏	❏	❏
5. Establishes history of recent weight loss	❏	❏	❏
6. Establishes family history of diabetes and thyroid disease	❏	❏	❏
7. Excludes eye, foot and other complications	❏	❏	❏
8. Establishes associated risk factors - alcohol, dietary excess and smoking	❏	❏	❏
9. Summarises the findings and makes the correct diagnosis	❏	❏	❏
10. Is able to discuss future management in an appropriate manner	❏	❏	❏

	Good	**Adequate**	**Poor/not done**
11. Does all in a fluent, professional manner	❏	❏	❏

Diagnosis

Newly diagnosed insulin dependent diabetes mellitus

Comment

Management plan
- Investigations: FBC, U+Es, glucose, HBA1c, lipids, urinalysis to exclude ketonuria, protein and glycosuria

- Examination: Full examination to include ophthalmoscopy and neurological assessment

- Treatment: Admit to hospital and start on insulin; Prior to discharge patient should be able to inject herself with insulin and have a reasonable understanding of the disease and possible complications.

Education principally from diabetic liaison nurse; reinforced by doctors; dietician assessment and education viz:
Dietary planning
Reduce/stop smoking and alcohol excess
Exercise

STATION 1.8

Patient history

I am 21 years old and I have just been told, three days ago, that I have diabetes mellitus. I have seen the dietician and the diabetic liaison sister, who have answered a lot of my questions. I have had a go at injecting myself with insulin but am not too confident as yet. I understand quite a lot about the disorder as my uncle is a diabetic, but he takes tablets. I would particularly like you to tell me:
- Will I always need to take insulin or will I one day be put on tablets instead?
- Will I be able to have children?
- I have heard that diabetics go blind and have strokes. Is this true?

Assessment	Good	Adequate	Poor/not done
1. Polite introduction; establishes rapport	❑	❑	❑
2. Establishes patient's current understanding of the disease	❑	❑	❑
3. Explains in a clear manner:			
What diabetes means	❑	❑	❑
Treatment with insulin	❑	❑	❑
Reinforcement of diet	❑	❑	❑
Blood or urine testing	❑	❑	❑
Possible complications	❑	❑	❑
Importance of compliance	❑	❑	❑
What to do for a 'hypo'	❑	❑	❑
Associated risk factors - alcohol excess and smoking	❑	❑	❑
4. Answers the questions in a satisfactory manner	❑	❑	❑
5. Does all in a fluent, professional manner	❑	❑	❑

STATION 1.9

Assessment	Good	Adequate	Poor/not done
1. Polite introduction; establishes rapport	❏	❏	❏
2. Observes neck of seated patient from front and requests patient to swallow (hands patient a glass of water)	❏	❏	❏
3. Standing behind patient palpates the thyroid gland with both hands, both lobes and isthmus	❏	❏	❏
4. Requests patient to swallow whilst palpating the thyroid gland	❏	❏	❏
5. Percusses manubrium for retrosternal extension and auscultates for bruit	❏	❏	❏
6. Palpates the triangles of the neck and supraclavicular fossae for lymph nodes	❏	❏	❏
7. Performs all in a fluent, professional manner	❏	❏	❏

Comment

Examination of the thyroid gland is an essential skill, which is critically assessed in any clinical examination. Following inspection from the front and side, palpation for the gland and cervical nodes must be commenced from behind. A positive 'swallowing test' must be elicited, as it confirms the swelling as part of the thyroid. Protrusion of the tongue would make a thyro-glossal cyst move upwards. Systemic signs of thyroid disease, including hands (sweaty palms, oncholysis, acropachy), pulse (atrial fibrillation, tachycardia /bradycardia), peripheral myopathy, eye signs (exophthalmos, lid lag, lid retraction, cranial nerve palsies, chemosis) and slow relaxing reflexes, should all be sought.

STATION 1.10

Answers

1. Figure 1.10a: Graves' disease (hyperthyroidism with exophthalmos)
   Figure 1.10b: Follicular carcinoma of thyroid with skull metastases

2. Radioisotope I^{131} scintiscan

3. Figure 1.10a: Exophthalmos-producing substance: a neuroendocrine transmitter secreted in the hypothalamus

   Figure 1.10b: A deposit of follicular carcinoma in the skull from a primary tumour of the thyroid gland

4. Figure 1.10a: Graves' disease: medical control with antithyroid agents with/without subtotal thyroidectomy

   Figure 1.10b: Follicular carcinoma of thyroid: total thyroidectomy with radio-iodine ablation of metastases

Comment

In Graves' disease, hyperthyroidism is due to IgG microsomal antibodies against TSH receptors on the thyroid follicular cell, stimulating thyroid hormone production and goitre formation. Long acting thyroid stimulating antibodies are also present but their role is uncertain.

In follicular carcinoma of the thyroid, blood-borne spread occurs early, and total thyroidectomy, even in the absence of goitre, enables tumour deposits to be targeted by radioiodine therapy.

STATION 1.11

Answers and explanations

1.   (a) False   (b) False   (c) True   (d) False   (e) False
This figure shows evidence of background diabetic retinopathy with blot and dot haemorrhages concentrated in the temporal quadrants. The nasal quadrants are relatively disease free, and the macula and optic disc are normal. These changes mark the onset of microvascular complications and are often associated with early renal damage, characterised by microalbuminuria. Papilloedema is not associated with background retinopathy and remains a sinister sign for which an underlying cause should be sought.

2.   (a) True   (b) False   (c) False   (d) True   (e) False
This figure shows background diabetic retinopathy with added maculopathy. There are blot and dot haemorrhages and several areas of hard exudate including the areas surrounding the macula. Hard exudates have well defined margins and represent lipid deposition within the retina.

3.   (a) True   (b) True   (c) False   (d) True   (e) False
This slide shows evidence of extensive retinal haemorrhage with exudates. There is also a 'long boat', subhyaloid (pre-retinal) haemorrhage and a macular 'star', formed by the exudates encircling the macular. This represents severe pre-proliferative diabetic retinopathy and maculopathy.

4.   (a) True   (b) True   (c) True   (d) False   (e) False
This slide shows pre-proliferative diabetic retinopathy with blot and dot haemorrhages, soft and hard exudates. Soft exudates (cotton wool spots) have ill defined, 'fluffy', margins as seen in the inferior temporal and upper nasal quadrants. They represent areas of impending ischaemic damage to the retina. The patient requires strict glycaemic control, through diet and medication, which may be oral hypoglycaemics rather than insulin.

5.   (a) True   (b) True   (c) True   (d) False   (e) False
This slide shows proliferative diabetic retinopathy, characterised by new vessel formation, neo-vascularisation. This is an attempt by the retina to overcome increasing ischaemia. Neovascularisation, worsening visual acuity, maculopathy and visual loss are all indications for referral to an ophthalmologist.

STATION 1.12

Answers and explanations

1. (c)
Long term steroid use causes suppression of endogenous steroid production and is the commonest cause of Addison's disease. Patients typically present with non-specific symptoms but may present in coma. In any patient who presents with coma and hyponatraemia, Addison's should always be considered and, if no obvious cause can be attributed, the patient should be given 100 to 200 mg of IV hydrocortisone 4 to 6 hourly for 24 hours, depending on the clinical response.

2. (d)
Hypothyroidism may cause hyponatraemia associated with a macrocytosis. The hyponatraemia is secondary to increased ADH secretion and reduced free water clearance. The macrocytosis may be secondary to the thyroid disease or to associated pernicious anaemia.

3. (e)
Atypical pneumonias, e.g. mycoplasma, are a common cause of the syndrome of inappropiate ADH. Other causes include:

- **Intracerebral**
  Head injury
  Meningitis
  Encephalitis
  Benign and malignant tumours

- **Pulmonary**
  Pneumonia
  Tuberculosis
  Small cell
  Tumours
  Abscess

- **Malignancies**
  Thymoma
  Prostatic
  Pancreatic
  Lymphoma

- **Drugs**
  Chemotherapeutic agents
  Chlorpropamide
  Carbamazepine
  Clofibrate

4.   (a)

Psychogenic polydypsia is an uncommon cause of hyponatraemia. It is important to exclude diabetes mellitus and insipidus which may also present with polyuria. Patients with psychogenic polydypsia have a hyponatraemia associated with a low serum osmolality and an appropriately low urine osmolality. The diagnosis is confirmed using a water deprivation test.

5.   (b)

The most common cause of hyponatraemia in the older patient is the use of diuretics. Other side-effects of loop diuretics include hypokalaemia, hypomagnesaemia and pre-renal impairment, causing a rise in urea and creatinine. SSRIs also commonly cause hyponatraemia in the elderly.

STATION 1.13

Answers

Hypokalaemia	Hyperkalaemia
Cushing's disease	Addison's disease
Frusemide infusion	Spironolactone
Type I RTA	Type IV RTA
Fanconi's syndrome	Acute renal failure
Ectopic ACTH	Lisinopril
Conn's syndrome	
Cardiac failure with secondary hyperaldosteronism	

Comment

Cushing's disease (pituitary dependent) and Cushing's syndrome, e.g. ectopic ACTH secretion, cause hypokalaemia. Ectopic ACTH secretion may cause a severe hypokalaemia associated with a metabolic alkalosis. It usually arises in association with a malignant tumour, most commonly a small cell carcinoma of the lung. Addison's disease causes a hyperkalaemia and hyponatraemia with an associated metabolic acidosis.

Loop and thiazide diuretics cause hypokalaemia, whereas spironolactone and amiloride cause potassium retention. Loop diuretics are often given in combination with amiloride to maintain normokalaemia. Lisinopril is one of the new generation of ACE inhibitors. They cause potassium retention through their effects on the renin-angiotensin system.

Conn's syndrome (primary hyperaldosteronism) and secondary hyperaldosteronism cause hypokalaemia and a metabolic alkalosis. Secondary hyperaldosteronism arises in oedematous states, e.g. cardiac, renal and hepatic failure.

Type I RTA and Fanconi's syndrome (associated with Type II RTA) cause hypokalaemia, whereas Type IV RTA causes hyperkalaemia.

STATION 1.14

Answers and explanations

Patient A
Plasma osmolality = 2[158 + 4.9] + 50 = 409.8
Anion gap = [158 + 4.9] - [12 + 102] = 48.9
The high anion gap is due to the very high lactate level. The patient's urinalysis suggests that she is suffering from a UTI.

Diagnosis
UTI sepsis leading to lactic acidosis and hyperglycaemic coma.

Patient B
Plasma osmolality = 2[145 + 4] + 14 + 45.3 = 357.3
Anion gap = [145 + 4] - [8 + 106] = 35
The high anion gap cannot be accounted for by the slightly raised lactate level. This patient's urinalysis suggests 'heavy' ketonuria in keeping with diabetic ketoacidosis (DKA).

Diagnosis
Pneumonia leading to diabetic ketoacidosis

Patient C
Plasma osmolality = 2[155 + 4.5] + 19 + 80 = 418
Anion gap = [155 + 4.5] - [25 + 110] = 24.5
The slightly elevated anion gap is due to the raised lactate level which may be due to tissue hypoxia in severe sepsis. However, compared to the other cases this patient has a relatively normal anion gap and, as shown by his plasma osmolality, is in a hyperosmolar, non-ketotic coma [HONK]

Diagnosis
Hyperosmolar, non-ketotic hyperglycaemic coma

Comment

If a diabetic patient is found unconscious in the street, you should always attempt to give them some glucose. After following the basic resuscitation rules of ABC, the easiest method is to dissolve a sachet of sugar or some honey under their tongue. (Attempting to force sweet drinks into a semiconscious or unconscious patient may lead to aspiration.)

STATION 1.15

Answers and explanations

A 3.   Primary hypothyroidism
The data indicates an extremely elevated TSH with low levels of T_3 and T_4. Common causes include autoimmune disease including Hashimoto's disease, post thyroidectomy, irradiation and radioactive iodine therapy for thyrotoxicosis and, in mountainous regions, iodine deficiency.

B 1.   Thyrotoxicosis
The data shows a supressed TSH level, with a raised T_3 and extremely raised T_4. This is the most common biochemical presentation of thyrotoxicosis. Causes of thyrotoxicosis include autoimmune thyrotoxicosis, benign and malignant thyroid masses, multinodular goitre and acute thyroiditis.

C 5.   Sick euthyroid syndrome
In acute illness, particularly severe systemic disease, abnormal production and binding of thyroid hormones and transport proteins lead to biochemical results which do not tally. In this case, the data initially suggests the patient may have hypothyroidism, with low T_3 and T_4. However, the TSH is low which suggests either hypothalamic/pituitary failure or the sick euthyroid syndrome. In moderate illnesses the free T_4 may be raised with a normal or raised TSH.

D 2. T_3 thyrotoxicosis
This is an uncommon cause of thyrotoxicosis. The patient has clinical symptoms and signs of thyrotoxicosis but has a T_4 in the normal range. The T_3, as in this case, is elevated.

E 4.   Euthyroid
The patient has normal T_3, T_4 and TSH.

STATION 1.16

Answers and explanations

1.   (E)   (f)
This woman has symptoms consistent with osteomalacia, i.e. proximal muscle weakness and pain. In childhood the lack of vitamin D and its metabolites leads to bony deformity, particularly of the lower limb bones, and the classical appearance of rickets. The bony abnormality arises due to ineffective osteoid mineralization.

2.   (F)   (e)
This is a classical history for sarcoidosis. Black American women, particularly in the Southern states of the USA have a very high incidence of the disorder. Sarcoid causes hypercalcaemia and hypercalciuria, leading to renal tract calcification and stones.

3.   (D)   (a)
The premature menopause suggests long term oestrogen deficiency, a primary risk factor for the development of osteoporosis. The disorder per se does not affect calcium levels and a raised calcium should make the physician think of associated malignancy, particularly myeloma, which may present in a similar fashion.

4.   (A)   (c)
This is a classical history of Paget's disease of the bone. The calcium and phosphate are unchanged by the disorder but the alkaline phosphatase is often greatly raised. This reflects the excessive bony turnover and increased osteoclastic activity. Complications of the disease include bony pain, pathological fractures, the classical anterior bowing of the tibia, cranial nerve compression, high output cardiac failure and rarely, osteosarcoma formation.

5.   (C)   (b)
Multiple myeloma is one of the most common causes of hypercalcaemia in the elderly. Clinically, it presents with bone pain. As well as hypercalcaemia, the patient has a raised ESR, often over 100, and a normochromic, normocytic anaemia. Other markers include the presence of a paraprotein in the serum, shown by plasma electrophoresis, and Bence Jones proteins in the urine. Lytic lesions present radiologically.

6. **(B)** **(d)**

Pseudohypoparathyroidism is a rare disorder due to end organ resistance to the effects of parathyroid hormone. The patients are dysmorphic, with a low IQ, and shortened 4th and 5th metacarpals. Biochemically, the patient appears to have hypoparathyroidism but parathyroid levels are normal. Pseudo-pseudohypoparathyroidism is the disorder of abnormal phenotype with normal calcium metabolism.

STATION 1.17

Answers and explanations

Patient A: Cranial diabetes insipidus

The data shows this patient to have a relatively high plasma osmolality with an inappropriately low urinary osmolality. During the eight hours of water deprivation the urinary osmolality remains very low suggesting an inability to concentrate the urine, i.e. no effective ADH. However, when the patient is given DDAVP, an ADH analogue, the urine concentrates with a fall in plasma osmolality. This indicates that the renal tubules have the capacity to react to ADH, i.e. the posterior pituitary is failing to secrete ADH appropriately. If the data had been unaffected by the ADH this would imply nephrogenic diabetes insipidus, where there is an insensitivity of the tubules to appropriate levels of ADH.

During a water deprivation test the patient's urine output and body weight are closely monitored. If the patient loses more than 3% of their initial body weight the test is immediately stopped and the diagnosis of diabetes insipidus is assumed.

Patient B: Normal control

The data is all within normal limits and is unenhanced with the addition of extra ADH. The patient concentrates their urine appropriately in an attempt to conserve water in the face of a prolonged period of water deprivation.

Patient C: Psychogenic polydipsia

Patients with this disorder present with polydipsia, polyuria and a normal plasma glucose. They are thought to have a psychiatric condition and are therefore often difficult to assess. A water deprivation test is used to exclude diabetes insipidus, although partial ADH insensitivity is difficult to differentiate. Classically, they have a low, or low normal, plasma osmolality with appropriately low urinary osmolality. When subjected to a prolonged period of water deprivation they will appropriately conserve water in response to ADH secretion and will thus raise their urinary osmolality. The effect of additional ADH is similar to the normal control.

STATION 1.18

Answers and explanations

1. (a) False (b) False (c) True   (d) False (e) True
This SXR shows an enlarged pituitary fossa (Figure 1.18A). The diagnosis may be made in 70-80% of cases of acromegaly. The classical double floor of the fossa should only be diagnosed when the clinoid processes are aligned. Other SXR changes that may be seen in this condition are an enlarged, protruding mandible (prognathism), which can be seen in this patient and increased interdental separation in the AP view.

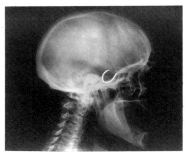

Fig. 1.18A

2. (a) False (b) True   (c) False (d) True   (e)False
This is an AP foot X-ray of a diabetic patient showing evidence of swelling and possible gas in the soft tissues, particularly over the right second toe. There is also destruction of the proximal phalanx of the second toe due to osteomyelitis. Note the vascular calcification which is a common sign in diabetes mellitus. Other radiological changes that may occur include Charcot (neuropathic) joints and digital amputation.

3. (a) True   (b) False (c) True   (d) True   (e) True
This lateral skull X-ray shows gross Paget's disease of the bone. (It is important to add 'of the bone' as Paget described disorders of the nipple and scrotum as well.) The radiograph shows evidence of platybasia, an invagination of the foramen magnum and skull base which is due to the remodelling. This produces pressure on the upper cervical cord, medulla and lower cranial nerves and may be responsible for the neural deafness. Four sites are classically affected; the skull, the pelvis, the tibia (sabre tibia), and other weight-bearing bones. Bony abnormalities include local warmth of the bones due to increased vascularity, pain, fractures and rarely osteosarcomatous change. Other complications include optic atrophy due to compression of the optic nerve and high output cardiac failure.

STATION 1.19

Answers and explanations

1.   (a) False   (b) False   (c) False   (d) False   (e) True
This is an AP view of the pelvis and hip joints showing multiple Looser's zones of osteomalacia (indicated by arrows in Figure 1.19a: page 18). The bones are of normal radiodensity. With such florid bone changes a patient would be expected to have a low serum calcium and raised alkaline phosphatase.

2.   (a) True   (b) True   (c) True   (d) False   (e) True
This AP thoracic inlet view of the chest shows soft tissue swelling and calcification on the right side of the neck consistent with a calcified thyroid nodular goitre. The trachea is deviated to the left. Further investigations should include an autoantibody screen, thyroid function tests, fine needle aspirate (FNA) and radioisotope scan of the thyroid.

3.   (a) True   (b) True   (c) True   (d) False   (e) True
This is an AP chest X-ray of a baby showing the 'sail' sign of a prominent thymus gland.

STATION 1.20

Answers and explanations

1. This is a radioisotope scan of the thyroid gland showing a 'toxic' or hot nodule in the right thyroid lobe with suppression of the rest of the gland. This most likely represents a solitary benign active nodule or may represent part of a multinodular goitre. Inactive or cold nodules represent areas of fibrosis, cysts or in 10% of cases a malignant tumour.

2. This is a pancreatic angiogram, the arrows defining the margins of a mass, which is most likely to be an insulinoma. Insulinomas are often very small tumours and may be difficult to define with other forms of imaging such as CT or MRI scan.

3. This is a CT scan taken through the orbits. The structures are:
   (A) thickened right medial rectus
   (B) right optic nerve
   (C) right lateral rectus
   (D) proptosed right eye
   The scan shows a proptosed right eye with a greatly thickened right medial rectus, (compare the left and right sides). These abnormalities are consistent with Grave's orbitopathy. Grave's thyroid disease is an autoimmune disease which may cause the patient to be hypo-, eu- or hyperthyroid. The classical triad of the disorder is thyroid acropachy, orbitopathy and pretibial myxoedema. Patients should have TFTs and thyroid autoantibodies and a general autoantibody screen.

STATION 1.21

Answers and explanation

1. AP view of the thoracic inlet shows marked displacement of the trachea to the right by a large goitre that extends to just below the sternal notch

2. Thyroid enlargement (goitre) extending to below the thoracic inlet

3. Lateral views of the neck and thoracic inlet
   Chest radiograph

4. Surgical removal of the goitre (a subtotal or total thyroidectomy)

Comment

Retrosternal goitres are uncommon and may compress the trachea, oesophagus and the jugular veins at the thoracic inlet. Emergency surgical decompression is rarely indicated, and thyroid and respiratory function must be assessed during work-up for thyroidectomy.

STATION 1.22

Answers

(A) Cerebral cortex
(B) Genu of Corpus callosum
(C) Suprasellar tumour extension
(D) Pituitary fossa and tumour

(E) Sphenoidal air sinus
(F) Collicular plate
(G) Fourth ventricle
(H) Cerebellar cortex

STATION 1.23

Answers

(A) Liver
(B) Adrenal adenoma
(C) Aorta
(D) Vertebral body

(E) Left crus of diaphragm
(F) Upper pole of left kidney
(G) Spleen
(H) Stomach with contrast and air bubble above fluid level

STATION 1.24

Answers

1. Radioisotope scan of the thyroid gland
    Radioactive iodine (^{131}I or ^{123}I) or technetium (^{99m}Tc)

2. Lower pole of left lobe contains a circumscribed lesion that does not take up the radioisotope - a cold spot

    A thyroid cyst
    An area of haemorrhage
    A thyroid adenoma
    A thyroid carcinoma

3. Ultrasound scan of the thyroid to determine if the lesion is solid or cystic and to enable a guided fine needle aspiration biopsy of the lesion. (The incidence of thyroid cancer in a solitary solid nodule is 12%)

Comment

A 'hot' nodule with its increased uptake of radio-iodine is usually diagnostic of a hyperactive nodule but occasionally a focus of follicular carcinoma may appear likewise. A thyroid cyst, which also appears as a 'cold' nodule on scintiscanning is readily distinguished on ultrasound scanning. Fine needle aspiration cytology is useful in confirming anaplastic tumours and bony metastatic deposits of follicular tumours.

STATION 1.25

Patient history

I am a 48 year old solicitor and have recently developed symptoms of the menopause. My last normal period was over seven months ago, although I have had 3 or 4 further scanty bleeds since. I have flushing, irritability and more recently dyspareunia secondary to vaginal dryness. I understand from magazines about the treatment and would like to start. I am a non-smoker and a keen walker. I am otherwise well and have had no serious illness in the past. My last smear was four years ago and was normal.

The questions I would like answered are:
- How long will I be on the treatment?
- Does it have any side-effects?
- Will it increase my risk of cancer?

Assessment	Good	Adequate	Poor/not done
1. Polite introduction; establishes rapport	❏	❏	❏
2. Establishes patient's last period and menopausal symptoms	❏	❏	❏
3. Establishes patient's understanding of the treatment	❏	❏	❏
4. Discusses the treatment in a clear, non-jargonistic manner	❏	❏	❏
5. Specifically mentions:			
Protection against osteoporosis	❏	❏	❏
Possible protection against IHD	❏	❏	❏
Stops symptoms of oestrogen deficiency	❏	❏	❏
Small risk of thrombo-embolic disease and benign breast disease	❏	❏	❏
Many treatments still cause cyclical blood loss	❏	❏	❏
Recommended treatment is for about five years	❏	❏	❏

Good Adequate Poor/not done

6. Establishes whether patient has
    had any gynaecological or breast
    malignancies   ❏   ❏   ❏
7. Establishes other risk factors for
    osteoporosis   ❏   ❏   ❏
8. Is able to answer the patient's
    questions in a reasonable
    manner   ❏   ❏   ❏
9. Does all in a fluent,
    professional manner   ❏   ❏   ❏

Comment

Over the last ten years hormone replacement therapy for post menopausal women has become both accepted and demanded by women. It has few contra-indications and although there are no long term studies on its effects, the short term therapy recommended at present seems to have major advantages and few disadvantages.

Treatment is recommended to post menopausal women for about five years. A definitive time period is as yet unknown. Therapy alleviates symptoms of oestrogen deficiency such as flushing and vaginal atrophy, delays the onset of bone loss, leading to osteoporosis, and increases HDL and decreases LDL levels.

There is an increased risk of thrombo-embolic disease but this is much smaller than that associated with the oral contraceptive pill, and should be viewed in relation to other risks such as smoking, previous thrombo-embolic events and obesity. Caution is also recommended in patients with previous breast and gynaecological malignancies, although there is no definitive evidence that HRT causes an increase in these cancers. However, benign breast changes do occur, making mammographic screening more difficult. Newer treatments with continuous therapy have meant that withdrawal vaginal bleeding does not occur. This makes it a more attractive prospect, particularly in elderly women who have not had periods for many years.

STATION 1.26

Answers and explanations

1. (C) (b)
Actrapid, as its name suggests, is a short acting insulin. It is used in QDS insulin regimes where it is used as the pre-prandial insulin. It is also commonly used intravenously with an insulin sliding scale. Insulin is principally manufactured through genetic engineering and therefore allergic reaction is rare. Local infection may occur at injection sites and lipoatrophy may also occur if the sites are not routinely rotated.

2. (E) (d)
Metformin is the only biguanide used today, as its sister molecule, Phenformin, caused severe lactic acidosis. Metformin may also produce this side-effect and must be used with caution in patients with unstable angina, hepatic and renal impairment, as these all predispose to increased levels of the drug and an acidosis occurring.

3. (A) (e)
Tolbutamide is a short acting sulphonylurea with a half life of 6–8 hours. The main side-effect of this group is hypoglycaemia and patients must be pre-warned about hypoglycaemic symptoms.

4. (B) (a)
Acarbose is an α glucosidase inhibitor which is principally used as an adjuvant therapy in NIDDM. The drug inhibits amylase, maltase and sucrase, thus decreasing carbohydrate absorption and reducing post-prandial hyperglycaemia. The side-effects of flatulence and bloating limit its use.

5. (D) (c)
Chlorpropamide is a long-acting sulphonylurea. It may cause SIADH, which was previously utilised in patients with diabetes insipidus, and flushing with alcohol, although this is rare. Glibenclamide and chlorpropamide should not be used in the elderly as their long half life and patients' renal impairment leads to increased risk of hypoglycaemia.

STATION 1.27

Patient history

I am 23 years old and work as a secretary. I was admitted to hospital four days ago with newly-diagnosed diabetes mellitus. I have been seen by the dietician and the diabetic liaison sister, who has explained the principles of insulin therapy to me. I have not as yet attempted to inject myself. The nurses have been showing me how to draw up the insulin and where and how to give the injections.

Assessment   **Good Adequate Poor/not done**

	Good	Adequate	Poor/not done
1. Polite introduction; establishes rapport	❏	❏	❏
2. Establishes the patient's understanding of the treatment	❏	❏	❏
3. Explains in a clear, non-jargonistic manner the following:			
Establishes patient has correct equipment	❏	❏	❏
Checks using correct insulin which is in date	❏	❏	❏
Uses clean syringe and needle for each injection	❏	❏	❏
Inverts the insulin and draws it up to the correct units required	❏	❏	❏
Cleans the injection site using an antiseptic wipe	❏	❏	❏
Forms a pinch of skin and injects through it at 90 degrees	❏	❏	❏
4. Establishes patient has understood by getting them to demonstrate the procedure	❏	❏	❏
5. Invites patient's questions and answers in an appropriate manner	❏	❏	❏
6. Stresses the importance of:			
Rotating injection sites between the abdomen, thighs and buttocks	❏	❏	❏
Never missing doses of insulin	❏	❏	❏
To seek medical attention if unable to take insulin or if unable to eat after insulin	❏	❏	❏
Tight glycaemic control leads to few complications	❏	❏	❏
Insulin should be administered approximately 30 minutes prior to a meal	❏	❏	❏
7. Does all in a fluent, professional manner	❏	❏	❏

STATION 1.28a

Patient history

I am a 19 year old nurse and recently underwent surgery for a pituitary tumour. I have had some of my new medicines explained to me by the consultant but have not really understood all the treatments. I would like to know the answers to the following questions:

- Will I be able to get pregnant on these hormones?
- Will I get big muscles with these steroid tablets?
- Is it true that I will probably have to take these tablets for life?

Assessment

		Good	Adequate	Poor/not done
1.	Polite introduction; establishes rapport	❏	❏	❏
2.	Establishes patient's current understanding of her treatment	❏	❏	❏
3.	Explains in a clear, non-jargonistic manner:			
	How the pituitary gland normally functions	❏	❏	❏
	The drugs being used are to replace naturally occurring hormones and will take over their function	❏	❏	❏
	It is essential she never misses doses of the drugs, particularly the hydrocortisone	❏	❏	❏
4.	Ensures the patient has been issued with a blue steroid card and has a medi-alert bracelet	❏	❏	❏
5.	If unwell needs to seek medical advice immediately	❏	❏	❏
6.	Invites patient questions and answers them in an appropriate manner	❏	❏	❏
7.	Does all above in a fluent, professional manner	❏	❏	❏

Answers to Specific Questions

- The removal of cyclical FSH/LH means it is very difficult for the patient to become pregnant. Although the FSH/LH replacement restores oestrogen activity, essential for cardiovascular and bone protection, it cannot reproduce a normal menstrual cycle. However, with ovulation and egg harvesting, for in vitro fertilisation and implantation, a pregnancy may be carried to term under endocrine therapy.

- No. The hydrocortisone replaces only the naturally occurring steroids of the body and should not cause any side-effects but in excess may lead to problems. It is therefore essential to have at least an annual assessment of hormone replacement.

- Yes. The hydrocortisone and thyroxine will be lifelong but the FSH/LH are principally needed to maintain normal menstrual/ovulatory function and may be withdrawn to induce a natural menopause.

STATION 1.29

Patient history

I have been having severe pain and swelling of both breasts, the left breast more so than the right for the past eight months. The pain is relieved during periods but gradually builds up afterwards. My breasts feel tender and lumpy, and I find it uncomfortable to lie on my side. I am finding it difficult to do my housework, particularly carrying the shopping and coping with my three-year-old toddler. I have two other children, all of whom were breast fed.

My breasts have not bothered me in the past, and I have been well all my life. I smoke about 4 or 5 cigarettes a day, and I like drinking coffee and drink alcohol only on social occasions.

My doctor gave me pain killers and water tablets, which have not been of much help. Two weeks ago, I started taking Evening Primrose Oil tablets, which were recommended by a friend who had the same problem; it has not had any effect.

Assessment	Good	Adequate	Poor/not done
1. Polite introduction; establishes rapport	❏	❏	❏
2. Establishes site, duration and periodicity of presenting symptoms	❏	❏	❏
3. Asks about other breast symptoms; past history of breast disease	❏	❏	❏
4. Establishes current treatment (if any)	❏	❏	❏
5. Asks about menstrual cycle, contraceptive use	❏	❏	❏
6. Establishes history of pregnancies, lactation, family history of breast disease (breast cancer)	❏	❏	❏
7. Social and/or professional status; smoking and drinking habits	❏	❏	❏
8. Makes a reasonable attempt at the diagnosis	❏	❏	❏
9. Does all in a fluent, professional manner	❏	❏	❏

Diagnosis
Mastalgia

Comment

Mastalgia is cyclical breast pain and is benign. It is associated with fibroadenosis or benign breast change. Fluid retention also causes breast pain. (The contraceptive pill and smoking are aggravating factors, and coffee consumption has been implicated.) Breast support during the day, and at night if necessary, with an oral diuretic may be sufficient as an initial measure. For persisting symptoms, Evening Primrose Oil or Starflower Oil may be prescribed. Danazol may be tried if the above measures fail to give relief after a 4 to 6 month trial with a gradually increased dosage.

STATION 1.30

Patient history

> I am single and work as a medical secretary. I am in good health and have had no trouble with my breasts, except for cyclical discomfort and swelling. I am currently not on the pill, and my periods are regular. My mother had breast cancer at the age of 38 and had a mastectomy. She is on long-term tamoxifen and is keeping well. My aunt (my mother's elder sister) developed breast cancer at the age of 52, and my cousin also had breast cancer, when she was 40. They both underwent surgery and chemotherapy.

Assessment	Good	Adequate	Poor/not done
1. Polite introduction; establishes rapport	❏	❏	❏
2. Establishes the presenting anxiety	❏	❏	❏
3. Establishes/excludes family history of cancer	❏	❏	❏
4. Establishes/excludes previous breast disease in patient	❏	❏	❏
5. Establishes menstrual history, pregnancy and lactation	❏	❏	❏
6. Establishes contraception/ hormone therapy	❏	❏	❏
7. Establishes social and professional history	❏	❏	❏
8. Does all in a fluent, professional manner	❏	❏	❏

Comment

> Only 1–2% of breast cancers are hereditary, and these are transmitted through the BRCA 1 and BRCA 2 oncogenes. These genes also transmit ovarian cancer. Hereditary breast cancer usually manifests itself before the fifth decade of life. Genetic counselling is advised if two or more first degree relatives had developed breast cancer before the age of 50 years. Genetic testing identifies the oncogene and, if it is present, the patient would require counselling with regard to close surveillance with periodic mammography. Prophylactic bilateral subcutaneous mastectomies with prosthetic reconstruction as a means of eliminating the risk should also be discussed.

STATION 1.31

Answers

True: 1, 2a, 2b, 2c, 3a, 3b.
False: 2d, 3c.

Comment

Breasts are rarely identically symmetrical in women. When one or both breasts are hypoplastic or rudimentary, breast augmentation is performed by expandable silicone implants. The short and long term complications of such implants must be discussed with the patient when obtaining consent. Hypertrophy of the breast is more common and may be corrected by reduction mammoplasty; nipple transfer and re-implantation precludes subsequent lactation.

STATION 1.32

Assessment	Good	Adequate	Poor/not done
1. Introduction and positioning of subject	❑	❑	❑
2. Inspection of breasts (subject seated with arms by the side; arms raised)	❑	❑	❑
3. Comments on symmetry, presence of scars or deformity	❑	❑	❑
4. Palpation of breasts with the subject supine, normal side first. Palpates with flat of hand, quadrant by quadrant	❑	❑	❑
5. Palpation of regional lymph nodes: *Palpates axillary and supraclavicular nodes.*	❑	❑	❑
Comments on axillary groups, i.e. apical, medial, lateral, basal and pectoral	❑	❑	❑

Comment

Breast examination begins with inspection of the breasts with the patient seated facing the examiner. She is asked to place her hands on her lap, raise her hands over the head and then to place her hands on the hips and to press in. Any deformity of the breast, irregularity of its contour, skin or muscle tethering would be observed.

Palpation of the breasts is best performed in the supine, semi-recumbent position with her hands by the side and then with the hands raised over her head.

STATION 1.33

Answers

1. Figure 1.33a: radioisotope bone scan
    Figure 1.33b: liver ultrasound scan

    Figure 1.33a: uptake of isotope by skeletal metastases in the left femur and pelvis.
    Figure 1.33b: discrete hypoechogenic deposits (3 in number) in the right lobe of the liver

2. Metastatic deposits are present in the bone and liver from the breast cancer.

3. Local excision or radiotherapy of the primary tumour if large or prone to local complications.
    Distal spread may be controlled by adjuvant chemotherapy and/or tamoxifen therapy.

Comment

Recurrent breast carcinomas must be staged, before treatment is planned, with chest radiography, and liver and bone scans. Local control of the recurrence is by surgical excision or radiotherapy to the chest wall. Control of systemic disease is by chemo- or endocrine therapy. Recurrence may be local, regional or systemic; local recurrence does not affect mortality but carries a significant morbidity, it must therefore be effectively managed.

STATION 1.34

Answers

1. Mammograms

2. Both investigations show focal radiological opacity, with discrete microcalcification and distortion of the surrounding breast tissue.

3. Breast carcinomas

4. Wire-guided excisional biopsy

5. The patient (in the presence of a relative and a breast nurse counsellor) is informed of the mammographic findings and the need to remove the lesion shown by means of a wire-guided biopsy for pathological examination. Confirmation of the presence of a tumour would lead to planning appropriate treatment.

Comment

Deposits of calcium in breast tissue may be in the form of macro- or microcalcification. The former are large calcium deposits, which are associated with benign change. Microcalcification, however, is linked to malignancy and, when present within a mass lesion, is suggestive of cancer.

STATION 1.35

Assessment	Good	Adequate	Poor/not done
1. Palpation of the marked lesion Cleanse skin	❑	❑	❑
2. Introduction of needle into lesion and withdrawal of plunger during repeated passes into lesion	❑	❑	❑
3. Covers puncture site with dressing	❑	❑	❑
4. Examines syringe contents Prepares smears (air-dried and in fixative)	❑	❑	❑
Empties remaining aspirate into container with fixative for cytospin smears	❑	❑	❑

Comment

Fine needle aspiration cytology is one of the diagnostic modalities of the triple assessment of a breast lesion. Smears are examined for cellular atypic and cellular adhesion. Benign cells are regular in shape and size and tend to adhere to one another in clumps. Neoplastic cells vary in size and show nuclear pleomorphism or mitotic activity; they do not show normal intercellular adherence and appear separate from each other. Aspirates from cysts require cytological assessment if blood-stained.

STATION 1.36

Assessment	Good	Adequate	Poor/not done
1. Polite introduction; establishes rapport with the couple	❑	❑	❑
2. Informs patient of result	❑	❑	❑
3. Answers questions on the diagnosis with care	❑	❑	❑
4. Answers questions on outcome in broad, optimistic terms	❑	❑	❑
5. Ascertains if patient wishes to be involved in management decisions	❑	❑	❑
6. Answers questions on treatment and side-effects	❑	❑	❑
7. Does all in a fluent, empathetic and non-jargonistic manner	❑	❑	❑

Comment

If the patient already suspects the diagnosis, it should be confirmed gently. If the patient is unaware of the diagnosis, the results should be conveyed, giving time for the information to be understood. Occasionally, on being informed of the diagnosis, the patient may go into denial, when further discussion should be postponed to a meeting with the breast nurse counsellor (and if required, a clinical psychologist). Further, if the patient's partner does not wish for her to be told of the diagnosis, this should be honoured as long as the patient does not actively seek information.

Should the patient not wish to be involved in management decisions, she must, nevertheless, be informed of the chosen protocol, its effectiveness and side-effects. If the patient is in denial of the diagnosis and rejects treatment, assistance from nurse counsellor, psychologist and the patient's family are required to bring her out of denial. Those patients who wish to participate in selecting treatment protocols must be given sufficient information and encouragement, as they will then be better prepared to tolerate the side-effects or to accept failures of treatment.

STATION 2.1

Patient history

I am a 24-year-old engineering student and I am normally fit and well. I have been revising hard for my final exams and have been very stressed. During the last three weeks I have had bloody diarrhoea. My bowels are open once or twice an hour and I am passing semiformed/loose stools with blood and mucous, mixed and separate to the stools. I have lost 5 kilogrammes in weight and have been too tired to play squash, which I normally do twice a week. I have tried eating normally but have felt too unwell most of the time to manage anything. There seems to be no relationship to my dietary intake and the diarrhoea. In the last week I have developed red, painful lesions on my shins, and have been feverish. I have not travelled abroad recently and no-one in my family has ever had anything similar. I have no risk factors for 'food poisoning'. I am not on any medication and do not drink alcohol. I smoke 10 cigarettes per day. No one in my family has bowel disease.

Assessment   **Good Adequate Poor/not done**

	Good	Adequate	Poor/not done
1. Polite introduction; establishes rapport	❏	❏	❏
2. Establishes duration of the illness	❏	❏	❏
3. Establishes normal bowel habit of the patient	❏	❏	❏
4. Establishes what the patient means by diarrhoea i.e. frequency and volume of stool	❏	❏	❏
5. Establishes how often the patient is opening their bowels in a 24-hour period	❏	❏	❏
6. Establishes the consistency of the motion	❏	❏	❏
7. Establishes the presence of blood and mucous in the stool	❏	❏	❏
8. Establishes/excludes weight loss	❏	❏	❏
9. Establishes associated gastrointestinal symptoms- vomiting and abdominal pain	❏	❏	❏
10. Asks about systemic features	❏	❏	❏
11. Establishes any other risk factors for diarrhoea e.g. foreign travel/ recent contacts	❏	❏	❏
12. Establishes/excludes family history of bowel disease	❏	❏	❏
13. Makes a reasonable attempt at the diagnosis	❏	❏	❏
14. Does all in a fluent, professional manner	❏	❏	❏

Diagnosis
Inflammatory bowel disease

STATION 2.2

Patient history

I have just returned from a 2 month trekking holiday in Nepal. I am normally fit and well and have never had any bowel problems before. In the last 10 days I have had bloody, watery diarrhoea, with urgency. I am opening my bowels every 2 to 3 hours, and immediately after eating or drinking anything. I have had no vomiting, but have had intense, cramping abdominal pains, particularly after food. In this period I have had a couple of episodes of fever and 'chills'. I think I may have 'picked up a bug' after a village feast I attended. I am not very keen on any investigations but would take medication if it was necessary.

A couple of other people on the trek were similarly unwell with fever and diarrhoea but my husband has been well. I am on no medications other than HRT after a premature menopause and I do not drink alcohol or smoke.

Assessment	Good	Adequate	Poor/not done
1. Polite introduction; establishes rapport	❏	❏	❏
2. Establishes duration of present illness and excludes similar episodes	❏	❏	❏
3. Establishes where the patient went on holiday and contact history	❏	❏	❏
4. Establishes how often the patient is opening her bowels	❏	❏	❏
5. Establishes the consistency of the stool	❏	❏	❏
6. Establishes the presence of blood in the stool	❏	❏	❏
7. Asks about the presence of mucous in the stool	❏	❏	❏
8. Establishes associated features, i.e. pain, vomiting, fever	❏	❏	❏
9. Establishes/excludes weight loss	❏	❏	❏
10. Asks about the likely source of the infection - water, dairy products, shell fish, meat	❏	❏	❏
11. Explains the diagnosis to the patient in a clear, non-jargonistic manner	❏	❏	❏
12. Explains the need for blood tests, stool culture and possible sigmoidoscopy and biopsy	❏	❏	❏
13. Invites questions and addresses any concerns the patient may have	❏	❏	❏
14. Does all in a fluent, professional manner	❏	❏	❏

Diagnosis

Infective diarrhoea. Amongst other organisms, amoebiasis and giardiasis should be excluded in this case.

STATION 2.3

Patient history

I am a 24-year-old legal secretary, and I was fit and well with a normal bowel habit until four months ago. Since then I have been passing offensive, pale, porridge-like stools up to 8 to 10 times per day. The stools float and are difficult to flush away.

During my illness I have lost 10 kilos in weight; have lost my appetite and feel extremely tired, to the point where I am missing a lot of time from work. I have no abdominal pain, nausea or vomiting and have not passed any blood or mucous PR. I have had no fever or systemic upset.

I have never been abroad and have had no recent contacts with anyone with similar symptoms. There is no family history of bowel problems. I drink 5–10 units of alcohol per week (mainly white wine) and smoke 20 cigarettes per day. I am on no medications other than the OCP.

Assessment

	Good	Adequate	Poor/not done
1. Polite introduction; establishes rapport	❏	❏	❏
2. Establishes duration and nature of presenting complaint	❏	❏	❏
3. Establishes normal bowel habit of the patient	❏	❏	❏
4. Establishes frequency and volume of diarrhoea	❏	❏	❏
5. Establishes stools have the characteristics of steatorrhoea	❏	❏	❏
6. Establishes/excludes the presence of blood and mucous PR	❏	❏	❏
7. Establishes the associated features of anorexia, weight loss and lethargy	❏	❏	❏
8. Establishes/excludes recent foreign travel or contacts	❏	❏	❏
9. Establishes/excludes family history of bowel disease	❏	❏	❏
10. Establishes the diagnosis of malabsorption and makes a reasonable attempt at the differential diagnosis	❏	❏	❏
11. Does all in a fluent, professional manner	❏	❏	❏

Diagnosis
Malabsorption secondary to coeliac disease

Comment

Differential diagnosis:
  Coeliac disease and dermatitis herpetiformis
  Infective - tropical sprue, bacterial overgrowth, Whipple's disease,
      Giardia, Cryptosporidium
  Small bowel lymphoma
  Pancreatic insufficiency
  Small bowel resection - short bowel syndrome, blind loop syndrome
  Iatrogenic - radiation enteritis, drugs, e.g. cholestyramine

STATION 2.4

Patient history

I am a 36-year-old with an 'alcohol problem' with repeated admissions with upper GI bleeds, secondary to oesophageal varices I have had an endoscopy, and on two or three occasions the varices have been injected. I have been out on a large alcoholic binge and started vomiting fresh blood about an hour ago. I have vomited twice, each time bringing up about a 'cup or two' of blood. I have some retrosternal and epigastric pain and feel nauseated. I have not had any melaena or blood PR. I do not take any NSAIDs and do not have any other risk factors for GI bleeding. I am generally very healthy but I do smoke moderately.

Assessment	Good	Adequate	Poor/not done
1. Polite introduction; establishes rapport	❏	❏	❏
2. Establishes nature of the haematemesis, i.e. fresh blood or coffee grounds	❏	❏	❏
3. Establishes the present number of haematemeses and the volume of each haematemesis	❏	❏	❏
4. Establishes the presence/absence of melaena stool and fresh blood PR	❏	❏	❏
5. Establishes previous episodes of haematemesis and hospital admissions	❏	❏	❏
6. Asks about associated symptoms, e.g. epigastric pain, recent weight loss, anorexia, dyspepsia	❏	❏	❏
7. Establishes or excludes the risk factors for upper GI bleed:			
Use of NSAIDs	❏	❏	❏
Alcohol excess, smoking	❏	❏	❏
Previous peptic ulcer disease	❏	❏	❏
✘ *Known oesophageal varices*	❏	❏	❏
Anticoagulant therapy – e.g. warfarin	❏	❏	❏
8. Makes a reasonable attempt at the diagnosis	❏	❏	❏
9. Does all in a fluent, professional manner	❏	❏	❏

Diagnosis
Alcohol related chronic liver disease with known oesophageal varices.

STATION 2.5

Patient history

I am a 32-year-old stockbroker and I am normally fit and well. Like all stockbrokers I suppose I drink and smoke too much and live on takeaways. (When pressed you admit to the exact amounts – 30 cigarettes per day and 30–40 units of alcohol per week in the form of lager and spirits).

In the past 6 months I have had increasing upper abdominal pain, which is particularly bad when I am under stress or have been on a bit of a binge. The pain is burning in nature and radiates through to my back and occasionally behind my breast bone. It is relieved with Rennies and Alka-Seltzers. It is usually worse when I am hungry and better after meals.

I have been otherwise well, with no other GI symptoms. My weight is stable and my appetite is fine. I have never vomited up blood but I did have some black stools one morning after a particularly bad episode a few weeks ago. I do not take any pain killers and have never had any peptic ulcers, hiatus hernias or gastritis in the past. I have had no symptoms suggestive of anaemia, e.g. shortness of breath, chest pain or faints, but have been feeling tired of late.

Assessment	Good	Adequate	Poor/not done
1. Polite introduction; establishes rapport	❑	❑	❑
2. Establishes onset of symptoms	❑	❑	❑
3. Establishes characteristics of the abdominal pain:			
Site and radiation	❑	❑	❑
Exacerbating factors	❑	❑	❑
Relieving factors	❑	❑	❑
4. Establishes/excludes haematemesis, melaena or fresh blood PR	❑	❑	❑
5. Establishes/excludes dyspepsia, retrosternal burning and water brash	❑	❑	❑
6. Establishes associated GI symptoms, e.g. weight loss, anorexia, nausea and vomiting	❑	❑	❑
7. Establishes risk factors for peptic ulcer disease and upper GI inflammation:			
Use of pain killers	❑	❑	❑
Alcohol excess	❑	❑	❑
Smoking	❑	❑	❑
Previous ulcer	❑	❑	❑
Known hiatus hernia or GI inflammation, e.g. gastritis	❑	❑	❑
8. Establishes/excludes symptoms of anaemia	❑	❑	❑
9. Makes a reasonable attempt at the diagnosis	❑	❑	❑
10. Does all in a fluent, professional manner	❑	❑	❑

Diagnosis
Peptic ulcer disease

STATION 2.6

Answers and explanations

1. **True:** this allows not only direct visual evidence of the cause but also the taking of biopsies and performance of a CLO test.
2. **False:** an iron deficiency anaemia is associated with a low plasma ferritin.
3. **True:** this is usually associated with chronic cases of iron deficiency.
4. **False:** a microcytic anaemia produces a low MCV
5. **True:** CLO = campylocbacter-like organism = *Helicobacter pylori*
6. **True:** triple therapy is used in ulcer healing and eradication of *Helicobacter pylori*.
7. **False:** it is usually given for 1–2 weeks.
8. **True:** clarithromycin is given with amoxycillin and a proton pump inhibitor.
9. **False:** cimetidine is an H2 antagonist.
10. **False:** he may require 3–6 months of treatment but, provided he stops smoking and reduces his alcohol intake, he should avoid recurrence. Maintenance or long term therapy with a proton pump inhibitor is only occasionally required.

STATION 2.7

Patient history

I am a 47-year-old carpet salesman with a long history of peptic ulcer disease and gastro-oesophageal reflux. I have a six month history of intermittent difficulty in swallowing solids. I can manage most foods most of the time but occasionally foods like bread and potatoes seem to stick 'behind the lower part of my breast bone'. I have lost a little weight, about 2 to 3 kilogrammes, but have had no other associated gastrointestinal symptoms.

I am generally well and have had no major illness or admissions to hospital in the past. I am a non-smoker and drink 5–10 units of alcohol per week, principally in the form of red wine.

Assessment

	Good	Adequate	Poor/not done
1. Polite introduction; establishes rapport	❑	❑	❑
2. Establishes duration and nature of the presenting illness	❑	❑	❑
3. Establishes level of the dysphagia, i.e. pharynx, upper, mid or lower oesophagus	❑	❑	❑
4. Establishes degree of dysphagia, i.e. solids/liquids	❑	❑	❑
5. Establishes rate and nature of progression	❑	❑	❑
6. Establishes/excludes presence of regurgitation	❑	❑	❑
7. Establishes history of peptic ulcer disease and reflux	❑	❑	❑
8. Establishes/excludes symptoms of GI bleeding - melaena, haematemesis, blood PR	❑	❑	❑
9. Establishes/excludes associated gastrointestinal features e.g. abdominal pain, nausea and vomiting, weight loss	❑	❑	❑
10. Excludes risk factors for oesophageal carcinoma	❑	❑	❑
11. Establishes any associated features of systemic diseases or relevant previous medical history	❑	❑	❑
12. Makes a reasonable attempt at the diagnosis	❑	❑	❑
13. Does all in a fluent, professional manner	❑	❑	❑

Diagnosis

Benign stricture secondary to long term gastro-oesophageal reflux disease (GORD).

STATION 2.8

Patient history

I am 33 years old and I have been unwell for about 2 months. Initially I thought I just had a touch of 'flu with a slight fever and aching joints and muscles. However, in the last week or so, I have developed yellow skin and eyes. I feel very lethargic and generally unwell.

(In response to questioning only)

I drink 20 to 30 pints of beer per week and an occasional whisky. In the past I have been an intravenous drug user and shared needles on occasions. Currently I am off drugs. A recent HIV test I had was negative.

I have not travelled abroad and have had no sexual contacts with prostitutes. I have had no homosexual contacts, no blood transfusions and no regular medications. I remember my mother saying I was born jaundiced but I have never had any further episodes. I have no other gastric symptoms although I have lost 4 kilogrammes in the past 6 months. My stools and urine are normal in colour and consistency. I am working in a sorting depot of a large Post Office and smoke 10 to 20 cigarettes per day.

Assessment	Good	Adequate	Poor/not done
1. Polite introduction; establishes rapport	❑	❑	❑
2. Establishes duration and nature of the presenting symptoms	❑	❑	❑
3. Establishes previous episodes of jaundice and cause	❑	❑	❑
4. Establishes risk/symptoms of infective hepatitis:			
Prodromal symptoms/fever	❑	❑	❑
Foreign travel	❑	❑	❑
Sexual contacts	❑	❑	❑
Recent contacts	❑	❑	❑
Intravenous drug abuse	❑	❑	❑
Previous transfusions	❑	❑	❑
5. Establishes alcohol consumption and duration	❑	❑	❑
6. Establishes colour and consistency of stools and urine	❑	❑	❑
7. Establishes medications	❑	❑	❑
8. Establishes systemic symptoms - weight loss, abdominal pain, diarrhoea, steatorrhoea	❑	❑	❑
9. Makes a reasonable attempt at the diagnosis	❑	❑	❑
10. Does all in a fluent, professional manner	❑	❑	❑

Diagnosis

This patient has risk factors for viral hepatitis complicated by possible alcoholic liver disease. He will need investigation to exclude viral causes including liver biopsy. He should be counselled about alcohol consumption.

STATION 2.9

Patient history

Three months ago I noticed dark blood mixed in my motions, which are hard but occasionally very loose with slime. My appetite is poor, I have lost a little weight and I am not eating well, as I feel bloated with crampy pains in the abdomen following meals. I had a severe attack of bowel cramps a few years ago. I had an X-ray of the bowels three years ago, which showed I had diverticulitis. I was placed on a course of tablets but have been constipated most of my life. I had my gall bladder removed for stones many years ago and am on water and blood pressure tablets. I live alone and I manage very well. I don't drink or smoke.

Assessment   **Good Adequate Poor/not done**

1. Polite introduction;
   establishes rapport   ❏   ❏   ❏
2. Establishes presenting complaint:
   Passage of blood/slime/melaena   ❏   ❏   ❏
   Constipation alternating with
   diarrhoea   ❏   ❏   ❏
   Tenesmus ?pruritus ?piles   ❏   ❏   ❏
3. Asks about poor appetite/
   weight loss   ❏   ❏   ❏
4. Asks about abdominal cramps
   and bloating   ❏   ❏   ❏
5. Establishes past history of bowel
   problems and outcome   ❏   ❏   ❏
6. Establishes current dietary habits
   and lifestyle   ❏   ❏   ❏
7. Makes a reasonable attempt at
   the diagnosis   ❏   ❏   ❏
8. Does all in a fluent,
   professional manner   ❏   ❏   ❏

Diagnosis
Inflammatory bowel disease

Comment

A long history of episodic diarrhoea with the passage of mucus and malaise is indicative of inflammatory bowel disease, although less severe symptoms may suggest an irritable bowel syndrome. Abdominal bloating and cramps point to subacute colonic obstruction, usually from a constricting tumour. This is a late presentation in tumours of the colon but may be the only symptom in tumours of the proximal colon. A long history of constipation and diverticular disease usually go hand-in-hand, and rectal bleeding from a focus of diverticulitis is not uncommon. Massive bleeding results from erosion of blood vessels at the base of a diverticulum, and is uncommon in an ulcerating tumour.

STATION 2.10

Patient history

I have suffered from piles on and off for the past 25 years. They now come out when I go to the toilet and sometimes I have to push them back. There is usually blood on the toilet paper and occasionally splashes of blood in the toilet bowl. I had the piles injected a few years ago and I use Anusol suppositories when they become troublesome. I am a long-distance lorry driver, and as I spend days on the road, my meals are not regular, and I tend to be constipated. I am generally healthy and have had no major illnesses. I am trying to get my weight down.

Assessment	Good	Adequate	Poor/not done
1. Polite introduction; establishes rapport	❏	❏	❏
2. Establishes presenting complaint	❏	❏	❏
3. Establishes duration of symptoms and treatment	❏	❏	❏
4. Establishes dietary and bowel habits: excludes passage of blood and mucus	❏	❏	❏
5. Establishes general lifestyle	❏	❏	❏
6. Makes a reasonable attempt at the diagnosis	❏	❏	❏
7. Does all in a fluent, professional manner	❏	❏	❏

Diagnosis
Haemorrhoids

Comment

Haemorrhoids are a common and benign ailment, affecting 10% of the population. Piles are associated with, and may indeed be precipitated by, poor dietary habit and constipation. Small piles (first degree haemorrhoids) may respond to a high residue diet alone. Large and troublesome piles that have responded poorly to sclerotherapy or rubber banding require surgery. It is important to bear in mind that piles may be a 'red herring' in patients with rectal bleeding caused by an occult colonic tumour.

STATION 2.11

Assessment	Good	Adequate	Poor/not done
1. Polite introduction; establishes rapport	❏	❏	❏
2. Examines hands and fingernails	❏	❏	❏
3. Examines conjunctiva, tongue and fauces	❏	❏	❏
4. Examines for supraclavicular nodes	❏	❏	❏
5. Exposes abdomen and identifies laparotomy scar and stoma	❏	❏	❏
6. Palpation for liver, spleen, kidneys and other abdominal masses	❏	❏	❏
7. Percusses and auscultates abdomen	❏	❏	❏
8. Does all in a fluent, professional manner	❏	❏	❏

Clinical note for assessor:

This is a 37-year-old woman who underwent a total colectomy and an ileostomy for Crohn's disease five years ago. She is currently well and in remission.

Comment

Examination of the abdomen must start with the hands for clubbing, pallor, liver palms and liver flap; then examine the conjunctiva and tongue for pallor. Supraclavicular nodes are classical sites for metastatic deposits from gastric and pancreatic cancers. Gentle abdominal palpation detects inflammation (local or generalised), organomegaly and pathological masses. Percussion detects gaseous distension and ascites, whilst auscultation is for bowel sounds.

Abdominal stomas: may be intubated (e.g. gastrostomy or caecostomy) or open (ileostomy or colostomy or ileal conduit). Cutaneous fistulae and sinuses take a number of forms but are distinguishable from stomas by the presence of surrounding abdominal wall distortion, scarring and soilage.

STATION 2.12

Answers

Figure 2.12a - Black hairy tongue 2, 3, 4, 6

Figure 2.12b - Fissured 1, 2, 6

Figure 2.12c - Leucoplakia 2, 4, 5

Figure 2.12d - Carcinoma 4

Comment

A white patch in the mouth is called leucoplakia. Approximately 3% of white patches undergo malignant change in 5 years. Biopsy is, therefore, essential. Erythroplasia (red patches in the mouth) have a higher predilection to malignancy. Carcinoma of the mouth is associated with smokers, and tobacco and betel nut chewers. Carcinoma of the tongue is treated by surgery or radiotherapy; cervical nodal spread requires a block dissection.

STATION 2.13

Answers

1. Figure 2.13a: Oesophageal varices
    Figure 2.13b: Raised polypoid mucosal lesion

2. (a) Oesophageal varices secondary to portal hypertension
        Gastric (antral) carcinoma
    (b) Multiple endoscopic mucosal biopsies for histological
        confirmation

3. (a) Cirrhosis of the liver due to alcoholic liver damage, hepatitis B
        or C, or Wilson's disease
    (b) Megaloblastic anaemia associated with achlorhydria

4. Figure 2.13a: Haematemesis, melaena
    Figure 2.13b: Dyspepsia, anorexia, tiredness and weight loss,
    melaena

Comment

Oesophageal varices are treated by endoscopic sclerotherapy, and
long-term endoscopic surveillance, with sclerosis of recurrences,
and propranolol therapy. Nutritional and lifestyle measures are
required to halt the progression of cirrhotic change.

Gastric cancers present insidiously, with vague dyspepsia and
anaemia. Dyspepsia of 8 weeks or more duration requires an
endoscopic assessment. Non-ulcer dyspepsia is common, and
antral mucosal biopsies usually reveal a type II gastritis associated
with *Helicobacter pylori* infection.

STATION 2.14

Answers and explanations

1. Figure 2.14a: oedematous, inflamed mucosa with haemorrhage and covered with yellow exudate or slough
   Figure 2.14b: sessile mucosal polyp

2. Figure 2.14a: acute pseudomembranous colitis
   Figure 2.14b: rectal polyp

3. (a) Long-term antibiotic therapy producing a superinfection
   (b) Rectal carcinoma

4. Figure 2.14a: IV fluid and electrolyte replacement
   Stop patient's current antibiotic regime
   Figure 2.14b: endoscopic excision and histological examination. If benign, place patient on colonoscopic surveillance; if malignant, surgical excision of rectum with preoperative radiotherapy

Comment

Figure 2.14a: pseudomembranous colitis is a potentially lethal complication of intermittent or long-term antibiotic therapy for infective or ulcerative colitis. It is also a complication of AIDS. The causative agent is *Clostridium difficile*.

Figure 2.14b: colorectal carcinoma is thought to evolve from adenomatous or dysplastic polyps and from the familial polyposis syndrome. In the latter, the entire colon is studded with polyps and, as malignant transformation is inevitable, prophylactic total colectomy is advised.

Colonoscopic biopsies would confirm the diagnosis in both cases.

STATION 2.15

Answers and explanations

1. (E) (d)
This patient has coeliac disease which causes malabsorption within the jejunum leading to folate deficiency, hypoalbuminaemia, hypo-calcaemia and hypomagnesaemia. Any patient in this age group presenting with a macrocytic anaemia should be screened for coeliac disease. This should include a duodenal biopsy which will show the classical pattern of subtotal villous atrophy. Anti-endomysial antibodies are the specific immune marker in this disease.

2. (D) (e)
Patients with alcohol-related liver disease may present with a pancytopenia, as in this case, due to the direct toxic effects of alcohol on the bone marrow. The macrocytosis may be due to the liver disease or the direct effect of the alcohol.

3. (A) (f)
All causes of upper and lower GI bleeding can present with a microcytic anaemia. However, acute bleeding is often associated with a thrombo-cytosis. Change in bowel habit in patients over the age of 40 requires further investigation and this patient should have a colonoscopy.

4. (F) (b)
Pernicious anaemia is associated with several autoimmune diseases, particularly hypothyroidism. The macrocytosis may be due to the hypothyroidism or the vitamin B12 deficiency of pernicious anaemia. Severe vitamin B12 deficiency, as in this case, causes bone marrow suppression leading to a pancytopenia. However, this occurs over a long period of time and leads to a very suppressed haemoglobin, which may often be surprisingly well tolerated. Treatment in this case should include thyroid replacement, vitamin B12 injections and upper GI endoscopy, as such patients are at increased risk of gastric carcinoma.

5. (C) (a)
This patient has a microcytic anaemia indicating a chronic bleeding problem but this is associated with a raised platelet count and melaena, both indicators of acute blood loss. He requires a 6 unit cross match and urgent upper GI endoscopy.

6. (B) (c)
Inflammatory bowel disease commonly causes a normochromic, normocytic anaemia. If associated with GI blood loss it may cause a microcytic anaemia and rarely terminal ileal Crohn's disease may lead to vitamin B12 deficiency.

STATION 2.16

Answers and explanations

1. (E) (c)
Carcinoma of the head of the pancreas causes an obstructive jaundice, the patient often presenting as 'severely' jaundiced both clinically and biochemically.

2. (B) (e)
Primary biliary cirrhosis is an autoimmune disorder of the liver which principally affects middle aged women. It has been postulated that there is a cross antigen reaction in childhood between *E. coli* and hepatocytes. Patients present with signs of chronic liver disease and may have a hepatitic jaundice.

3. (A) (b)
Coeliac disease is also an autoimmune disease of the small bowel. It may present at any age but principally affects young female adults. It rarely causes derangement of the liver function tests but causes general malabsorption leading to folate deficiency, hypocalcaemia, hypo-magnesaemia and hypoalbuminaemia.

4. (D) (a)
Colonic carcinoma commonly metastasises to the liver and the skeleton. There is derangement of the liver function tests with a raised alkaline phosphatase. This may indicate both liver and bony metastases as it is produced in both tissues, but the raised calcium infers bony metastases.

5. (C) (d)
Gallstones within the lower common bile duct may produce an obstructive jaundice with an acute pancreatitis. An amylase over 1000 may be caused by an acute pancreatitis, a perforated viscus and a leaking abdominal aortic aneurysm. The low calcium is indicative of acute pancreatitis.

STATION 2.17

Answers and explanations

1. (D) (e)
Chronic viral hepatitis is a principal risk factor for developing a hepatoma. All patients with decompensating chronic disease should be screened for a hepatoma using the marker alpha fetoprotein and ultrasound scan. Hepatoma may be amenable to surgical resection or radiological embolization.

2. (C) (f)
This patient has developed liver metastases from a primary colonic carcinoma. Although CEA is requested in many hospitals as a screening tool for colonic carcinoma, the pick-up rate has been disappointingly low. It should be used mainly after surgical resection as a marker of secondary disease, so that aggressive therapy may be instituted.

3. (E) (a)
This patient has developed primary haemochromatosis, an autosomal recessive disorder of iron metabolism. Excess iron is laid down in the liver leading to cirrhosis and its secondary sequelae. The suntanned appearance is due to melanin excess in the skin, and not iron. Treatment is by regular venesection, some patients also requiring the chelating agent desferrioxamine. All first degree relatives should undergo screening.

4. (B) (c)
This patient has primary biliary cirrhosis, an autoimmune disorder of the liver which principally affects middle aged women. It is thought to be a cross antigen reaction between *E. coli* and hepatocytes, as these patients have been shown to be susceptible to *E. coli* UTIs in childhood. Immune markers of the disease include antimitochondrial antibodies and, less commonly, antismooth muscle and antinuclear antibodies.

5. (F) (b)
Autoimmune hepatitis (previously termed autoimmune or lupoid chronic active hepatitis) has now been divided into 2 separate disorders by the different autoantibodies present. **Type 1** is characterised by non organ specific autoantibodies and liver specific autoantibodies. Non organ specific autoantibodies are a heterogeneous group, the commonest being the dsDNA antibodies. The principal of these is in antismooth muscle antibodies with anti-actin specificity. The most

219

specific of the liver antibodies is AntiASGP-R (asialoglycoprotein receptor). **Type 2** is characterised by the presence of circulating antiliver/ kidney microsomal antibodies (anti-LKM), which have been subdivided into 3 distinct antibodies: anti-LKM 1, 2 and 3.

6. (A) (d)

Wilson's disease is a rare autosomal recessive disorder which leads to an inability to metabolise copper normally. The copper is deposited in various sites: the liver, leading to cirrhosis, the brain, particularly the basal ganglia, and the cornea, leading to the pathognomonic Kayser-Fleischer ring. The disorder leads to a dyskinetic syndrome or bradykinetic/rigidity syndrome (Parkinsonism). There is an associated progressive cognitive impairment. The disease effects may be retarded by the use of oral penicillamine. All relatives should have genetic counselling and screening.

STATION 2.18

Answers and explanations

1. False	7. True
2. True	8. True
3. False	9. True
4. False	10. False
5. True	11. True
6. False	12. False

Patient (a) - This patient has evidence of acute viral replication (aHBc IgM positive) and high infectivity risk (HBe aGen positive) indicating acute viral hepatitis.

Patient (b) - The presence of HBs antibody shows previous exposure to the hepatitis B virus with subsequent development of immunity. This may occur after vaccination or after the resolution of an acute infection.

Patient (c) - This patient continues to express HBv DNA which has become encoded within their own genome (HBs aGen positive). However the expression of aHBc IgG shows no ongoing viral replication. The patient remains HBe aGen positive which means they are still at high risk of passing on the infection and must be warned about sexual and drug taking practices.

Patient (d) - This patient is a chronic carrier but is at low risk of passing on the infection and does not have evidence of ongoing viral replication. However these patients are still not allowed to give blood in the UK.

STATION 2.19

Answers

1.	(E)	(d)	4.	(F)	(b)
2.	(D)	(e)	5.	(C)	(a)
3.	(A)	(f)	6.	(B)	(c)

STATION 2.20

Answers

1. Figure 2.20a: supine view of the abdomen
    Figure 2.20b: erect antero-posterior (AP) view of the abdomen

2. Dilatation of stomach and jejunal, and ileal bowel loops (2.20a);
    with air fluid levels (2.20b)

3. Acute small bowel obstruction

4. Place patient on a 'drip and suck' regime
    Assess serum urea and electrolytes and replace fluid and electrolyte
    deficit
    Hourly naso-gastric aspiration
    Ascertain cause of bowel obstruction and organise surgical relief if
    required
    Intramuscular analgesia for pain relief

Comment

Small bowel obstruction usually presents acutely, whilst large bowel
obstruction is insidious in onset. Relief of small bowel obstruction
must be immediate to prevent perforation or gangrene. Exceptions
are sub-acute obstruction due to adhesions, or a bolus obstruction
which may resolve with its passage. Fluid and electrolyte depletion
from vomiting and third compartment loss is life-threatening and
must be replaced through IV access.

STATION 2.21

Answers

1. Barium enema examination

2. Instil liquid barium into the rectum under hydrostatic pressure not exceeding 30 cm water. Tilt the patient as required to demonstrate the colon.

3. A segment of colon showing an intra-luminal obstruction from an intussusception of the large bowel

4. Surgical reduction of the intussusception if the bowel is viable, or resection of the involved loops of the bowel if the viability is in doubt.

Comment

Intussusception is a cause of bowel obstruction in infants during weaning, but is rare in adults. It is, however, a cause of insidious bowel obstruction in AIDS and is associated with bowel lymphoma and Kaposi's sarcoma. Contrast-enhanced CT scan of the abdomen is the preferred method of diagnosing this condition in these patients, who may have co-existing symptoms from chronic enteric infections.

STATION 2.22

Answers and explanations

1.   (a) True   (b) False   (c) True   (d) True   (e) True
This is an erect CXR showing gas below the right hemidiaphragm. The principal cause of this appearance is perforation of a hollow viscus such as the bowel. Free air under the diaphragm is expected for 48 hours post laparoscopy but would indicate a perforation post ERCP. The initial management of a patient with perforation is intravenous antibiotics, e.g. metronidazole and cefuroxime, intravenous fluids and NG suction. This is colloquially known as 'drip and suck'. In patients unable to have operative intervention this conservative management may allow time for the perforation to be 'walled off' and heal, if it is small and the contamination limited.

2.   (a) True   (b) False   (c) False   (d) True   (e) False
This is a plain, supine film showing large bowel obstruction. Small bowel is differentiated from large bowel by the plica circulares which extend across the entire small bowel width. The large bowel is defined by the haustration of its wall. Two grossly dilated lengths of large bowel fill the length of the abdomen. Fluid levels are a feature of an erect film and are therefore not seen in this X-ray. The ground glass appearance in the right iliac fossa is produced by faecal loading. Adhesions commonly cause small bowel obstruction but are a relatively rare cause of large bowel problems. Common causes include diverticular disease, tumours, abscesses, volvulus and extrinsic compression from pelvic tumours.

3.   (a) False   (b) False   (c) True   (d) True   (e) False
Figure 2.22C is an erect CXR showing a large, probably incarcerated rolling hiatus hernia: showing stomach shadow and probable small gut loop. The 'double' left cardiac border is a result of the retrocardiac hernia. The hernia contains an air-fluid level which raises the possibility of the hernia being obstructed. Patients with a large hiatus hernia may have insidious gastro-intestinal blood loss leading to a microcytic anaemia.

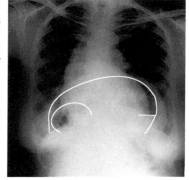

Fig. 2.22C

STATION 2.23

Answers and explanations

1. **(a) False** **(b) True** **(c) False** **(4) True** **(5) True**
This is a barium swallow showing a long, smooth stricture, consistent with a benign lesion. Common causes are oesophageal reflux and corrosives. Presbyoesophagus, ('cork screw oesophagus') is a benign condition of old age and a diagnosis is made on video fluoroscopy. It must be differentiated from malignancy.

2. **(a) True** **(b) False** **(c) False** **(4) False** **(5) True**
This barium swallow shows a grossly dilated lower oesophagus with a classical 'bird beak' deformity in the distal segment. There is abundant food residue within this dilated segment. These appearances are consistent with achalasia. This is an idiopathic disorder which is caused by an aganglionic segment of the lower oesophagus, (similar to Hirschsprung's disease of the rectum). It is an important diagnosis as it is a pre-malignant condition.

3. **(a) False** **(b) False** **(c) True** **(4) False** **(5) True**
On comparing the stricture in the barium swallow in Figure 2.23a with this examination, it is clear that the strictured segment is very irregular and is diagnostic of a carcinoma. Oesophageal carcinoma is related to cigarette smoking, heavy alcohol intake and spicy foods. Predisposing conditions include achalasia, tylosis, Plummer-Vinson syndrome and Barrett's oesophagus.

STATION 2.24

Answers and explanations

1.   (a) True   (b) True   (c) False   (d) True   (e) False
This is a barium meal and follow-through
(into the small bowel) study showing a large
3 cm ulcer crater on the posterior wall of the
body of the stomach (Figure 2.24A). The
smooth margins indicate its probable benign
nature. There is almost complete loss of the
normal gastric rugae (folds) which indicates
gastric atrophy and raises the possibility of
pernicious anaemia. In the follow-through
there is evidence of incidental duodenal and
jejunal diverticulae and radio-opaque
gallstones are also outlined.

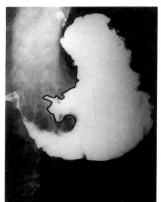

Fig. 2.24A

2.   (a) False   (b) False   (c) True   (d) False   (e) True
This is a barium meal showing a large ulcer
on the lesser curvature of the antrum and
body of the stomach. Its irregular margins
(comparing it to the example above) indicate
it is probably a malignant ulcer. Carcinoma
of the stomach is associated with the
presence of *H. pylori* and pernicious
anaemia. It is therefore advisable that early
eradication therapy is given to younger
patients presenting with peptic ulcer disease
and that patients with pernicious anaemia
have endoscopic follow up.

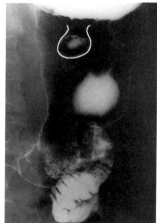

Fig. 2.24B

3.   (a) True   (b) False   (c) True   (d) True   (e) True
This is a barium meal and follow-through showing a grossly shrunken,
poorly distended stomach. The oesophagus and duodenum are within
normal limits. This appearance is due to diffuse mucosal infiltration by a
gastric carcinoma. This appearance is termed a 'leather bottle' stomach
or linitis plastica.

STATION 2.25

Answers and explanations

1. (a) True (b) False (c) True (d) False (e) False
This is a barium enema taken with the patient lying on their right as witnessed by the fluid levels. The study shows multiple diverticulae throughout the colon. Diverticular disease is related to a low fibre, Western diet and is rarely seen in black Africans. The disorder is unrelated to inflammatory bowel disease.

2. (a) False (b) True (c) False (d) False (e) True
This is a double contrast barium study showing loss of the haustral pattern in the distal two thirds of the transverse colon and the descending colon. This appearance is termed 'lead piping' and is a feature of ulcerative colitis. The small indentations are pseudopolyps and not diverticulae. The incidence of inflammatory bowel disease is similar in the two sexes. The incidence of colonic carcinoma is greatly increased in patients with ulcerative colitis for 10 years or greater and they should be under colonoscopic surveillance.

3. (a) True (b) False (c) True (d) False (e) True
This is a double contrast study showing a classical 'apple core' stricture of the proximal transverse colon (Figure 2.25C). This appearance is classical of colonic cancer. Patients present with weight loss, change in bowel habit and bleeding and mucous per rectum. Colonic carcinoma usually presents in the 6th to 7th decade.

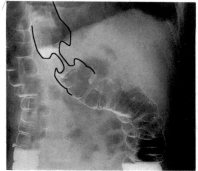

Fig. 2.25C

STATION 2.26

Answers

(A) Liver   (E) Ribs
(B) Spleen   (F) Right crus of the diaphragm
(C) Lumbar vertebra   (G) Liver metastases
(D) Abdominal aorta

STATION 2.27

Answers and explanations

1. (a) This is an ERCP (endoscopic retrograde cholangiopancreatogram).
   (b) It shows a markedly dilated common bile duct and biliary tree and a filling defect at the lower end of the bile duct. No gallstones are identified. At operation, a carcinoma of the ampulla of Vater was identified and resected.

2. (a) This is a selective coeliac axis arteriogram which is principally used to delineate small tumours of the pancreas, e.g. insulinomas.
   (b) The arteriogram shows normal splenic, left gastric and hepatic arteries but the gastro-duodenal arteries show a blush at their distal ends, with encasement and narrowing of the pancreatico-duodenal artery proximally. These appearances suggest a pancreatic carcinoma.

3. (a) This is an ultrasound scan of the liver.
   (b) Ultrasound is a relatively simple, safe, non-invasive procedure which is extremely useful in visualising the intra-abdominal viscera. Indications for its use include hepatobiliary disease, particularly the investigation of jaundice. Structures that may be visualised include liver metastases, gallstones and other causes of obstruction of the hepatobiliary tree. Pancreatic visualisation is more difficult due to overlying gastric and duodenal gas, and ultrasound has been superseded in many respects by CT scanning to visualise the pancreas. Other intra-abdominal indications include investigations of any mass, visualising the renal tract and the pelvic organs. Ultrasound may be used to define an aortic aneurysm but in the acute situation dissection can only be truly excluded at operation or

by aortogram. This scan shows multiple, heterogeneous lesions within the liver, consistent with metastases.

4. This is a right decubitus view of a barium enema showing the classical appearance of the twisted neck of a sigmoid volvulus. The sigmoid colon has become twisted with resulting gross dilatation. The initial treatment is to attempt to pass a flatus tube across the twisted segment into the obstructed sigmoid loop. If this is successful, the flatus tube should be left in for 24 to 48 hours. If this fails, a limited barium enema should be attempted which may cause the volvulus to untwist. Urgent surgical intervention is usually required, involving sigmoid colectomy.

5. This is an erect CXR showing a calcified mass in the right upper quadrant. This patient had a hydatid cyst, but many chronic conditions produce calcification within the liver, e.g. tuberculosis; arterio-venous anomalies, aneurysms, hepatoma and metastases.

STATION 2.28

Answer and explanation

This woman has a duodenal ulcer which is proven to be associated with *Helicobacter pylori*. She should therefore be started on a course of eradication and ulcer healing therapy. As yet there is no single agreed regimen. Eradication therapy combines one or two antibiotics with an antisecretory drug. For full ulcer healing the antisecretory drug may need to be continued for a further 1–2 months. The regimen chosen must be relatively 'user friendly' as the biggest problem is often poor patient compliance. Recently therefore, one week regimes have been advocated using higher doses of the drugs.

Suggested combinations are shown below (as per Prescriber's Journal 1996, Vol.36 No 3).

One week:
Triple therapy – eradication rates vary from 80–90%
Amoxycillin 750 mg tds + Metronidazole 400 mg tds + Ranitidine 300 mg nocte
Amoxycillin 500 mg tds + Metronidazole 400 mg tds + Omeprazole 20 mg bd or Lansoprazole 30 mg bd
Amoxycillin 1g bd + Clarithromycin 500 mg bd + Omeprazole 20 mg bd or Lansoprazole 30 mg bd
Clarithromycin 250 mg bd + Metronidazole 400 mg bd + Omeprazole 20 mg bd or Lansoprazole 30 mg bd

Two week:
Dual therapy – eradication rates vary from 60-80%
Amoxycillin 1 g bd + Omeprazole 20 mg bd or Lansoprazole 30 mg bd
Clarithromycin 500 mg tds + Omeprazole 40 mg mane

The correct prescription should be filled in with any of the regimens suggested above, ensuring the patient details are all correct, the drugs, doses and frequencies are clearly stated and the duration of therapy is written below. The prescription must be signed, with your name printed and dated.

STATION 2.29

Answers and explanations

1. False
He is likely to be in a catabolic state due to sepsis and multiple trauma.

2. False
He has a disproportionately raised creatinine compared to his urea. This suggests he has renal cellular damage, as well as any pre-renal impairment.

3. True
To calculate his corrected calcium = calcium + (standard albumin [40 mmol/l] – serum albumin) x 0.02 = 1.9 + ([40-19] x 0.02) = 2.12 mmol/l.

4. False
40 mmol is the normal daily requirement. This patient has marked hypokalaemia and therefore requires 100–200 mmol.

5. True
If peripheral or central venous access is becoming difficult, the insulin may be given in the TPN bag. However, under normal circumstances, an IV sliding scale insulin regime should be maintained.

6. True
Although he has a low albumin he cannot have a very high protein concentration in his TPN because of his renal impairment.

7. False
His BMI = weight (kg)/height (metres)^2 = 80/3.24 = 24.69 (normal = 20–28).

8. True
He can receive all his fluid replacement through the TPN.

9. False
He will require increased calories because of the catabolic effects of the sepsis.

10. True
Although a 'dedicated' line is better.

STATION 2.30

Answers and explanations

1. False   2. True   3. False
Instrument A is a rigid sigmoidoscope used to view the first 15–25cm of distal large bowel. It is used to view the bowel mucosa to exclude local inflammation, tumours and bleeding sites. Biopsy forceps may be inserted through the sigmoidoscope in order to biopsy mucosa or tumours. Sigmoidoscopy should be nothing more than 'uncomfortable' and is carried out without sedation.

4. False   5. True   6. True
Instrument B is a Sengstaken-Blakemore tube. Although endoscopy has allowed direct access to sources of both upper and lower gastrointestinal bleeding, the Sengstaken tube may still play a vital role in containment of a bleeding site in the lower oesophagus or stomach. It is particularly useful in controlling bleeding from oesophageal varices. A tennis ball or similar soft object is often attached to the proximal end of the tube, cushioned and tied against the face, to stop the patient swallowing the entire tube! After an initial examination, sigmoidoscopy precedes proctoscopy to avoid misinterpretation of any hyperaemia produced in the rectum by the proctoscope: treatment of local perianal conditions can also be undertaken through the proctoscope, with the knowledge that proximal rectal pathology has already been excluded. Proctoscopy must be undertaken routinely after any sigmoidoscopy.

7. True   8. False   9. False
Instrument C is a proctoscope used to look at local disease within the rectum. It may be used with a sigmoidoscope but it is often used independently. Sigmoidoscopy usually precedes proctoscopy so that erythema produced by the latter is not misinterpreted as inflammation, and that therapeutic measures, such as injection of piles, can be undertaken, knowing that there are no contraindications pertaining to the rectum

10. False 11. True   12. False
Instrument D is a liver biopsy needle. The patient must be able to lie flat on their back and hold their breath for approximately ten seconds to allow the biopsy to be taken. Apart from being unable to do either of these, other contraindications include local skin sepsis, deranged clotting or thrombocytopaenia, gross ascites and extrahepatic

cholestasis. The patient should have a FBC and clotting screen prior to the procedure and full informed consent should be obtained. The procedure is usually performed with local anaesthetic.

13. False 14. True 15. False

Instrument E is an endoscope used to view the upper and lower bowel. It has now been shown that coeliac disease may be diagnosed from duodenal biopsies and this has made the use of the Crosby-Kugler capsule unnecessary. ERCP is performed through a slightly modified endoscope. Pneumomediastinum is a relatively rare complication of an upper GI endoscopy. It may arise due to force being applied to the endoscope or through biopsying areas of the oesophagus, causing tears in the mucosa. Small tears will cause few problems and will heal over with no further intervention. Large tears, however, need surgical repair.

16. True 17. True 18. False

Instrument F is a nasogastric tube used to feed and hydrate patients who are having difficulty maintaining their nutritional input. This may be due to a decreased level of consciousness or mechanical swallowing problems, both of which may occur in a stroke patient. The feeding of patients using the gut is known as enteral feeding. Parenteral feeding is the use of specialised feeding lines inserted into a vein. The tube is radio-opaque to allow its position to be seen on a chest radiograph. Its position may be checked clinically by pushing 50mls of air from a syringe down the tube whilst listening with a stethoscope over the stomach, or by aspirating fluid back along the tube and then testing to see if it is acidic with litmus paper.

STATION 3.1

Patient history

I am 18 years old and, for the last 5 years, I have been getting recurrent urinary symptoms. I have had multiple urinary infections, blood in my urine and, more recently, dull pain in my lower back. In the last 18 months I have also had recurrent headaches and visual disturbance. My mother and grandmother both had kidney disease and my mother died of a bleed inside the brain. Each episode of infection is relieved for a week or two by antibiotics but I have had to self-medicate from time to time to stop them coming back so frequently. Each infection lasts for 5 to 6 days with frequency, as well as pain and blood when I pass urine. I have been admitted on three occasions with severe infections with associated fever and rigors.

I have never been further investigated because I am terrified of the possible diagnoses and have always taken my own discharge before the hospital has had time to do any secondary investigations. I have also moved around a lot because of my father's job in the Navy.

Assessment	Good	Adequate	Poor/not done
1. Polite introduction; establishes rapport	❑	❑	❑
2. Establishes duration of urinary problems	❑	❑	❑
3. Establishes symptoms of urinary tract infection	❑	❑	❑
4. Establishes associated fever and rigors	❑	❑	❑
5. Establishes symptoms of polycystic kidney disease:			
UTIs	❑	❑	❑
Loin pain	❑	❑	❑
Haematuria	❑	❑	❑
Features of hypertension	❑	❑	❑
Establishes family history of renal disease	❑	❑	❑
6. Establishes mother died of subarachnoid haemorrhage	❑	❑	❑
7. Makes reasonable attempt at a diagnosis	❑	❑	❑
8. Does all in a fluent, professional manner	❑	❑	❑

Diagnosis
Recurrent urinary tract infection secondary to adult polycystic kidney disease

STATION 3.2

Patient history

I am 24 years old and am normally fit and well. I have come to the Accident and Emergency Department with severe left-sided pain in my lower back. I have had the pain now for 8 hours and it has gradually increased in intensity and is now unbearable. The pain comes and goes in waves and has no radiation. I have had two similar episodes in the last year, but these were not as severe. I have not had any symptoms of urinary infection, fever or rigors, or pain on passing urine.

Assessment	Good	Adequate	Poor/not done
1. Polite introduction; establishes rapport	❏	❏	❏
2. Establishes duration of present illness	❏	❏	❏
3. Establishes left-sided loin pain	❏	❏	❏
4. Establishes character and nature of the pain	❏	❏	❏
5. Establishes history of two similar but less severe episodes	❏	❏	❏
6. Excludes symptoms of UTI	❏	❏	❏
7. Asks about passage of renal stones	❏	❏	❏
8. Makes a reasonable attempt at a diagnosis	❏	❏	❏
9. Talks competently about the management options	❏	❏	❏
10. Does all in a fluent and professional manner	❏	❏	❏

Diagnosis
Renal colic secondary to renal stones

Comment

Renal stones produce intense, acute pain, causing the patient to roll around in agony. The most important acute treatments are adequate analgesia, with either pethidine or voltarol, and IV fluids. When using pethidine, or if vomiting is present, an anti-emetic should also be given. Initial management should include FBC, U+Es, LFTs, amylase and calcium, plain AXR, IV access and IV fluids. An USS of the renal tract and/or an IVU should be organised as soon as possible.

Small stones may pass spontaneously and the patient may have noticed previous stones passed in the urine. Larger stones may require surgical removal or may be disintegrated using lithotripsy.

STATION 3.3

Patient history

I am the wife of the patient, who is 55 years old and a diabetic. He has non-insulin dependent diabetes mellitus and hypertension, and was recently started on an ACE inhibitor by his local GP on the advice of the hospital.

In the last week he has become increasingly confused and unwell. He has been vomiting and has had severe hiccups. He is continually scratching and I have not seen him pass any urine for over 48 hours. His ankles are becoming increasingly swollen. He does not have any other systemic symptoms. He is known to have slight kidney problems due to diabetes and his high blood pressure. As well as the ACE inhibitor he is on gliclazide and bendrofluazide.

Assessment	Good	Adequate	Poor/not done
1. Polite introduction; establishes rapport and the woman's identity	❑	❑	❑
2. Establishes premorbid problems of the patient	❑	❑	❑
3. Establishes recent addition of ACE inhibitor therapy	❑	❑	❑
4. Establishes duration of present illness	❑	❑	❑
5. Establishes/excludes symptoms of uraemia and renal failure:			
Nausea and vomiting	❑	❑	❑
Pruritus	❑	❑	❑
Hiccups	❑	❑	❑
Oliguria in last week	❑	❑	❑
Peripheral oedema	❑	❑	❑
6. Makes a reasonable attempt at a diagnosis	❑	❑	❑
7. Discusses the management in a competent manner	❑	❑	❑
8. Does all in a fluent and professional manner	❑	❑	❑

Diagnosis
Uraemic precoma, secondary to acute on chronic renal failure. The recent addition of the ACE inhibitor has precipitated the dramatic acceleration of his renal impairment.

STATION 3.4

Patient history

I am a 53-year-old bank manager and I was fit and well until 5 months ago. Initially I noticed occasional episodes of blood mixed with my urine but, more recently, I have had several episodes of passing blood. This is associated with a dull pain in my left loin and I have also noticed a slight swelling in this area. I have lost several kilogrammes in weight and have a poor appetite. I have had no energy to do anything and feel continually tired. In the last few weeks I have also had a fever, particularly at night, and have woken on several occasions drenched in sweat.

Assessment	Good	Adequate	Poor/not done
1. Polite introduction; establishes rapport	❏	❏	❏
2. Establishes the duration of the presenting illness	❏	❏	❏
3. Establishes the nature of the haematuria, i.e. frank blood	❏	❏	❏
4. Establishes frequency of the haematuria	❏	❏	❏
5. Establishes associated dull left loin pain and swelling	❏	❏	❏
6. Establishes associated malaise, lethargy, anorexia and weight loss	❏	❏	❏
7. Establishes history of night sweats	❏	❏	❏
8. Makes a reasonable attempt at a diagnosis	❏	❏	❏
9. Is able to discuss the possible further management in a clear and competent manner	❏	❏	❏
10. Does all in a fluent, professional manner	❏	❏	❏

Diagnosis
Malignant renal tumour

Comment

Any patient over 40 years old with painless haematuria must have malignancy of the renal tract excluded. Blood tests should include an FBC to exclude anaemia secondary to haematuria or polycythaemia, which is a rarer presentation. U+Es may be abnormal, particularly in bilateral disease. The ESR is often raised. A CXR, USS of the renal tract and an IVU should be routinely performed to assess the tumour and its spread.

Renal tumours are often extremely vascular and may be demonstrated using renal arteriography. A staging CT scan of the abdomen should also be performed in this situation.

Unilateral tumours are generally treated by surgical excision. Radiotherapy and chemotherapy are also used, particularly in bilateral and metastatic disease.

STATION 3.5

Patient history

I am 37 years old and have had SLE for the last 6 years. I have recently noticed my ankles and calves swelling up, to such an extent in the last few weeks that I now cannot get my shoes on. In the last ten days I have not passed very much urine, despite drinking a lot of fluids and I have also become breathless on exertion. Other than the SLE I have had no serious illnesses and have never had any problems with my heart. At present I am taking azathioprine and steroids for the SLE.

Assessment	Good	Adequate	Poor/not done
1. Polite introduction; establishes rapport	❑	❑	❑
2. Establishes the presenting complaint	❑	❑	❑
3. Establishes the duration of the presenting illness	❑	❑	❑
4. Establishes associated history of exertional dyspnoea	❑	❑	❑
5. Establishes history of poor urine output for several days	❑	❑	❑
6. Excludes previous cardiac history and symptoms	❑	❑	❑
7. Establishes drug treatment of SLE	❑	❑	❑
8. Makes a reasonable attempt at a diagnosis	❑	❑	❑
9. Does all in a fluent, professional manner	❑	❑	❑

Diagnosis
Nephrotic syndrome secondary to SLE

STATION 3.6

Patient history

I have been having increasing difficulty holding my water for the past year and I wet myself more and more often. I leak when I am up and about walking or gardening and sometimes when I cough or sneeze. I don't drink and wear a pad when I am going out to avoid embarrassing situations. I have no children and live alone and have been healthy all my life, except for attacks of cystitis when I was young. I am not on any drugs except for oestrogen patches to prevent hot flushes and to keep my bones healthy.

Assessment	Good	Adequate	Poor/not done
1. Polite introduction; establishes rapport	❑	❑	❑
2. Establishes presenting complaint	❑	❑	❑
3. Establishes duration and associated features	❑	❑	❑
4. Establishes current medication	❑	❑	❑
5. Establishes urinary tract/pelvic infections	❑	❑	❑
6. Establishes/excludes history of abdominal surgery and/or obstetric injuries	❑	❑	❑
7. Makes a reasonable attempt at a diagnosis	❑	❑	❑
8. Does all in a fluent, professional manner	❑	❑	❑

Diagnosis
Stress incontinence

Comment

Stress incontinence in the female is caused by pelvic floor flaccidity and is usually associated with multiple pregnancies or previous obstetric trauma. Treatment is with pelvic floor exercises, to improve muscle tone. Surgical reconstruction of the pelvic floor, or implantation of a muscle stimulator, may be tried in the refractory patient.

Stress incontinence is also associated with motor neurone disease and must be distinguished from detrusor muscle instability, where the treatment is with anticholinergics.

STATION 3.7

Answers

1.	Testicular torsion	Fig. 3.7d
2.	Varicocele	Fig. 3.7e
3.	Haematocele	Fig. 3.7b
4.	Testicular tumour	Fig. 3.7c
5.	Vaginal hydrocele	Fig. 3.7a

B.

Clinical condition (diagnosis)	History	Symptoms	Signs	Treatment
1. Testicular torsion	3a	3b	1c	5d
2. Varicocele	4a	5b	4c	3d
3. Haematocele	1a	4b	2c	1d
4. Testicular tumour	2a	2b	5c	2d
5. Vaginal hydrocele	5a	1b	3c	4d

Comments

Testicular torsion occurs in childhood and is accompanied by nausea, vomiting and fever. The pain radiates to the lower abdomen.

A varicocele is caused by engorgement of the testicular venous plexus and is associated with subfertility. A haematocele is bleeding into the testicular substance, and the tunica vaginalis, usually due to blunt trauma. Evacuation of the haematoma may be necessary.

Testicular tumours produce painless enlargement: early diagnosis is essential to enable curative treatment to be initiated.

A vaginal hydrocele is a collection of fluid between the coverings of the testis and may occasionally be secondary to a testicular tumour.

STATION 3.8

Answers and explanations

1. **True:** The raised haemoglobin and haematocrit are consistent with polycythaemia
2. **True:** Adult polycystic kidney disease and renal carcinoma may both produce excessive eythropoietin causing polycythaemia
3. **False:** This is suggestive of lower urinary tract infection and may be associated with symptoms of cystitis
4. **False:** These results are consistent with a normochromic, normocytic anaemia
5. **True:** Chronic renal disorders are commonly associated with an anaemia of chronic disease
6. **False:** Anaemia of chronic disease is associated with a normal plasma ferritin

7. **True:** In this case malignancy of the renal tract must be excluded
8. **False:** These results are suggestive of an ongoing bleeding disorder. This would be in keeping with a renal tract problem causing chronic haematuria e.g. polycystic kidney disease or renal carcinoma. Renal abscesses do not usually present in this manner
9. **True:** The raised platelet count in association with the microcytic anaemia is consistent with an active bleeding problem

10. **True:** This patient has results consistent with multiple myeloma. The four investigations of choice are plasma calcium (raised), plasma electrophoresis (monoclonal bands), ESR >100, urinary Bence-Jones proteins.
11. **False:** Myeloma is associated with hypercalcaemia
12. **False:** The plasma cells noted are seen in the peripheral blood film of 15% of patients with myeloma

STATION 3.9

Answers and explanations

1. **False**: The results are suggestive of pre-renal impairment. The urea is raised disproportionately higher than the creatinine
2. **True**: A GI bleed will cause hypovolaemia, leading to pre-renal impairment. It will also cause a rise in the urea due to the absorption of protein from blood in the gut

3. **False**: The low urea is not compatible with dehydration
4. **False**: This blood result is consistent with blood drawn from a vein proximal to a dextrose infusion. There are no suggestions of renal impairment despite the hyperglycaemia

5. **True**: The patient has diabetic nephropathy. The raised HBA1c suggests poorly controlled diabetes. The low bicarbonate shows a metabolic acidosis which would be consistent with chronic renal disease
6. **True**: This is the classical lesion of diabetic glomerulosclerosis

7. **True**: Initial treatment of the hyperkalaemia should be with insulin and dextrose. However this is a short term solution and, in view of the patient's renal failure, the best treatment would be dialysis
8. **False**: The patient has acute on chronic renal failure with a low serum calcium. This data does not support a diagnosis of myeloma. Renal failure in myeloma may result from a nephrotic syndrome, obstruction of the nephrons due to heavy light chain excretion, amyloidosis, myelomatous infiltration of the kidneys and the associated hypercalcaemia and hyperuricaemia

9. **False**: This patient has obstructive nephropathy secondary to prostatic carcinoma
10. **True**: This is an important investigation in a patient with prostatic carcinoma which commonly metastasises to bone

STATION 3.10

Answers and explanations

Sample Patient
1.   (E)
E. coli is a common organism causing urinary tract infections. Other common causes of UTI include Proteus, *Staphylococcus saprophyticus* or *epidermis* and Klebsiella.

2.   (A)
This urine culture has grown acid fast bacilli, proving this woman has renal tract tuberculosis. This requires at least 6 months antituberculosis treatment.

3.   (D)
This microscopy shows renal red cell casts which are indicative of renal disease. The history is suggestive of renal failure with a possible nephrotic syndrome.

4.   (C)
This patient has renal colic secondary to recurrent stones. The specimen shows a sterile pyuria. Other causes include interstitial nephritis, papillary necrosis and tuberculosis of the renal tract.

5.   (B)
Although there is significant growth of pseudomonas, the white cell count indicates this is most likely to be a contaminant. Unless the patient is unwell this should not be treated with antibiotics.

STATION 3.11

Answers and explanations

1.   (E)   (b)
The malar rash is characteristic of SLE as are the Anti-ds DNA antibodies. Several other auto-antibodies are found in SLE which have now been linked to specific subsets within the disease, (see Rheumatology and Dermatology chapter) e.g. anticardiolipin antibody, anti-ro and anti-la. SLE is commonly associated with renal involvement and may present with asymptomatic proteinuria or an acute glomerulonephritis with nephritic or nephrotic syndrome.

2.   (D)   (a)
The significance of the hepatitis B antigen in PAN is still unclear. It occurs in a small percentage of patients with the disorder and is thought to indicate a possible environmental association with the vasculitis.

3.   (A)   (e)
Systemic sclerosis (scleroderma) has now been reclassified into 2 separate sub-groups. **Limited cutaneous**, previously called the CREST syndrome, is most readily identified by the anticentromere antibody, whereas diffuse cutaneous is associated with the anti-Scl 70 antibody. Patients with diffuse disease commonly develop renal involvement, principally manifested as severe hypertension and worsening cardiac failure.

4.   (B)   (c)
The patient has signs of both renal and lower respiratory tract involvement consistent with glomerular basement membrane disease or Goodpasture's disease. With the advent of immunofluorescence microscopy it became evident that the original syndrome described by Goodpasture in the USA after the influenza epidemic in 1918 was in fact common to several disorders including the systemic vasculitides. The antibody shares a common antigen in the glomerular basement membrane and the alveolar basement membrane. This has now been localised to type IV collagen which is a major component of both membranes.

5. (C) (d)

Antineutrophil cytoplasmic antibodies (ANCA) are subdivided into cANCA (c = cytoplasmic) and pANCA (p = perinuclear) according to their pattern of indirect immunofluorescence. cANCA is closely linked to Wegener's granulomatosis and, more recently, has been specifically linked to the antigen proteinase 3. The presence of antiproteinase 3 antibodies is now regarded as diagnostic of Wegener's. pANCA is associated with microscopic PAN and has been linked to the antigen myeloperoxidase. This is not as specific as the association of cANCA and proteinase 3; it is seen in several other disorders, including inflammatory bowel disease and autoimmune hepatitis.

STATION 3.12

Answers and explanations

1.   (a) True   (b) False   (c) True   (d) True   (e) False
This is a plain abdominal X-ray of the abdomen showing grossly enlarged renal outlines (Figure 3.12A). The normal kidneys should be no more than 3 lumbar vertebrae in length. Causes of bilaterally enlarged kidneys include polycystic kidney disease, bilateral malignant tumours and hydronephrosis. The lower pole of the right kidney has a clear area of calcification which, under normal circumstances, should be considered malignant until proven otherwise. This patient has polycystic kidney disease and this appearance may be caused by calcification of haemorrhage into one of the cysts. However, renal ultrasound, IVP and urinary cytology should be performed.

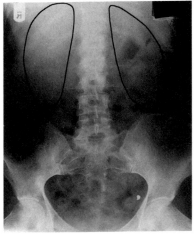

Fig. 3.12A

2.   (a) False   (b) False   (c) True   (d) False   (e) True
This plain abdominal X-ray shows a large staghorn calculus in the pelvis of the right kidney. Such calculi are associated with recurrent UTIs particularly with Proteus infections. These organisms hydrolyse urea and so cause alkalysation of the urine which in turn favours stone formation. The majority of renal stones are composed of calcium oxalate and phosphate, the others being composed of uric acid, cystine and magnesium ammonium phosphate.

3.   (a) True   (b) False   (c) False   (d) True   (e) True
This view from an IVP shows a huge vesical calculus within the bladder. The two ureters are dilated (hydroureters) due to the bladder obstruction being caused by the stone. The right pelvicalyceal system in particular shows evidence of 'clubbing' also resulting from the obstruction. Bladder stones formation is related to foreign bodies, e.g. indwelling catheters, within the bladder and bladder outflow tract obstruction. The majority of patients have stagnation of urine within the bladder and significant bacteruria.

STATION 3.13

Answers

1. Right-sided stag-horn renal calculus

2. Obstruction to drainage of the renal pelvis and progressive destruction of the renal parenchyma from pressure and infection

3. Fragmentation with shockwave lithotripsy or surgical removal of the calculus, together with treatment of any underlying infection. Nephrectomy may be required if the kidney is irretrievably damaged

Comment

Staghorn calculi are shaped by, and virtually fill, the entire pelvi-calceal system. Symptoms such as back pain and renal colic occur when the calculi obstruct one or more calyces or the renal pelvis.

Most renal calculi are visible on plain radiography; only pure uric acid stones and the rare xanthine and 'protein matrix' stones are radiolucent.

STATION 3.14

Answers

1. Radio-opaque vesical (bladder) calculi

2. Dietary factors
    Metabolic (hereditary) cause
    Chronic cystitis

3. Transurethral removal of the calculus after crushing with a lithotrite or fragmentation with shock-wave lithotripsy

Comment

Calcium-containing urinary stones are far more frequently encountered in Western society than uric acid or phosphate stones. Metabolic evaluation is undertaken if active stone disease is suspected, i.e. evidence of new stone formation, stone growth or passage of gravel within one year. Absorptive hypercalcaemia is associated with an altered bowel response to Vitamin D, leading to increased absorption of calcium, elevated serum calcium levels and depression of parathyroid function, with increased urinary excretion of calcium. Renal hypercalcaemia is due to the inability of the kidney to conserve calcium, due to a tubular functional defect. This leads to a low serum calcium level, resulting in stimulation of parathyroid hormone secretion and increased synthesis of vitamin D, with increased absorption of calcium from the bowel and resorption from bone.

STATION 3.15

Answers

1. Intravenous urogram (IVU)

2. Bilateral duplex kidneys and ureters

3. Retrograde uretero-pyelogram

4. A urinary tract infection in the pelvi-calceal system; other possibilities include ureteric calculus originating in the abnormal pelvi-calyceal system

Comment

Pelvi-ureteric congenital abnormalities are not uncommon and range from complete absence to duplication or triplication of the renal pelvis and ureter. They may cause obstruction requiring urgent treatment, or they may be asymptomatic and of no clinical significance. Obstruction at the pelvi-ureteric junction is due to a developmental abnormality that requires surgical correction. Obstruction at the uretero-vesical junction is four times more common in boys than in girls. Surgery is usually indicated, with excision of the distal ureter and uretal reimplantation.

STATION 3.16

Answers

1. Intravenous urography (pyelography)

2. Hydrocalyces and hydropelvis of right kidney
   Obstruction at the pelvi-ureteric junction

3. Surgical reconstruction of the pelvi-ureteric junction

4. Pressure necrosis of the renal cortex, with or without pyelonephritis

Comment

On presentation this patient would have had a KUB (plain radiograph) followed by an ultrasound scan of the right collecting system. The latter is usually diagnostic in obstructive uropathies. An IVU demonstrates the anatomic details of the site of obstruction for surgical reconstruction.

STATION 3.17

Answers and explanations

1. (a) This is a renal angiogram showing a downwardly displaced left kidney with a highly vascularised area above it. These appearances may be due to a malignant tumour or polycystic disease.

    (b) Indications for this investigation include suspected renal artery stenosis, intrarenal arterial disease, e.g. polyarteritis nodosa, which causes intrarenal aneurysms, and defining the presence and extent of a renal tumour.

    Important questions to ask the patient prior to starting this procedure should include identifying the patient, the procedure they are to have and the reason for it, identifying previous allergies to contrast media and drug allergies.

2. (a) This is an IVU showing calcification in the upper pole of the right kidney.
    (b) Common causes of renal calcification include:
    Diffuse: Medullary sponge kidney, hypercalcaemia and renal tubular acidosis.
    Medullary: diffuse papillary necrosis
    Cortical: Acute cortical necrosis, chronic transplant rejection
    Focal areas: tuberculosis, renal carcinoma, polycystic disease and amyloidosis.

3. (a) This is an IVU
    (b) It shows a right pelvic kidney without functioning normal kidneys. The bones of the pelvis show evidence of renal osteopathy.
    (c) These abnormalities indicate a renal transplant following chronic renal failure.

    There are two tablets in the stomach. The bone changes associated with renal failure are termed 'renal osteodystrophy'. Renal osteodystrophy initially arises due to osteomalacia associated with chronic renal failure. Hypocalcaemia leads to secondary and subsequent tertiary hyperparathyroidism. The classical 'rugger jersey spine' of tertiary hyperparathyroidism, which is alternating hypo- and hyperdense bands within the vertebrae, is not apparent in this film.

STATION 3.18

Answers and explanations

(b) Shows a downwardly displaced left-sided kidney. The right kidney is not as well visualised but is within normal limits as is the bladder. This appearance may be caused by a large renal mass displacing the kidney. Examples include renal cell carcinoma, large renal cysts and polycystic renal disease.

(c) The left renal pelvi-calceal system is grossly dilated. This appearance is consistent with pelvi-ureteric obstruction. This may be caused by a functional abnormality arising due to an inelastic ring of tissue at the junction, strictures, transitional cell carcinoma and calculi.

(d) This is a bilateral abnormality demonstrating a horseshoe kidney. Both pelvicalyceal systems are rotated through 90°, appearing to be 'end on'. This is characteristic and arises due to an embryonic failure of the developing kidneys to split apart as they ascend along their development pathways in the abdomen to their normal positions. The disorder may affect a small area, such as the lower poles or may include the kidney's entire length.

(e) This IVU shows an irregular area at the insertion of the right ureter into the bladder with no visible ureter or kidney above it. This implies a non-functioning right kidney due to obstruction within the bladder. Further investigation revealed a transitional cell carcinoma of the bladder.

STATION 3.19

Answers

(a)

A - Lumbar vertebra
B - Abdominal aorta
C - Inferior vena cava
D - Left kidney

E - Small bowel
F - Liver
G - Spleen
H - Right renal tumour

STATION 3.20

Answers

1. Urodynamic (pressure-flow) studies
2. Detrusor instability
    Prostatic hyperplasia
    Bladder neck hypertrophy
    Neurogenic bladder

3. Figure 3.20A shows the completed labelled trace

4. Voluntary micturition commences at X and ends at Y

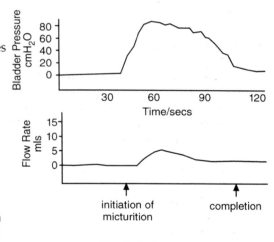

Fig. 3.20A

Comment

The patient has a double-lumen indwelling catheter; one for filling the bladder and the other for pressure measurement. A catheter in the rectum monitors abdominal pressure changes. The latter is subtracted from the bladder pressure recording to give the true intravesical pressure.

The bladder catheter is removed prior to voiding and a flow meter attached to the commode monitors the volume of urine voided and computes the flow rate in ml/sec.

STATION 3.21

Answers and explanations

1. Enalapril, bumetanide, amoxycillin, aspirin and diclofenac – penicillins and NSAIDs may cause an acute tubulo-interstitial nephritis. This patient has evidence of mild renal impairment and has known IHD which may point to an element of atherosclerotic renal artery stenosis. This should make one wary about adding on an ACE inhibitor to this patient's regime.

2. Gliclazide (sulphonylurea), acarbose (alpha glucosidase inhibitor).

3. Amoxycillin, omeprazole, aspirin and diclofenac may all be directly contributing to her nausea.

4. Enalapril, bumetanide and GTN spray may all cause postural hypotension. Aspirin and diclofenac may lead to acute and chronic gastrointestinal blood loss, indirectly contributing to her hypotension.

5. FBC – to exclude anaemia
   Glucose and HBA1c – diabetic control
   Lipid profile – if not checked recently
   Calcium and phosphate – essential in chronic renal impairment
   USS of the renal tract – principally to exclude obstruction
   Urinalysis – to exclude red cell casts
   MSU – to exclude urinary tract infection. This may be contributing to her worsening renal function.

STATION 3.22

Answers and explanations

1. (D) (c)
Benign prostatic hyperplasia (BPH), is a histological diagnosis which may be inferred from a patient's history and a normal PSA, but must be confirmed by cystoscopic biopsy of the prostate. If symptoms are mild or the patient is not fit for surgical intervention a 5α reductase inhibitor, such as finasteride may be used. 5α reductase is an enzyme required for the production of testosterone, which is known to worsen BPH.

2. (F) (e)
Patients with chronic renal failure commonly suffer with a normo-chromic/normocytic anaemia. This anaemia is frequently due to loss of erythropoietin production in the failing kidneys. Although this is a common disorder amongst this group of patients not all respond to erythropoietin replacement. All such patients should have haematinics, i.e. vitamin B12, folate and ferritin to exclude other, more readily treatable causes. It should be noted that erythropoietin treatment was one of the first drugs to be withdrawn on financial reasoning alone.

3. (B) (e)
Prostatic carcinoma is a common malignancy of older men, although it can occur from age 40. The diagnosis is inferred on history, examination, which may show a 'craggy', abnormal prostate, and investigation may show deranged U+Es and raised PSA. Metastatic disease may be apparent on CXR, USS of the liver and on bone scan. Diagnosis is confirmed on prostatic biopsy. Treatment is principally surgical resection with or without bilateral orchidectomy. Antiandrogens such as cyproterone, are commonly used in inoperable cases, as are other treatments to lower circulating testosterone, e.g. Stilboestrol and LHRH injections.

4. (C) (f)
Urinary incontinence may have many causes, one of which is detrusor instability, leading to poor bladder sphincter control. This disorder is readily treated with anticholinergics such as oxybutynin. However, the treatment should not be instituted until a postmicturition residual bladder volume has been measured. If this is greater than 150 to 200 mls, the addition of an anticholinergic will worsen the condition as they can cause urinary retention, stagnation and infection.

5.   (A)   (d)
Diabetic patients, particularly those with hypertension, should be treated with an ACE inhibitor. The newer generation of ACE inhibitors, e.g. quinapril, lisinopril and perindopril, retard and possibly reverse both microvascular changes and atherosclerotic disease.

6.   (E)   (b)
Patients with myelo- and lymphoproliferative disorders are particularly at risk of gout due to the massive turnover of cells in these conditions. Allopurinol is often given prophylactically to these patients to stop overt clinical gout arising. It should be remembered that hyperuricaemia is 20–30 times more common than clinical gout.

STATION 3.23

Assessment	Good	Adequate	Poor/not done
1. Cleaning and draping of the region	❑	❑	❑
2. Catheterization technique (non-touch; use of lubricant)	❑	❑	❑
3. Ensure the catheter tip is in the bladder by drawing out urine before blowing up the balloon	❑	❑	❑
4. Checks balloon volume size; blows up catheter balloon with the appropriate amount of saline	❑	❑	❑
5. Connects catheter to drainage bag	❑	❑	❑

Comment

When catheterizing to relieve acute or acute on chronic urinary retention, choosing the smallest gauge self-retaining catheter (CH 9, 10 or 12) minimises urethral mucosal trauma. Check the balloon volume size before commencing. When blowing up the balloon in a Foley catheter ensure that the catheter tip is well into the bladder to avoid blowing up the balloon in the urethra.

STATION 3.24

Answers

1. A: Puncture needle
    B: Catheter with sleeve
    C: Adaptor – clamp

2. Percutaneous suprapubic catheterization

3. Urinary retention (usually acute)

4. A distended, readily palpable urinary bladder

Comment

This is a bed-side surgical procedure undertaken under local anaesthesia, to relieve acute or chronic retension, often following failed transurethral catheterization. A fully sterile technique must be adopted and the procedure must not be undertaken if the bladder is not palpable.

STATION 3.25

Patient histories

Husband: I am a 35-year-old sales representative for a pharmaceutical firm. We have been married for four years and have two children. We do not wish to add to our family, and my wife and I have discussed the various methods of birth control between ourselves and with our GP; vasectomy is the procedure we have agreed on. I am healthy and fit and am on no medication. Ten years ago I was treated for TB of the lung and made a full recovery; a right sided groin hernia was repaired four years ago.

Wife: I am 28 years old and a housewife. Our children are one and three years of age. I have a seven-year-old daughter from a previous marriage, and she lives with her father and stepmother. My husband and I have completed our family and do not want any more children. I tried the birth control pill many years ago and suffered side-effects. I used a birth control coil after my last child but had to have it removed 6 months ago, as it caused heavy and painful periods. My husband and I have talked about the vasectomy operation for some time now, and our GP agrees that this operation would be the best for us.

Assessment	Good	Average	Poor/not done
1. Greetings and introductions	❑	❑	❑
2. Obtains request for sterilization from both partners	❑	❑	❑
3. Ascertains reason for request:			
Completed family	❑	❑	❑
Other methods ineffective	❑	❑	❑
4. Ascertain other methods of contraception tried			
Side effects: groin haematoma, sperm granuloma	❑	❑	❑
Failures: sterility is not immediate recannalisation - rare	❑	❑	❑
5. Establishes understanding of irrevocable nature of the procedure	❑	❑	❑
Re-confirms both partners understand the procedure	❑	❑	❑

Comment

When filling in a consent form for vasectomy both (married) partners must be in agreement in wishing to have the procedure carried out. They must also understand the irreversible nature of the operation. Sterility is not assured until three consecutive semen samples taken over 3 months after the vasectomy are azoospermic. This fact must be emphasised during consent, and for an alternative form of contraception to be used in the interim period.

STATION 4.1

Patient history

I have been married for three years and I work full-time as an administrative officer for a pharmaceutical company. My husband is a civil engineer with a road construction firm. My father has diabetes, which recently affected his eyesight and kidneys. I had a miscarriage two years ago and was admitted as an emergency and received a blood transfusion.

I was on the birth control pill until a few months ago, when we decided to start a family. My last period was 10 weeks ago and they have always been regular and of normal duration. I have been feeling sick and dizzy most mornings but am getting over it now. I don't smoke but took sleeping tablets at night until recently, when I found out that I was pregnant.

Assessment	Good	Adequate	Poor/not done
1. Polite introduction; establishes rapport	❏	❏	❏
2. Establishes:			
LNMP	❏	❏	❏
Symptoms of early pregnancy	❏	❏	❏
Recent febrile illnesses, e.g. *German measles*	❏	❏	❏
Any current medications	❏	❏	❏
Alcohol cunsumption/smoking	❏	❏	❏
Indulgence in recreational drugs	❏	❏	❏
3. Establishes history of previous pregnancies (number)	❏	❏	❏
Full term deliveries and/or premature labour	❏	❏	❏
Abortions or miscarriages	❏	❏	❏
Ante-partum haemorrhage, hypertension, heart disease, diabetes, UTI or eclampsia during pregnancy	❏	❏	❏

	Good	Adequate	Poor/not done
4. Establishes past medical history: *Major medical illnesses & treatment*	❏	❏	❏
Surgical operations & outcome	❏	❏	❏
Gynaecological problems and outcome	❏	❏	❏
Smoking habit	❏	❏	❏
5. Establishes whether the patient works and if so, what kind of work.	❏	❏	❏
6. Establishes if the patient is married or in a long-term relationship	❏	❏	❏
Fertility treatment	❏	❏	❏
Number of children, birth weights	❏	❏	❏
Birth defects (if any)	❏	❏	❏
Establishes whether children were breast-fed	❏	❏	❏
7. Does all in a fluent, professional manner	❏	❏	❏

Comment

The history must include: home circumstances and lifestyle, any fertility treatment, multiple pregnancies and/or birth defects, pelvic inflammatory disease and treatment, smoking history, past medical history and family history of heart disease, hypertension and diabetes. Past obstetric complications indicate the need for close monitoring of current pregnancy, to prevent recurrence.

STATION 4.2

Patient history

I have not seen my periods for 10 weeks and am worried that I am pregnant, as I did not plan to be. I work full-time as a producer for a local TV and cable company. I am single and have no plans to marry. I have been on the contraceptive pill for the past eight years or so but came off it a few months ago when I saw one of your partners in the practice because of my painful breasts. I was diagnosed as having a benign breast condition and was advised to stop taking the pill.

My breasts feel full and sore at present, and I feel sick in the mornings. I am getting up at night to pass water and am going more frequently during the day. My periods have always been regular, and I have never been pregnant. I have always been healthy and fit except for a bad attack of malaria when I was in Africa recently working on a wildlife documentary.

Assessment | **Good Adequate Poor/not done**

Assessment	Good	Adequate	Poor/not done
1. Polite introduction; establishes rapport	❑	❑	❑
2. Establishes symptoms of early pregnancy	❑	❑	❑
3. Establishes menstrual history	❑	❑	
Establishes contraceptive practice	❑	❑	❑
4. Family and social history	❑	❑	❑
5. Establishes attitude to pregnancy/need for counselling	❑	❑	❑
6. Establishes gynaecological history, including infection	❑	❑	❑
7. Establishes current and past general health	❑	❑	❑
8. Does all in a fluent, professional manner	❑	❑	❑

Comment

The patient is anxious and worried, and the pregnancy needs confirmation. She must, therefore, be questioned sympathetically, and she should develop confidence that she would be supported and cared for in her present situation. A positive pregnancy test may require counselling on the care provided at home and in hospital.

STATION 4.3

Patient history

I have not been pregnant before, and this news is most unexpected and worrying. I have not told my partner, who is responsible for my pregnancy, and I do not know how he would react to the news. My parents would like me to marry and settle down, but I am not sure if I am ready for this, and my partner and I have never discussed marriage. My work involves a good deal of foreign travel, and I have a full work schedule for the next year or so. Taking time off for this would mean professional sacrifices but with the support of my partner and my family, I may think of going through with the pregnancy. If I decide on termination, how much time do I have? Where can I have it done? Would it affect my health in any way? I am confused and unable to decide right now but need your advice and help in arriving at a decision.

Assessment	Good	Adequate	Poor/not done
1. Establishes empathy and shows sympathy and understanding	❑	❑	❑
2. Emphasizes positive aspects of pregnancy and childbirth, i.e. a sense of fulfilment	❑	❑	❑
3. Explains antenatal support during pregnancy and social service support following birth	❑	❑	❑
4. Explains procedures for surgical termination of pregnancy	❑	❑	❑
5. Explains that termination in first trimester is done as a day procedure and carries negligible risks to health and fertility	❑	❑	❑
6. Stresses importance of involvement of partner in counselling	❑	❑	❑
7. Does all in a fluent, professional and sympathetic manner	❑	❑	❑

Comment

The doctor has to guide the patient through a highly emotive and sensitive decision-making process with underlying socio-religious implications. Counselling of the patient and her partner should be directed towards the support available to take her safely through her pregnancy, confinement and antenatal care and, on the patient's request, the safety of pregnancy termination in a hospital setting. The doctor should refrain from expressing his/her personal, moral or ethical views.

STATION 4.4a

Patient history

I have always been fit and well, although overweight, and I am 12 weeks pregnant with my first child. I am 1.54m and 64 kilogrammes. I have come for the results of a glucose tolerance test I had five days ago. This was because at my first antenatal visit, blood and urine tests showed a possibility of sugar diabetes. My great aunt has diabetes, which is controlled with diet and tablets, and I am hoping, if needs be, I can go on these.

I have stopped smoking and drinking alcohol since finding out that I am pregnant but I have 'a very sweet tooth' and tend to eat boxes and boxes of chocolates. Nobody has explained the results or the implications of diabetes, and I have no concept of what this will mean to me or the baby. Apart from a bit of morning sickness, I have been well in the last few weeks.

Assessment	Good	Adequate	Poor/not done
1. Polite introduction; establishes rapport	❏	❏	❏
2. Establishes patient identity and reason for attendance	❏	❏	❏
3. Establishes patient's understanding of the investigation and the possible diagnosis	❏	❏	❏
4. Explains the investigation results and diagnosis in a clear non-jargonistic manner	❏	❏	❏
5. Explains the implications of the diagnosis on the pregnancy			
Complications to the mother	❏	❏	❏
Complications to the foetus	❏	❏	❏
6. Explains the treatment alternatives – diet or insulin; no tablets may be used	❏	❏	❏
7. Establishes the patient's present dietary intake, height and weight	❏	❏	❏
8. Excludes other risk factors: smoking and alcohol	❏	❏	❏

	Good	Adequate	Poor/not done
9. Explains about regular blood monitoring	❏	❏	❏
10. Invites patient's questions and answers appropriately	❏	❏	❏
11. Does all in a fluent, professional manner	❏	❏	❏

Diagnosis
Gestational diabetes

Comment

Management of diabetes during pregnancy
Pre-existing diabetics should optimise their glycaemic control prior to pregnancy and should be cared for by an obstetrician and a diabetologist.

Gestational diabetes is thought to be a marker of susceptibility to type II diabetes in later life, with the 'stress' of pregnancy causing alterations in glycaemic control. (A small percentage of women diagnosed as having new onset diabetes during pregnancy will have insulin dependent diabetes).

Patients may be managed with a strict diabetic diet, but if this fails, the only option is to use insulin. Patients are usually started on small doses of mixtard insulin, on a bd regime, e.g. 8 units mane, 4 units nocte. If this fails to maintain normoglycaemia, a qds regime may be adopted, using pre-meal actrapid and an evening dose of an intermediate acting insulin. Doses are titrated upwards according to the patient's glycaemic control, which they must be taught to monitor using BM stix.

Complications of hyperglycaemia during pregnancy

Maternal: Infections, e.g. vaginal candidiasis, UTIs
Polyhydramnios
Pre-eclampsia and eclampsia

Foetal: Intrauterine death and neonatal mortality are both greatly increased
Macrosomia (large baby)
All birth defects are increased

STATION 4.5a

Patient history

I am 42 years old and have always been fit and well, and am 34 weeks pregnant with my third child. My previous two pregnancies were without problems and both babies were born at full term by normal vaginal delivery. I had slightly raised blood pressure during my last pregnancy but it settled with rest at home.

I was told by both the doctor in the hospital and the GP that my blood pressure has again been slightly high but I have been taking it easy and when the community midwives checked it, it has been okay. I realise I may have to be admitted to hospital but am not very keen because of caring for my other children. My partner is very supportive but works 6 days a week and at present cannot afford to take time off. My mother-in-law has offered to come and stay to look after the children but I am not very keen on this as her health is rather fragile.

Assessment   **Good Adequate Poor/not done**

1. Polite introduction;
    establishes rapport   ❏   ❏   ❏
2. Establishes patient's understanding
    of her blood pressure problem
    and its implications   ❏   ❏   ❏
3. Establishes previous obstetric
    history and history of pregnancy
    induced hypertension   ❏   ❏   ❏
4. Explains the risk of eclampsia to
    mother and foetus in a clear,
    non-jargonistic manner   ❏   ❏   ❏
5. Explains that patient requires
    admission – bed rest, treatment
    of blood pressure, possible
    caesarian delivery   ❏   ❏   ❏
6. Establishes and discusses reasons
    why patient is reluctant to be
    admitted   ❏   ❏   ❏
7. Invites patient's questions and
    answers appropriately   ❏   ❏   ❏
8. Does all in a fluent
    and professional manner   ❏   ❏   ❏

Diagnosis
Pregnancy induced hypertension; patient is now pre-eclamptic requiring admission

Comment

Pre-eclamptic toxaemia is one of the leading causes of mortality in the UK. Possible crises include eclampsia, HELP syndrome, placental abruption, renal failure and cerebral haemorrhage. The spectrum of the condition includes uteroplacental insufficiency and intrauterine growth retardation is commonly associated.

The patient requires admission for close monitoring of the blood pressure, biochemistry and foetal well-being. Indications for delivery include foetal compromise, inability to control maternal blood pressure, and the development of maternal symptoms suggesting impending crisis, e.g. right upper quadrant pain.

STATION 4.6

Assessment	Good	Adequate	Poor/not done
1. Polite introduction; establishes rapport	❑	❑	❑
2. Establishes patient identity and reason for attendance	❑	❑	❑
3. Establishes patient's present understanding of the situation	❑	❑	❑
4. Explains the ultrasound results in a clear, non-jargonistic manner	❑	❑	❑
5. Explains the need for delivery by caesarean section	❑	❑	❑
6. Invites patient's questions and answers appropriately	❑	❑	❑
7. Does all in a fluent, professional manner	❑	❑	❑

Comment

Placenta praevia describes the condition where the placenta lies in the lower uterine segment. It is associated with multiple foetuses e.g. twins, triplets, an abnormally large placenta, uterine structural abnormalities, benign and malignant tumours and previous uterine surgery, e.g. caesarean section.

Classification: Grade I – The lower margins of the placenta do not reach the os.

Grade II – The lower margins reach but do not cover the os.

Grade III – The lower margins cover the os when closed, but not when dilated.

Grade IV – The os is totally covered by the overlying placenta.

STATION 4.7

Patient history

My baby is due in two months' time and I hear that it is always difficult and painful with the first baby. I cannot stand much pain and the thought of a difficult labour and having an episiotomy is frightening. I need to know how you are going to deal with the pain, because if I am going to feel any pain I want to be asleep during labour and until it is all over. My sister had a long and difficult labour last year and had to have stitches. As my mum also had problems, I am scared that this may run in the family. Do you think a caesarian section would be safer for me and the baby?

Assessment	Good	Adequate	Poor/not done
1. Polite introduction; establishes rapport	❏	❏	❏
2. Establishes how the patient reached her understanding of childbirth and whether she has read the educational literature or had discussions with the midwives	❏	❏	❏
3. Reassures her that unreliable information is misleading and often based on ignorance	❏	❏	❏
4. Establishes whether the patient or her partner attend antenatal classes or group therapy sessions, where labour is explained, to reduce fear and anxiety	❏	❏	❏
5. Reassures the patient that complete analgesia is achieved by regional block, always available in the labour room; will also make any episiotomy pain free	❏	❏	❏
6. Reassures the patient on the safety of caesarian section, when this is necessary	❏	❏	❏
7. Does all in an empathetic and professional manner	❏	❏	❏

Comment

Other forms of pain relief available are:

Transdermal electrical nerve stimulation (TENS) via surface electrodes placed on a patient's back and used in early labour: the strength and frequency of impulses can be adjusted for comfort.
Opiates: pethidine in the form of patient-controlled analgesia system (PCAS); morphine or diamorphine IV during prolonged labour.
Inhalation analgesia: Entonox by face mask is controlled by the patient.

STATION 4.8

Assessment	Good	Adequate	Poor/not done
1. Polite introduction; establishes rapport	❏	❏	❏
2. Invites questions from the couple	❏	❏	❏
(1) A definitive answer cannot be given unless there is an obvious cause of death or until postmortem findings are available. However, a postmortem may fail to reveal any abnormality and the cause may have to be attributed to antenatal hypoxia.	❏	❏	❏
(2) This must be answered with caution, with emphasis on the positive aspects of care. If a result of an internal enquiry is pending, the couple should be advised accordingly.	❏	❏	❏
(3) Reassures the couple that recurrent stillbirths are rare, except in some congenital abnormalities.	❏	❏	❏
(4) Answers supportively, i.e. whenever the couple feel they are ready. The outlook should be positive, and a new pregnancy should be embarked upon in anticipation and not fear.	❏	❏	❏

		Good	Adequate	Poor/not done
(5)	Advises the patient to book early for hospital antenatal care, with regular ultrasound monitoring and later combined with cardio-topographic monitoring in the third trimester. Hospital admission should be offered to 'carry her over' the time of the past stillbirth or closer to delivery for greater reassurance.	❏	❏	❏
3.	Does all in an empathetic and professional manner	❏	❏	❏

STATION 4.9

Assessment

		Good	Adequate	Poor/not done
1.	Polite introduction; establishes rapport	❏	❏	❏
2.	General examination: pallor jaundice and dependent oedema	❏	❏	❏
3.	Pulse, BP, cardiac assessment, lung expansion and breath sounds	❏	❏	❏
4.	Palpation for uterine size, foetal lie and presentation	❏	❏	❏
5.	Palpation for engagement of foetal head	❏	❏	❏
6.	Auscultate for foetal heart rate	❏	❏	❏
7.	Does all in a fluent, professional manner	❏	❏	❏

Comment

In-patient monitoring may be required for anaemia or jaundice, diastolic BP of >90 mm Hg after 26th week of pregnancy, multiple pregnancy (detected earlier by USS), abnormalities in foetal heart rate, proteinuria or glycosuria, endocrine abnormalities, e.g. hypo- or hyperthyroidism.

STATION 4.10

Assessment	Good	Adequate	Poor/not done
Figure 4.10a Normal CTG in labour; normal variation of foetal heart rate with uterine contractions (120-140 per min)	❑	❑	❑
Figure 4.10b Type 1 or early deceleration due to compression of the foetal head or cord during contractions; careful monitoring is required to detect any delay in recovery following contractions	❑	❑	❑
Figure 4.10c Complete loss of variability of foetal heart rate (flat CTG) during labour indicates severe foetal distress requiring urgent delivery	❑	❑	❑

Comment

Antenatal cardiotocography is used to monitor women at high risk in the last days of pregnancy to determine the best time to deliver the baby, a decision taken in conjunction with other parameters of the pregnancy. The normal foetal heart rate in the waking state shows baseline variability due to normal physiological stimuli (Figure 4.10a). Reduced variability results in a flat trace showing a heart not responding to such stimuli (Figure 4.10c). It may be caused by hypoxaemia due to reduction in placental blood flow. Sleep patterns also produce similar traces which revert to normal on waking the baby.

STATION 4.11

Apgar Scores

	0	1	2
Colour	Blue or pale	Blue extremities	Completely pink
Heart rate	Absent	< 100/min	> 100/min
Respiratory effort	Absent	Irregular	Good/crying
Muscle tone/ movement	Limp	Some flexion	Active movement
Reflex response	Absent	Minimal	Normal

Comment

The Apgar score denotes viability at birth. The need for immediate resuscitatory measures and/or transfer to an intensive care unit for monitoring is indicated with an Apgar score of 7 or less. Immediately life-threatening foetal abnormalities are also detected during the examination.

STATION 4.12

Assessment	Good	Adequate	Poor/not done
1. General inspection; facies and eyes	❏	❏	❏
2. Examination of mouth, ears and neck	❏	❏	❏
3. Examination of head and back	❏	❏	❏
4. Examination of chest and peripheral pulses	❏	❏	❏
5. Examination of abdomen, external genitalia, anus, hips and legs	❏	❏	❏
6. Does all in an efficient and professional manner	❏	❏	❏

Comment

Looks for obvious general abnormalities and assesses alertness, posture, movement and reflexes, eye anomalies and facial features suggestive of chromosomal abnormalities.

Examines mouth to exclude palatal and glossal abnormalities. External ear and meatal defects, thyroid enlargement, sternomastoid tumour.

Palpates fontanelles, checks for scalp haematoma (chignon), measures head circumference, examines back for signs of neural cord defects.

Auscultates for heart murmurs and breath sounds, examines for chest wall abnormalities, e.g. pectus excavatum, clavicular dislocation. Absent peripheral pulses suggest aortic coarctation.

Abdomen: normal to feel liver edge, kidneys/spleen; check cord stump, exclude exomphalos and imperforate anus.
External genitalia: In male: hypospadias, testicular descent. In female: labial fusion. Examines lower limbs for congenital hip dislocation, tallipes.

STATION 4.13

Assessment	Good	Adequate	Poor/not done
1. Tilts manikin head down Aspirates airway; 100% O_2 by face mask	❑	❑	❑
2. Monitor heart rate: if rate <100/min, intubates and ventilates Sets up venous access via umbilical vein	❑	❑	❑
3. In absence of heart beat after above, carries out external cardiac massage Counteracts acidosis by sodium bicarbonate (5 mmol/Kg wt) via umbilical vein catheter	❑	❑	❑
4. Keeps neonate warm with heating pad and space blanket	❑	❑	❑
5. Does all in an efficient and professional manner	❑	❑	❑

Comment

The long-held assumption that acidosis complicates cardiac arrest and may perpetuate arrhythmias has recently been challenged. Acidosis as measured by arterial and/or central venous blood gases probably bears little relationship to myocardial intra-cellular values; the passage of carbon dioxide across the cell membrane can lower intracellular pH, whilst the alkaline residue of the metabolized bicarbonate increases the extracellular pH. The development of an iatrogenic alkalosis may be even less favourable than the metabolic acidosis to the myocardium; and there is no good empirical evidence in favour of sodium bicarbonate during the early stages of cardiac arrest.

STATION 4.14

Patient history

I was previously a fit and well 19-year-old engineering student. I started having periods when I was 11–12 years old and these have been regular until 8 months ago: my normal cycle was 3–5/24–26. My periods have been irregular for the past 4 months. I was involved in a long term relationship until 6 months ago when I split up with my boyfriend because he was seeing other girls. I was devastated. We used to use condoms and I have never been on the OCP.

I have never been pregnant and have not had any other gynaecological problems. I have been relatively well, but lost 4–5 kilogrammes after the break-up of my relationship. (I have put some weight back on recently) I have been struggling at college and feel quite lonely and depressed. I have been sleeping poorly but have been eating a lot better recently. I have started smoking 10–20 cigarettes per day. I drink 20–30 units of alcohol per week. I am not on any regular medication, and have never suffered from anorexia or hormone imbalance.

Assessment	**Good**	**Adequate**	**Poor/not done**
1. Polite introduction; establishes rapport	❑	❑	❑
2. Establishes age of menarche	❑	❑	❑
3. Establishes normal menstrual cycle and last normal cycle	❑	❑	❑
4. Asks about sexual activity: establishes last sexual intercourse/ excludes symptoms of pregnancy	❑	❑	❑
5. Establishes present method of contraception, if any	❑	❑	❑
6. Establishes absence of an obstetric history	❑	❑	❑
7. Establishes/excludes other gynaecological symptoms: *dyspaeunia, pelvic pain, galactorrhoea, post coital bleeding, premenstrual symptoms*	❑	❑	❑

	Good	Adequate	Poor/not done
8. Establishes/excludes symptoms of differential causes:			
Endocrine disorders	❏	❏	❏
Anorexia/gross weight loss	❏	❏	❏
General systemic disorders – thyroid disease, anaemia, diabetes	❏	❏	❏
9. Enquires of social history, personal and family relationships leading to amenorrhoea	❏	❏	❏
10. Establishes smoking and alcohol history	❏	❏	❏
11. Establishes not on any medications	❏	❏	❏
12. Summarises findings; gives appropriate differential diagnosis	❏	❏	❏
13. Does all in a fluent, sensitive professional manner	❏	❏	❏

Diagnosis

Secondary amenorrhoea due to stressors of university course and personal relationship break-up.

STATION 4.15

Patient history (from wife)

We have been married for three years. We both work, he is a solicitor, and I am an estate agent. We own the house we live in and have no financial worries. My husband has a 5-year-old child from a previous marriage, whom he supports. I have never been pregnant and we are both healthy and fit. I had an operation for an ovarian cyst five years ago, when my right ovary was removed. My periods were regular when I was on the Pill but since I came off it over two years ago when we started trying for a baby, they come every six weeks or so and are occasionally heavy.

I have no other gynaecological history of note. I am a non-smoker and drink 3 to 4 glasses of wine each week.

Assessment	Good	Adequate	Poor/not done
1. Polite introduction; establishes rapport	❏	❏	❏
2. Establishes duration of marriage/ cohabitation	❏	❏	❏
3. Establishes history of previous pregnancies	❏	❏	❏
4. Establishes if there are any children from previous relationships	❏	❏	❏
5. Asks about occupations of couple	❏	❏	❏
6. Asks about home circumstances	❏	❏	❏
7. Establishes past/present health of husband	❏	❏	❏
8. Establishes past/present health of wife	❏	❏	❏
9. Establishes/eliminates history of gynaecological conditions	❏	❏	❏
10. Discussion of ovarian problem, hormonal therapy and in vitro fertilisation	❏	❏	❏
11. Does all in a fluent, sensitive professional manner	❏	❏	❏

Comment

Infertility problems should be considered as a couple's problem, rather than individual within a relationship. Infertility should only be diagnosed after the couple have been having a full sexual relationship, trying for a child, for one year. After the initial interview with the couple together, it may be appropriate to interview them separately, but all management decisions should be made in open discussion and with the agreement of both partners.

The loss of an ovary reduces the chances of normal conception by half, as the remaining (healthy) ovary ovulates once in every two menstrual cycles. Menstrual irregularities may result from sub-optimal endogenous oestrogen/progesterone production. Endocrine therapy may stimulate normal ovulation and conception, provided there are no tubal or uterine abnormalities. In vitro fertilization may be considered, with implantation during an artificially-induced progestational phase.

STATION 4.16

Patient history

I am single and work as an actress in theatre and TV productions. I want to have my tubes tied, as I do not wish to have a family. I am in a stable relationship, and my partner, who also works in the theatre, is not keen on children. We do not plan to marry at present. My job involves a good deal of time away from home, and involves working on productions in Europe.

I have had two early terminations (of pregnancy) in the past 10 years. I was on the pill until I developed thrombosis of my leg veins, following surgery for a serious kidney infection a year ago. My GP has not advised me against having children, as my kidneys are now working normally. However, I would not wish to stress them by becoming pregnant.

I do not think I would miss having children of my own, as my partner and I have nephews and nieces, and we wish to put all our efforts into our careers.

Assessment   **Good Adequate Poor/not done**

1. Polite introduction;
    establishes rapport   ❏   ❏   ❏
2. Establishes social and family
    history   ❏   ❏   ❏
3. Establishes reasons for wanting
    sterilisation   ❏   ❏   ❏
4. Establishes past medical and
    O&G history   ❏   ❏   ❏
5. Presence of chronic/long-standing
    illness that may contraindicate
    pregnancy   ❏   ❏   ❏
6. Enquires into partner/husband's
    wishes and the possibility of
    wanting children in the future   ❏   ❏   ❏
7. Does all in a fluent,
    professional manner   ❏   ❏   ❏

Comment

Counselling on sterilisation, particularly to a woman who does not have children, should explore the possibilities of a change of mind in the future, due to changes in social or economic circumstances. The stability of personal relationships and socio-economic factors affecting the patient should be explored in order to make an informed decision. Reversal of tubal ligation has a success rate of approximately 50%.

STATION 4.17

Patient history

I am having severe lower abdominal cramps just before my periods, and they subside only when my period ends. The pain is severe and radiates to my back and down my thighs: I have to spend the worst day or two in bed. I am single and work as a flight attendant and am having to alter my flight schedule virtually every month as a result. My periods tend not to be regular, and I get 'spotting' before they start. They are occasionally heavy, and I had put it down to experimenting with different birth control pills in the past. I have been off the contraceptive pill for over a year but my symptoms have simply got worse.

I began my periods when I was 14 years old but they became very painful about 9 months ago. I have never been pregnant and never had a pelvic infection. I am a very healthy and active person and am not on any medication except for the standard painkillers I take during menstruation.

Assessment	Good	Adequate	Poor/not done
1. Polite introduction; establishes rapport	❑	❑	❑
2. Establishes the characteristics of the pain:			
Severity, site & radiation	❑	❑	❑
Duration in relation to cycle	❑	❑	❑
Effect on daily activities	❑	❑	❑
3. Establishes menstrual history	❑	❑	❑
4. Establishes history of gynaecological ailments & general health	❑	❑	❑
5. Establishes any past pregnancies & outcome	❑	❑	❑
6. Asks about birth control pill or hormone therapy	❑	❑	❑
7. Does all in a fluent, professional manner	❑	❑	❑

Comment

The patient probably has secondary dysmenorrhoea: this is usually associated with demonstrable pelvic pathology, i.e. uterine hyperplasia, pelvic inflammatory disease, pelvic tumours, endometriosis, adenomyosis and cervical or vaginal stenosis. The dysmenorrhoea may be relieved symptomatically or by treatment of the underlying lesion.

STATION 4.18

Patient history

I have been having prolonged periods lasting for 6 days, with the passage of clots, for the past 6 months. I am having to change tampons over 10 times a day. I am not married and work as a senior executive in a publishing company. My general health has always been good and I have been on the pill intermittently for over 20 years. I had a full-term normal pregnancy over 20 years ago, and the child was given up for adoption. I currently live with my long-term partner. When I had a cervical smear test a year ago I was told that I had fibroids but they have not bothered me.

I would like to know if the problem is the fibroids or the approaching menopause.

Assessment	Good	Adequate	Poor/not done
1. Polite introduction; establishes rapport	❏	❏	❏
2. Establishes menstrual history:			
Frequency	❏	❏	❏
Duration	❏	❏	❏
Blood loss	❏	❏	❏
Associated pain or cramps	❏	❏	❏
Regularity	❏	❏	❏
3. Establishes gynaecological history	❏	❏	❏
4. Establishes obstetric history	❏	❏	❏
5. Establishes current medications	❏	❏	❏
6. Establishes any history of hormone therapy	❏	❏	❏
7. Establishes present health and past illnesses	❏	❏	❏
8. Establishes social and/or professional history	❏	❏	❏
9. Makes a reasonable attempt at the diagnosis	❏	❏	❏
10. Does all in a fluent, sensitive, professional manner	❏	❏	❏

Diagnosis

Menorrhagia for investigation

Comment

The normal menopause is signalled by reduced periods, with increasing intervals between them. Dysfunctional uterine bleeding at the time of the climacteric suggests a uterine pathology rather than a tubal or ovarian lesion.

STATION 4.19

Patient history

I am a sales representative with a marketing firm, and my work involves travelling and meeting clients. I have been constantly staining my underwear for the past six months or so, with itching of the surrounding skin; this is embarrassing when I am in company. The discharge is whitish, and I don't think it smells. I am having to wash and change my underwear constantly to be hygienic. I am worried with all the publicity on the dangers of cervical cancer and the need to see the doctor early.

My periods started in my late teens and are regular. I had a termination about 10 years ago when I was at college and needed a course of antibiotics afterwards but antibiotics have not sorted out the present problem. I've been on the Pill since college but stopped it with the current problems: as I have just started a new relationship I am very anxious to be sorted out.

Assessment   **Good Adequate Poor/not done**

		Good	Adequate	Poor/not done
1.	Polite introduction; establishes rapport	❏	❏	❏
2.	Characteristics of discharge:			
	Colour	❏	❏	❏
	Odour	❏	❏	❏
	Quantity (number of pads used)	❏	❏	❏
	Frequency	❏	❏	❏
3.	Associated factors:			
	Contraceptive pill	❏	❏	❏
	Recent pregnancy/miscarriage	❏	❏	❏
	Pelvic infection	❏	❏	❏
	Antibiotic use	❏	❏	❏
4.	O & G history:			
	Age at menarche	❏	❏	❏
	Menstrual problems	❏	❏	❏
	Vaginal infections	❏	❏	❏
	Use of contraception	❏	❏	❏
	Recent pregnancy	❏	❏	❏
	Number of sexual partners	❏	❏	❏
	Sexually transmitted diseases	❏	❏	❏
	Attendance at a special (GU) clinic	❏	❏	❏
5.	Recent pregnancy	❏	❏	❏
6.	Use of contraceptive pill	❏	❏	❏
7.	Does all in a fluent, sensitive professional manner	❏	❏	❏

Comment

The aetiological factors for the type of discharge the patient describes are:

Recent pregnancy
Use of the contraceptive pill
Vaginal infections

The last requires information on sexual exposure (number of partners), previous episodes and treatment and whether the patient had attended a special (GU) clinic. An uncommon cause is surgical termination of pregnancy.

STATION 4.20

Patient history

I am a school teacher, and am returning for the results of a cervical smear test I had several weeks ago. My previous smear, five years ago, was normal, and I have no anxieties about the results of this test.

(When told about the results)
I am very concerned about what you've just said.
Does this mean I have cancer?
Will I need a hysterectomy?

Assessment   **Good**   **Adequate**   **Poor/not done**

		Good	Adequate	Poor/not done
1.	Polite introduction; establishes rapport	❑	❑	❑
2.	Establishes patient identity and reason for attendance	❑	❑	❑
3.	Explains in a non-jargonistic manner the results of the smear test, communicating appropriately the seriousness of the condition	❑	❑	❑
4.	Explains the need for colposcopy and biopsy	❑	❑	❑
5.	Explains the procedure for colposcopy	❑	❑	❑
6.	Mentions possible need for local treatment of the cervix	❑	❑	❑
7.	Checks patient's understanding of explanation	❑	❑	❑
8.	Invites patient's questions and answers appropriately	❑	❑	❑
9.	Does all in a fluent, sensitive professional manner	❑	❑	❑

Comment

Management of CIN III - Women with CIN III require colposcopy and biopsy. Local treatment includes cryotherapy, laser treatment and electrodiathermy and the patient requires annual review with cervical smears. If microinvasion occurs or the squamocolumnar junction is breached, cone biopsy is required, which offers a total cure.

When giving the results of an abnormal cervical smear, counselling is essential to avoid emotional problems and possible delay in diagnosis and treatment.

STATION 4.21

Patient history

For the past 5 to 6 months I have had a constant sensation of something coming down in the pit of my stomach and a feeling of fullness in the vagina. I am in constant discomfort during the day and get backache when I am up and about; I have difficulty coping with the housework. I have 5 children, the first two were breech presentations with difficult births. I had no problems when the other three were born. I find that I have difficulty holding my water and wet myself if I do not get to the toilet in time. I tend to be constipated and have to take opening medicine from time to time. I had my gall bladder removed five years ago for gallstones, and am currently on blood pressure tablets.

Assessment   Good Adequate Poor/not done

Assessment	Good	Adequate	Poor/not done
1. Polite introduction; establishes rapport	❑	❑	❑
2. Establishes sensation of bearing down			
Site	❑	❑	❑
Duration	❑	❑	❑
Whether felt a vaginal mass	❑	❑	❑
Associated symptoms:			
Urinary tract	❑	❑	❑
Bowel	❑	❑	❑
3. Establishes any menstrual irregularities	❑	❑	❑
4. Number of children and any birth difficulties	❑	❑	❑
5. Obstetric/pelvic operations	❑	❑	❑
6. Past illnesses (medical & surgical)	❑	❑	❑
7. Current medication	❑	❑	❑
8. Makes a reasonable attempt at the diagnosis	❑	❑	❑
9. Does all in a fluent, professional manner	❑	❑	❑

Diagnosis
Uterovaginal prolapse

Comment

A clinical diagnosis of uterovaginal prolapse may be made on a good history alone, pelvic examination being carried out for confirmation. Prolonged or difficult labour and delivery, and perineal tears are the main predisposing factors. Occasionally the adjacent bladder or rectal walls may bulge into the anterior or posterior vagina. Post-natal pelvic floor exercise regimes help to strengthen pelvic musculature and may prevent the later development of prolapse.

Prolapse may be treated symptomatically with a vaginal pessary support. The surgical approach of anterior or posterior colporrhaphy involves butressing the anterior or posterior aspects of the pelvic floor musculature.

STATION 4.22

Assessment	Good	Adequate	Poor/not done
1. Puts on gloves	❑	❑	❑
2. Inspects the vulva commenting on appearance and any abnormalities	❑	❑	❑
3. Parts labia	❑	❑	❑
4. Performs bimanual examination correctly	❑	❑	❑
5. Comments correctly on:			
Position of the uterus	❑	❑	❑
Size of the uterus	❑	❑	❑
Mobility of the uterus	❑	❑	❑
Presence of adnexal pathology	❑	❑	❑
6. Does all in a fluent, gentle professional manner	❑	❑	❑

Comment

A vaginal examination requires sensitivity, gentleness and skill. It is carried out in the presence of a chaperone, after counselling the patient, in a calm, secluded environment. The examination has access to all pelvic organs and is able to assess their consistency, size, extent and mobility, and the origin, of any pelvic pathology.

STATION 4.23

Answers

1. A: Bivalve Cuscoe's or duckbill speculum
   B: Sim's speculum

2. Bivalve speculum demonstrates the cervix and vaginal vaults. (Lithotomy or left lateral position)
   Sim's speculum demonstrates the vaginal walls (left lateral position with knees drawn up)

3. A. Cervical erosions and cervical polyp
   B. Rectovaginal and rectovesical prolapse

Comment

Speculum examination requires skill and gentleness, as incautious introduction or removal of the instrument causes considerable discomfort and distress to the patient. Speculum examination should not be attempted when the hymen is intact, or in vaginal stenosis. The duckbill speculum is used to examine the vaginal vault and cervix, and obtaining cervical smears. The Sim's speculum enables the examination of the integrity of the vaginal wall, to diagnose prolapse, and other lesions, such as rectovaginal fistula.

STATION 4.24

Assessment	Good	Adequate	Poor/not done
1. Checks all items required to take smear are present: speculum, microscope slide, fixative, Ayer's spatula, pencil (Figure 4.24)	❏	❏	❏
2. Puts on gloves	❏	❏	❏
3. Positions patient	❏	❏	❏
4. Examines vulva and comments on appearance	❏	❏	❏
5. Ensures speculum is warm and in working order	❏	❏	❏
6. Parts labia and inserts speculum correctly	❏	❏	❏
7. Locks speculum with cervix well demonstrated	❏	❏	❏
8. Inserts smear spatula and rotates through 360° of the cervix	❏	❏	❏
9. Removes spatula, and gently closes and removes the speculum	❏	❏	❏
10. Spreads smear over the microscope slide and fixes it correctly using fixative	❏	❏	❏
11. Records patient's details on the slide correctly	❏	❏	❏
12. Does all in a fluent, gentle and professional manner	❏	❏	❏

Comment

Cervical screening is one of two current UK population screening programmes (the other being mammography). Cervical smears must be obtained and fixed in the prescribed manner to obviate variations in technique so that the cytologist can accurately interpret cellular changes of dysplasia (CIN I), pre-malignant changes; (CIN III) and frank neoplasia.

STATION 4.25

Answers

1. Figure 4.25a: Trichomonas vaginalis
    Figure 4.25b: Candida albicans (Monilia)

2. Fresh smear from a high vaginal swab, diluted with normal saline and spread on a slide with a coverslip, and examined microscopically.

3. Figure 4.25a: Metronidazole (200 mg tds orally for 7 days) or Nimovazole (2 mg orally od after a meal for 7 to 10 days). Also treat the partner.

    Figure 4.25b: Topical anti-fungal agents: clotrimazole, miconazole or nystatin in the form of pessaries and cream

    Recurrent infections may require systemic anti-fungal agents

4. Both these organisms are sexually transmitted. Thrush (monilia) is also associated with pregnancy, diabetes, oral contraceptive use or oestrogen therapy and occasionally as a superinfection following prolonged antibiotic therapy.

STATION 4.26

Answers

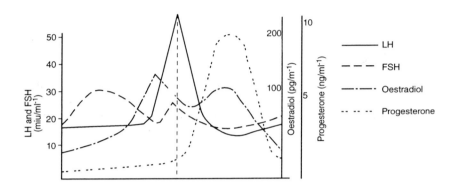

Figure 4.26A relates the normal changes in hormone levels to the menstrual cycle.

Comment

The monthly menstrual cycle starts with the onset of bleeding which leads to the development of new ovarian follicles producing increasing quantities of oestrogen which stimulates regeneration and growth of the endometrium.

The corpus luteum develops following ovulation and secretes both oestrogen and progesterone. If implantation does not occur the corpus luteum regresses with a rapid fall in the hormone levels. The endometrial lining becomes detached with resultant bleeding.

Hormonal contraception by daily synthetic oestrogen and progestin is through feed-back inhibition of FSH and LH secretion to suppress ovulation. Preparations containing only progestin produce alterations in the cervical mucus and endometrial lining inhibiting fertilization and implantation.

STATION 4.27

Answers

1. Hysterosalpingogram

2. Infertility due to tubal abnormalities

3. A: Uterus B: Fallopian tube
    The procedure is explained to the patient and any concerns addressed.

4. The conscious patient is positioned in the lithotomy position on the X-ray table and the cervix exposed by means of a bivalve speculum. A cannula is introduced into the cervix and contrast medium is injected into the uterine cavity. Serial exposures of the pelvis are then taken with an image-intensifier. (Patient sedation may be required.)

Comment

Blockage or stenosis of the Fallopian tubes is a common cause of secondary infertility resulting from chronic pelvic infection. Identifying and treating any residual infection may result in resolution of the inflammation and re-establishing tubal patency. Blockage caused by fibrosis and scarring from past infections would require tubal reconstruction. In-vitro fertilization and intra-uterine implantation may be feasible if pregnancy is desired when tubal surgery is not possible.

STATION 4.28

Answers

1. Hydatidiform mole
   Invasive mole (chorioadenoma detruens)
   Choriocarcinoma (malignant trophoblastic disease)

2. Discrete rounded ('cannon ball') opacities in lung parenchyma
   Diagnosis: Pulmonary metastases from choriocarcinoma.

3. Chemotherapy with methotrexate alone or in combination with vincristine, cyclophosphamide and/or actinomycin D.
   Local complications from a large primary tumour such as uterine perforation or severe bleeding may require a hysterectomy.

Comment

Trophoblastic disease follows pregnancy; a hydatidiform mole represents a degenerating pregnancy where villi have become hydrophic with trophoblastic proliferation. The villi locally invade the myometrium in the invasive mole; in choriocarcinoma the trophoblastic elements also invade and later metastasise.

Diagnosis of a molar pregnancy before the 12th week is suggested by a rapid increase in uterine size, vaginal bleeding and/or passage of grape-like molar tissue. Confirmation is by ultrasound scanning of the uterus and elevated urinary HCG titres.

Evacuation of a hydatidiform mole following detection is followed up with serial urinary HCG measurements and chest radiographs to exclude malignant progression. Contraception is necessary over the medium term as surveillance may be compromised by pregnancy.

STATION 5.1

Patient history

I am a 23-year-old woman and I was fit and well until 3 months ago. Initially I had joint pains, particularly in my fingers and toes, but more recently I have had swelling and severe pain in the small joints of my hands. The arthritis affects both hands identically and is associated with feeling generally unwell, tiredness and fever. I have also had painful red eyes and chest pain when I breathe in, over the past few weeks. I have not had any large joint swelling or pain, and no back pain. I am generally otherwise well and have had no bowel, gynaecological or urogenital symptoms. I am on the oral contraceptive pill but no other medications. I do not know anyone else in my family who has had arthritis.

Assessment	Good	Adequate	Poor/not done
1. Polite introduction; establishes rapport	❏	❏	❏
2. Establishes presenting complaint and duration of symptoms	❏	❏	❏
3. Establishes the characteristics of the arthritis:			
Symmetrical versus asymmetrical involvement	❏	❏	❏
Small joint involvement - proximal or distal	❏	❏	❏
Large joints involved - upper and lower limbs	❏	❏	❏
Spine - cervical, thoracic, lumbar, sacroiliac	❏	❏	❏
Features of acute arthritis - swelling, pain, increased temperature, erythema	❏	❏	❏
Early morning stiffness	❏	❏	❏

	Good	Adequate	Poor/not done
4. Establishes/excludes systemic associations:			
Eye/visual problems	❏	❏	❏
Bowel - upper/lower GI symptoms	❏	❏	❏
Respiratory symptoms	❏	❏	❏
Urogenital symptoms	❏	❏	❏
Skin, nail and hair problems	❏	❏	❏
General systemic symptoms - fever, malaise, arthralgia, myalgia	❏	❏	❏
5. Establishes/excludes family history of arthritis	❏	❏	❏
6. Establishes medication history	❏	❏	❏
7. Establishes previous medical history - particularly autoimmune disease	❏	❏	❏
8. Makes a reasonable attempt at the diagnosis	❏	❏	❏
9. Does all in a professional, fluent manner	❏	❏	❏

Diagnosis

Acute rheumatoid arthritis with episcleritis and pleuritic chest pain.

STATION 5.2

Patient history

I am 16 years old and still at school. I was fit and well until about 3 or 4 months ago when I started to get lower back pain. Initially I put it down to increased rugby training. The pain is in my lower back and upper buttocks and radiates down the upper thighs to my knees. It is a dull ache, which is much worse in the mornings, and is associated with stiffness, particularly on getting out of bed and after sitting on the 45 minute bus ride to school. The pain has been eased by aspirin tablets and I find that the stiffness eases through the day. I have noticed more recently that my neck is also starting to feel stiff. There are no other joints involved and I have been otherwise well. I have had no eye, breathing, bowel or urinary symptoms.

I have only previously been in hospital once, for a tonsillectomy. I am on no other medications other than the aspirin and do not drink any alcohol or smoke cigarettes. My mother has psoriasis and my grandfather had severe back pain associated with his Crohn's disease.

Assessment

	Good	Adequate	Poor/not done
1. Polite introduction; establishes rapport	❏	❏	❏
2. Establishes nature and duration of presenting complaint	❏	❏	❏
3. Establishes the characteristics of the back pain:			
Site - cervical, thoracic, lumbar, sacroiliac	❏	❏	❏
Radiation - excludes radiation down the lower limbs	❏	❏	❏
Exacerbating and relieving factors	❏	❏	❏
Early morning stiffness	❏	❏	❏
4. Establishes/excludes peripheral joint involvement	❏	❏	❏
5. Establishes/excludes associated systemic symptoms:			
Diarrhoea and GI symptoms	❏	❏	❏
Eye/visual problems	❏	❏	❏
Respiratory symptoms	❏	❏	❏
Urogenital symptoms	❏	❏	❏
General systemic symptoms	❏	❏	❏
6. Establishes family history - particularly of arthritis, IBD and psoriasis	❏	❏	❏
7. Establishes medication history	❏	❏	❏
8. Establishes previous medical history	❏	❏	❏
9. Makes a reasonable attempt at the diagnosis	❏	❏	❏
10. Does all in a fluent, professional manner	❏	❏	❏

Diagnosis
Ankylosing spondylitis

STATION 5.3

Patient history

I am 27 years old and am usually fit and well but I have developed a red, raised rash over both my cheeks in the past 4 to 5 months. The rash is slowly enlarging across the cheeks but has not spread to any other sites. The rash is not itchy or painful. I did have a nasty sunburn at the start of the summer but this has not recurred, mainly as I have avoided the sunlight. I have had painful joints in both my hands and feet but have not had any acute swelling or other signs of acute arthritis. No other joints are affected.

I have been feeling generally weak and tired, and have noticed over the last few weeks that my ankles, hands and face are swelling. I have also had a dull but persistent headache. I have been passing very little urine over the past week. I've had no eye, breathing or stomach problems.

I've had 2 or 3 DVTs in my legs over the past 5 years and am on long-term warfarin treatment. I have been married for 4 years and have had 3 miscarriages since. I am otherwise well and have had no admissions to hospital. Other than the warfarin, I only take paracetamol for my headache. There are no family medical problems of note.

Assessment	Good	Adequate	Poor/not done
1. Polite introduction; establishes rapport	❑	❑	❑
2. Establishes duration and nature of symptoms	❑	❑	❑
3. Establishes characteristics of the rash: site, spread appearance, pruritus	❑	❑	❑
4. Establishes nature of the joint involvement:			
Excludes symptoms of acute arthritis	❑	❑	❑
Establishes joints involved	❑	❑	❑

	Good	Adequate	Poor/not done
5. Establishes/excludes:			
Systemic symptoms	❏	❏	❏
Eye/visual symptoms	❏	❏	❏
Respiratory symptoms	❏	❏	❏
Upper and lower GI symptoms	❏	❏	❏
Urogenital symptoms	❏	❏	❏
General symptoms: headache peripheral oedema, malaise	❏	❏	❏
6. Establishes family history	❏	❏	❏
7. Establishes previous medical history – particularly recurrent DVT and several miscarriages	❏	❏	❏
8. Establishes medication history	❏	❏	❏
9. Makes a reasonable attempt at the diagnosis	❏	❏	❏
10. Does all in a fluent, professional manner	❏	❏	❏

Diagnosis

Systemic lupus erythematosus with anticardiolipid antibody. Symptoms suggest nephrotic syndrome and hypertension.

Comment

Various syndromes within the broader diagnosis of SLE have now been characterised by the presence of specific antibodies.

Syndrome	Antibody
Photosensitivity (subacute cutaneous lupus)	Anti-Ro/Anti-La
Photosensitivity, nephritis and serositis e.g. pleurisy or pericarditis	Anti-dsDNA
Neonatal lupus syndrome – splenomegaly, rashes, thrombocytopenia and complete heart block	Anti-Ro/Anti-La
Arterial and venous thrombosis, recurrent miscarriage, thrombocytopenia, central nervous syndromes – psychosis, cranial nerve palsies, headaches and atypical migraine	Antiphospholipid Lupus anticoagulant
Drug induced lupus	Antihistone
Overlap syndrome – Raynaud's, myositis, cardiorespiratory features	Anti-RNP

STATION 5.4

Patient history

I am a 37-year-old woman and I have been unwell for about 8 months. Last winter I noticed that my fingers and, to a lesser extent, my toes began to get extremely painful and changed colour in the cold weather. They went pale, and then red and painful. Over the last 2 months my fingers have begun to swell and the skin has felt very tight. During the last 3 months I have also noticed increasing problems with my swallowing. Initially this felt like a slight blockage to solids, such as bread and potatoes but has now progressed to liquids, and I am finding it increasingly difficult to eat and drink. I have had increasing shortness of breath on exertion and my exercise tolerance has reduced to 400 to 500 metres on the flat. I have had no other respiratory symptoms.

I have no other stomach symptoms, gynaecological or urinary problems. I do not have pain in my joints or arthritic problems. I do have pain in my muscles and feel generally weak. I have not noticed any furrowing around my mouth or small spots around my face. I have recently developed a dull, generalised headache and some blurring of my vision, but have put this down to feeling tired. In my family history my mother had a similar problem with her fingers but she is still alive and otherwise well. I am on no medications and do not drink or smoke.

Assessment	Good	Adequate	Poor/not done
1. Polite introduction; establishes rapport	❑	❑	❑
2. Establishes duration and nature of symptoms	❑	❑	❑
3. Establishes characteristics of Raynaud's syndrome: *Colour changes and pain on exposure to cold*	❑	❑	❑
4. Establishes character and level of dysphagia to solids and liquids	❑	❑	❑

University Of London Whitechapel
Library
CheckOut Receipt

13/06/05
05:09 pm

Item:OSCEs for medical undergraduates .
volume 2
54009000168308

Due Date: 20/06/2005

Thank You for using
the 3M SelfCheck System!

Good Adequate Poor/not done

5. Establishes/excludes other
    features of systemic sclerosis
    and connective tissue disease:

	Good	Adequate	Poor/not done
Swelling of fingers	❏	❏	❏
Respiratory symptoms	❏	❏	❏
Urogenital symptoms	❏	❏	❏
Acute arthritis	❏	❏	❏
Skin changes/rashes	❏	❏	❏
Lower GI symptoms	❏	❏	❏
Muscle pain and weakness	❏	❏	❏
Hypertension - visual disturbance and headache	❏	❏	❏

6. Establishes family history,
    particularly rheumatological
    disease   ❏   ❏   ❏
7. Establishes medication history   ❏   ❏   ❏
8. Makes a reasonable attempt at
    the diagnosis   ❏   ❏   ❏
9. Does all in a fluent,
    professional manner   ❏   ❏   ❏

Diagnosis
Diffuse cutaneous systemic sclerosis

Comment

The initial advice to all patients with either primary or secondary Raynaud's phenomenon should be to avoid cold exposure where ever possible and, when it is not, to advocate the prophylactic use of heated gloves and socks. The patients should be advised to stop smoking and avoid beta blockers. Short, uncomplicated attacks may be treated with fish oil or evening primrose oil. Longer, more frequent attacks may require the use of various therapeutic agents including calcium channel blockers, transdermal nitratres, Ketanserin, a selective $5HT_2$ receptor antagonist and ACE inhibitors. Severe attacks, which often are associated with ulceration, gangrene and secondary infection, require hospitalisation and Prostacyclin infusion, surgical debridement and even amputation. Occasionally digital or cervical sympathectomy are required.

STATION 5.5

Patient history

I am 25 years old and have just returned from a holiday in Spain. After a bout of food poisoning about a week ago, I developed a hot, swollen left knee, which I am now unable to put weight on. I have no other joint swelling, but my buttocks and lower back are very tender and painful. My eyes have also been painful, gritty and red, and the lids are stuck together when I wake up. I have not had any visual loss. I have also had pain on passing urine, but no discharge, pain in the heels and ulcers, both in my mouth and on the end of my penis. I have not had any rashes or other systemic upset.

My mother has Crohn's disease but there is no other family illness of note. I have had one similar episode to this one about 2 years ago, when I had a sexually transmitted disease after sleeping with a girl at a party. In the last 18 months I have been monogamous.

Assessment	Good	Adequate	Poor/not done
1. Polite introduction; establishes rapport	❑	❑	❑
2. Establishes duration of symptoms and precipitating illness, i.e. food poisoning	❑	❑	❑
3. Establishes pattern of joint involvement, excluding sacroiliitis	❑	❑	❑
4. Establishes nature of eye problems, confirming conjunctivitis	❑	❑	❑
5. Establishes/excludes other symptoms of Reiter's syndrome:			
Urethritis, dysuria and discharge	❑	❑	❑
Achilles tendonitis	❑	❑	❑
Keratoderma blennorrhagicum	❑	❑	❑
Circinate balanitis	❑	❑	❑
Oral ulceration	❑	❑	❑
Plantar fasciitis	❑	❑	❑
Fever/malaise	❑	❑	❑

	Good	Adequate	Poor/not done
6. Establishes sexual history and recent sexual contacts	❑	❑	❑
7. Establishes/excludes previous similar episodes – defining the precipitating cause	❑	❑	❑
8. Establishes family history, particularly of HLA B27 disorders	❑	❑	❑
9. Makes a reasonable attempt at a diagnosis	❑	❑	❑
10. Does all in a fluent, professional, manner	❑	❑	❑

Diagnosis

Reiter's syndrome

Comment

Reiter's syndrome is an HLA B27 related disorder, which is classically made up of the triad of arthritis, urethritis and conjunctivitis. Other features include plantar fasciitis, achilles tendonitis, keratoderma blennorrhagicum, circinate balanitis, oral ulceration, acute anterior uveitis and fever.

The common precipitating factors are gastrointestinal and urogenital infections, including Salmonella (not typhi or paratyphi), Campylobacter, Shigella, Yersinia and Chlamydia.

STATION 5.6

Patient history

I am 65 years old and have been unwell for about 2 months. Initially I developed a dull, constant headache which was principally over the temples in nature but has become more generalised in recent weeks. The headache is poorly relieved with paracetamol but I have not noticed any particular exacerbating factor. When I have the headache I also get a very tender scalp, which I notice particularly when I am combing my hair. Over the last month I have also developed a painful, tender and stiff shoulder and upper thigh muscles. The stiffness is particularly bad in the mornings and I've had to roll out of bed in the last few weeks. Sometimes my husband has to help me. I have not noticed any weakness or wasting of my muscles.

I have been getting pain in my jaw and tongue when I talk and while eating. I have not had any visual disturbances, angina, abdominal pain or cerebrovascular symptoms. Over the past month I have lost my appetite and have lost 5 kilogrammes in weight. I have had no other systemic symptoms.

Assessment	Good	Adequate	Poor/not done
1. Polite introduction; establishes rapport	❏	❏	❏
2. Establishes duration of presenting complaint	❏	❏	❏
3. Characterises the headache:			
Site: bitemporal	❏	❏	❏
Radiation	❏	❏	❏
Chararacter: dull, constant	❏	❏	❏
Exacerbating/relieving factors	❏	❏	❏
Scalp tenderness	❏	❏	❏
4. Establishes pain, tenderness and stiffness in the shoulders and thighs	❏	❏	❏
5. Excludes muscle weakness and wasting	❏	❏	❏

	Good	Adequate	Poor/not done
6. Establishes/excludes joint involvement	❏	❏	❏
7. Establishes/excludes symptoms of giant cell arteritis:			
Jaw claudication	❏	❏	❏
Angina	❏	❏	❏
Limb claudication	❏	❏	❏
Cerebrovascular symptoms	❏	❏	❏
Mesenteric/abdominal pains	❏	❏	❏
Visual loss	❏	❏	❏
Anorexia, weight loss, malaise	❏	❏	❏
8. Makes a reasonable attempt at the diagnosis	❏	❏	❏
9. Does all in a fluent, professional manner	❏	❏	❏

Diagnosis
Giant cell arteritis with features of polymyalgia rheumatica

Comment

The diagnosis of temporal arteritis should be confirmed by a temporal artery biopsy. However the risk of complications, particularly blindness, means that steroids should be started immediately. There is a 48 hour window between starting steroids and loss of pathological changes in a biopsy.

The recommended treatment is prednisolone 30–40 mg od until the ESR normalises, then gradual reduction depending on the ESR and symptoms.

STATION 5.7

Answers and explanations

1. True   2. False   3. True   4. False   5. False

This patient has a macrocytic anaemia and thrombocytopenia. The white cell count is normal but a differential should always be sought. The macrocytosis is associated with a reticulocytosis and hyper-bilirubinaemia which indicates haemolysis. SLE is associated with an autoimmune haemolytic anaemia. The thrombocytopenia is usually due to autoimmune destruction as well.

6. False   7. True   8. True   9.True   10. False

The data suggests this patient has acute on chronic renal failure. The hyperkalaemia is an acute marker whereas the metabolic acidosis, shown by the low bicarbonate, indicates chronic renal failure. The disproportionately raised creatinine to urea indicates renal rather than pre-renal impairment. SLE is associated with several different types of glomerulonephritis including rapidly progressive. The nephrotic syndrome is the triad of hypoalbuminaemia, significant proteinuria and oedema.

11. True   12. False 13. True   14. True   15. False

The data suggests the patient has a hepatitic jaundice which may be due to drug therapy or an autoimmune phenomenon. Gallstones classically cause an obstructive jaundice. The patient should have an ultrasound scan of the liver, biliary tree and renal tract in the first instance and then, depending on the results, a liver and renal biopsy.

STATION 5.8

Answers

1. (D) (f)
2. (E) (c)
3. (F) (b)
4. (A) (d)
5. (C) (a)
6. (B) (e)

STATION 5.9

Answers

1. (D) (e)
2. (E) (b)
3. (A) (c)
4. (B) (a)
5. (C) (d)

STATION 5.10

Answers and explanations

1. (D) (c)
Meningococcal bacteraemia usually causes a reactive, aseptic arthritis but may rarely cause a septic arthritis with evidence of bacteria within the joint.

2. (E) (a)
The aspiration from a gouty joint is normally aseptic with negatively birefringent crystals under polarised light microscopy.

3. (B) (e)
Pyrophosphate arthropathy or 'pseudogout' also gives an aseptic joint aspiration with positively birefringent crystals under polarised light microscopy. Radiographs may show intra-articular calcification.

4. (A) (b)
Spontaneous haemarthrosis is a relatively common complication of haemophilia, and prior to Factor VIII transfusion caused severe deformity, sepsis and even death. Whether a haemarthrosis is spontaneous or traumatic one should never aspirate the joint unless under strict aseptic technique, and some would advocate only in the operating theatre. Introducing infection into a bloodied joint provides a perfect culture medium for a severe septic arthritis.

5. (C) (d)
Reiter's syndrome causes an aseptic arthritis with a neutrophilia. The disorder principally affects the weight bearing joints of the lower limb, particularly the knee. It is usually asymmetrical.

STATION 5.11

Answers and explanations

1. **(a) True** **(b) False** **(c) False** **(d) False** **(e) True**
This is a radiograph of rheumatoid hands. There is a symmetrical erosive arthropathy principally affecting the MCP and PIP joints. The MCP joints are mostly subluxed and there is evidence of periarticular erosion and osteopenia. There is also gross erosion and destruction of the carpus.

2. **(a) False** **(b) True** **(c) False** **(d) False** **(e) True**
This radiograph shows gross changes of tophaceous gout. The arthropathy is asymmetrical and has caused destruction of the terminal phalanx of the right hand, with destruction and cystic changes at several of the DIP joints. The proximal interphalangeal joints are relatively spared.

3. **(a) True** **(b) True** **(c) True** **(d) False** **(e) False**
This radiograph shows changes consistent with osteoarthritis. There is periarticular sclerosis and loss of joint space at the right middle MCP joint and ring and middle DIP joints. There are also changes at both first carpometocarpal joints. The PIP joints are spared. Arthritis mutilans is a gross destructive arthropathy seen in psoriatic and rheumatoid disease.

STATION 5.12

Answers and explanations

1.   **(a) False**   **(b) True**   **(c) True**   **(d) False**   **(e) False**
This radiograph shows gross degenerative changes of the right knee joint consistent with osteoarthritis. There is loss of joint space, periarticular sclerosis and osteophytes at the margins of the joint. The patello-femoral joint is almost totally fused (ankylosed).

2.   **(a) True**   **(b) True**   **(c) False**   **(d) False**   **(e) True**
This radiograph of a left knee shows intra-articular calcification. The principal cause of this appearance is pyrophosphate arthropathy which is a crystal deposition disorder, presenting in a similar manner to gout. The two are differentiated by their crystals. Pyrophosphate crystals are positively birefringent under polarised light, whereas urate crystals are negatively birefringent. Other causes of intra-articular calcification include trauma and hyperparathyroidism.

3.   **(a) False**   **(b) True**   **(c) False**   **(d) False**   **(e) True**
This radiograph of a right hip joint and hemipelvis shows cortical thickening and trabeculation consistent with Paget's disease of the bone. There is no evidence of fracture. The patient would be expected to have a normal serum calcium and phosphate, with a raised alkaline phosphatase. Hypercalcaemia may arise due to fracture or concomitant malignancy. Cranial nerve palsies due to skull changes may occur and this may lead to deafness.

STATION 5.13

Answers and explanations

1. (a) True (b) True (c) True (d) True (e) False
This is a lateral radiograph of the cervical spine clearly showing the 7th cervical and 1st thoracic vertebrae. There is loss of the disc space at C5/6 and C6/7. There are small anterior osteophytes and evidence of degenerative changes in the lower apophyseal joints. These changes are consistent with osteoarthritis.

2. (a) False (b) False (c) True (d) True (e) True
This radiograph of the cervical spine shows atlanto-axial subluxation. The patient has rheumatoid arthritis and this is a well recognised complication. The patient requires neurosurgical stabilisation of the cervical vertebrae.

3. (a) False (b) True (c) True (d) False (e) False
This AP film of the lumbar spine and pelvis shows fusion (ankylosis) of the sacroiliac joints and syndesmophytes causing the classical 'bamboo spine' of ankylosing spondylitis. Such patients also suffer with ossification of the central spinous ligament, leading to the tramline appearance. This disorder is associated with HLA B27.

STATION 5.14

Answers and explanations

1. **(a)** This investigation is a technetium 99, radioisotope bone scan.
   (b) It shows multiple 'hot' spots throughout the thoracolumbar spine, ribs and left scapula. This patient had metastatic breast cancer.
   (c) The aim of treatment at this stage of disease is palliation. Bony pain may be treated with local radiotherapy and/or appropriate analgesia. Hormonal therapy with tamoxifen or arimidex also offers good palliation. Other symptoms arising from the malignancy and its metastatic effect should be addressed.

2. **(a)** This is a plain (AP) radiograph of the pelvis, hip joints and proximal femurs.
   (b) It shows multiple lytic metastases in the pelvis and right femur. This patient also had metastatic breast cancer
   (c) Lytic lesions are commonly associated with multiple myeloma and cancer of the breast, bronchus, thyroid and kidney. Prostatic carcinoma produces both osteolytic and sclerotic secondaries.

3. **(a)** This is a plain (AP) radiograph of the lower lumber spine and pelvis.
   (b) It shows a sclerotic wedged or collapsed fifth lumbar vertebra. There is also loss of definition of the pedicle on the right, probably due to destruction. This appearance is due to metastatic disease. There is a calcified mass lying to the right of the vertebra which probably represents a calcified lymph node.
   (c) Common causes of oesteosclerotic lesions include localised Paget's disease of the bone, multiple myeloma and metastases from prostatic and colonic primaries.

STATION 5.15

Answers

1.	(D)	(g)
2.	(E)	(f)
3.	(F)	(e)
4.	(A)	(b)
5.	(G)	(c)
6.	(C)	(a)
7.	(B)	(d)

Comment

In the treatment of rheumatic disease penicillamine and gold have a similar action and common side-effects such as skin reactions, mouth ulcers and blood dyscrasias.

Azathioprine and methotrexate are used to treat psoriatic arthropathy and are nephrotoxic and may produce lung complications.

Hydroxychloroquine and sulphasalazine produce liver and renal toxicity and hypersensitivity reactions including Stevens-Johnson syndrome (erythema multiforme). Hydroxychloroquine is avoided in pregnancy and lactation.

STATION 5.16

Patient history

I am 36 years old and normally I am fit and well. However, I have not been well for the last week. Initially I developed a sore throat but this quickly spread to my chest and I am now coughing up thick yellow sputum and have a fever. Over the last 24 to 48 hours I have developed a severe rash all over my body. At first the rash was red and hot but has now started to blister. The rash started over my hands and feet and has now spread to cover much of my back and abdomen. I have also noticed that there are blisters in my mouth, which has become very painful, and my eyes have felt gritty and sore. I have never had the rash before and have had no contact with a similar rash. I am on no medications, other than the contraceptive pill and have no drug allergies, although I am allergic to nickel.

I have no previous medical history of note and no other systemic upset.

Assessment   Good Adequate Poor/not done

	Good	Adequate	Poor/not done
1. Polite introduction; establishes rapport	❑	❑	❑
2. Establishes duration and nature of symptoms	❑	❑	❑
3. Establishes characteristics of the rash:			
Initial site of the rash	❑	❑	❑
Sites of spread and effect	❑	❑	❑
Specific sites - mucous membranes and eyes	❑	❑	❑
Macular/papular/vesicular	❑	❑	❑
Associated erythema and heat	❑	❑	❑
Pruritus	❑	❑	❑
Blistering	❑	❑	❑
4. Establishes systemic upset – respiratory, gastrointestinal and urogenital	❑	❑	❑
5. Establishes medications and allergies	❑	❑	❑
6. Establishes previous episodes of similar rash	❑	❑	❑
7. Establishes/eliminates recent contacts with similar rash	❑	❑	❑
8. Establishes previous medical history – inflammatory bowel disease or rheumatological disease	❑	❑	❑
9. Makes a reasonable attempt at the diagnosis	❑	❑	❑
10. Does all in a fluent, professional manner	❑	❑	❑

Diagnosis

Erythema multiforme/Stevens-Johnson syndrome secondary to a chest infection.

STATION 5.17

Patient history

I am 24 years old and work as a travel agent. I have been fit and well, although I am now very worried about a freckle on my left thigh. I first noticed it about 3 to 4 months ago when I seemed to catch it as I put on my jeans. The freckle seems to have got a lot bigger since then and has become more irregular and darker; the surface now feels quite rough. It is becoming increasingly itchy and because I scratch it, it has started to bleed. The freckle is now surrounded by other smaller but similar freckles but I have not noticed any distant similar lesions. (If asked: I do think that the glands in my groin seem quite swollen as well.)

Over the last year I have been taking part in body building competitions and as a result have spent 4 to 5 hours a week under a sunbed. I have always been a real sun worshipper and sunbathe when I can. I take at least 3 holidays a year, always to a sunny place and spend all the time I can on the beach. I have recently felt tired and run down but have been otherwise well.

Assessment

Assessment	Good	Adequate	Poor/not done
1. Polite introduction; establishes rapport	❑	❑	❑
2. Establishes when patient first noticed lesion/change in lesion	❑	❑	❑
3. Establishes specific characteristics of the lesion:			
Increased size	❑	❑	❑
Change in margins/shape	❑	❑	❑
Change in surface	❑	❑	❑
Change in colour	❑	❑	❑
Bleeding from lesion	❑	❑	❑
Pruritus	❑	❑	❑
Satellite lesions	❑	❑	❑
Distant lesions	❑	❑	❑
Local lymphadenopathy	❑	❑	❑
4. Establishes the degree of previous and recent UV exposure	❑	❑	❑
5. Explains to patient concerns and reasons for referral to dermatologist	❑	❑	❑
6. Invites questions, and answers appropriately	❑	❑	❑
7. Does all in a fluent, professional manner	❑	❑	❑

Diagnosis

Malignant melanoma

Comment

Malignant change in a pre-existing mole is difficult to assess. However, a change in size, itchiness or bleeding, should arouse clinical suspicion. Delayed or missed diagnosis may result in dissemination.

STATION 5.18

Answers and explanations

1.   (a) False   (b) True   (c) True   (d) True   (e) False
This slide shows clubbing of the fingernails. There is loss of the nail angle and the nail bed is boggy or fluctuant. The nail demonstrates increased curvature in both transverse and longitudinal planes.

2.   (a) False   (b) False   (c) True   (d) True   (e) True
This patient has onycholysis which is a transverse splitting of the nail as it grows. The defect is associated with HLA B27 diseases and hypothyroidism.

3.   (a) False   (b) True   (c) False   (d) False   (e) True
This slide demonstrates onychogryphosis, which is an overgrowth of the nail. It is often associated with trauma, but may be caused by neglect, or rarely, ischaemia. It is a benign disorder.

4.   (a) True   (b) False   (c) False   (d) True   (e) True
The nails shown in this slide demonstrates the characteristic features of psoriatic changes. Abnormal growth leads to pitting and ridging and onycholysis. The patient may have plaques over the flexor surfaces but subcutaneous nodules are associated with rheumatoid arthritis.

STATION 5.19a

Assessment	Good	Adequate	Poor/not done
1. Polite introduction; establishes rapport	❑	❑	❑
2. Establishes patient identity and present understanding of the treatment	❑	❑	❑
3. Explains the elements of PUVA treatment: *Psoralen – tablet sensitises the skin to UV radiation*	❑	❑	❑
4. UVA – similar radiation to the sun; delivered by sun lamp	❑	❑	❑
5. Explains the course of treatment: frequency of sessions, duration of each session, duration of course	❑	❑	❑
6. Explains benefits of treatment – few side-effects, easy to deliver, few long term effects if all directions followed	❑	❑	❑
7. Explains side-effects – short term and long term	❑	❑	❑
8. Invites questions, and answers appropriately	❑	❑	❑
9. Does all in a fluent, non-jargonistic manner	❑	❑	❑

The OSCE marking scheme

Traditionally, academic assessment has been 'norm' referenced, whereby candidates are compared to one another and are ranked from the best to the worst. In recent years the value of 'norm' referencing has come under question and 'criterion' referencing has become more accepted.

Criterion-referenced assessment is not new, the most obvious examples being the driving test and swimming life saving assessments. In both these examples a candidate must demonstrate a 'minimum competency level' for the given skills, i.e. driving a motor vehicle or saving a drowning person. Unlike traditional, norm-referenced assessment, there is no division of candidates into excellent, good, average, unsatisfactory and poor; there is only pass (competent) and fail (not competent).

Criterion referencing is easily applied to the OSCE format. A committee of examiners meets several months prior to the examinations and, through discussion, sets a minimum competency score, i.e. a passing score, for each given station. This score reflects what a candidate taking the OSCE should be reasonably expected to achieve, given their expected core knowledge, the time restrictions and the stress of the examination. These, in turn, should be reflected in the validity of the OSCE.

In volumes 1 and 2 the checklists are divided into three columns headed **Good, Adequate** and **Poor/not done**. These headings subdivide students into good, average and poor, where poor candidates do not demonstrate an acceptable level of competence, i.e. fail. However, in many medical establishments, the division of good and average candidates is regarded as old fashioned, regressing back to norm referencing and therefore the headings may read **Adequate or competent, Attempted but unsatisfactory** and **Not done.**

Some medical colleges apply weighting of individual items within a checklist. For instance, the initial item on each checklist – 'Polite introduction; establishes rapport', may have a maximum score of two marks if performed well, whereas another item, e.g. auscultating the four areas of the heart correctly, may carry 5 marks if performed well. Both would be given a lesser mark if performed adequately and 0 marks if not done at all. We have chosen not to weight individual items in our checklists. This is because:

(i) We feel that weighting of items in this way does not improve the discriminatory power of the examination.
(ii) We think students should be discerning enough to realise which are the important key points that will be more heavily weighted in a checklist.

We have, therefore, generally used 3 columns for our checklists, **Good, Adequate** and **Poor/not done**, carrying 3, 2 and zero marks respectively. Certain checklists, however, only have 2 columns, i.e. **Adequate** and **Not done**. These are typically items which are required to be named, e.g. risk factors for a DVT or contraindications to a given treatment. One can only mention them or not and for this reason a 'good column' is not applicable. In such cases 1 mark is given for adequate column and zero for the Poor/not done column.

To obtain the total score
For each station, minimum competency or pass mark is calculated by a committee of examiners/experts. If a candidate scores each item as 'adequate' this will equate to the 'pass' mark. A candidate should therefore aim to get an adequate or good for each item. If one scores adequate or poor/not done in the majority of items, this implies a lack of knowledge or areas of weakness and should be used to direct the student's learning.

In most OSCEs the stations are deemed to be as important as one another, so that the mean pass mark of the total number of stations is taken as the pass mark for the overall examination. If individual stations are important in terms of 'must pass', a weighting system may be applied to calculate the overall pass mark.

We have used one other style of marking whereby the station poses a series of questions to the student regarding an investigation, e.g. an abdominal radiograph, or a given scenario, e.g. management of a head injury patient. Examiners may consider that such answers should also carry serious consequences for the candidate, such as an outright failure on that question.

Establishing rapport with a patient is essential in a doctor-patient relationship. At the initial meeting, greetings and introductions help to put the patient at ease and ensure patient co-operation with the history and/or examination. In these stations, therefore, marks are allocated for such interaction. Positive criteria include empathy, putting a patient at their ease and establishing their confidence by careful listening and responding to verbal and non-verbal cues.

APPENDIX B: REVISION CHECKLIST

Use the checklist to monitor your revision. Mark off the sections you have covered so that key topics are not left out.

Endocrinology and Breast
- ☐ Diabetes mellitus
- ☐ Diabetes insipidus
- ☐ Toxic and non-toxic goitre
- ☐ Parathyroid disease
- ☐ Acromegaly
- ☐ Addison's disease
- ☐ Conn's syndrome
- ☐ Cushing's disease
- ☐ Breast cancer

Gastroenterology
- ☐ Tongue – leukoplakia and cancer
- ☐ Parotid gland swellings
- ☐ Oesophageal stricture and hiatus hernia
- ☐ Peptic ulcer disease
- ☐ Gastric cancer
- ☐ Acute abdomen
- ☐ Viral hepatitis
- ☐ Portal hypertension
- ☐ Cholecystitis
- ☐ Pancreatitis
- ☐ Inflammatory bowel disease
- ☐ Diverticular disease
- ☐ Colonic polyps and cancer
- ☐ Piles, fissures and fistulae
- ☐ Herniae

Urology and Renal Medicine
- ☐ Renal calculus disease
- ☐ Glomerulo nephritis and nephrotic syndrome
- ☐ Diabetic nephrology
- ☐ Renal failure
- ☐ Urothelial tumours
- ☐ Prostatism and urinary retention
- ☐ Urinary infections
- ☐ Testicular descent and tumours

Obstetrics, Newborn and Gynaecology
❑ Antenatal care
❑ Hypertension and diabetes in pregnancy
❑ Ante- and post-partum haemorrhage
❑ Eclampsia
❑ Assessment of newborn
❑ Foetal distress
❑ Infertility
❑ Ectopic pregnancy
❑ Hydatidiform mole
❑ Endometriosis
❑ Fibroids and uterine cancer
❑ Cervical erosions and cancer
❑ Vaginal infections

Rheumatology and Dermatology
❑ Rheumatoid and osteoarthritis
❑ Infective arthritis
❑ Lupus erythematosis
❑ Systemic sclerosis
❑ Systemic vasculitides
❑ Dermatological manifestations of systemic disease
❑ Nail and hair disorders
❑ Eczema
❑ Psoriasis
❑ Skin malignancies

APPENDIX C: RECOMMENDED READING LIST

Medical Texts

Hutchinson's Clinical Methods: Hutchinson R and Swash M, 20th edition, W B Saunders, 1995.

Davidson's Principles and Practice of Medicine: Edwards CRW, Bouchier IAD, Haslett C and Chilvers ER (editors), 17th edition, Churchill Livingstone 1995.

Clinical Medicine: Kumar P and Clark M, 4th edition, Balliere Tindall 1998.

Lecture Notes on Dermatology: Graham-Brown RAC, Burns T, 7th edition, Blackwell Science 1996.

Examining Patients: An Introduction to Clinical Medicine: Toghill PJ (editor), 2nd edition, Edward Arnold 1994.

Lecture Notes on Clinical Medicine: Bradley JR, and Wayne D, 5th edition, Blackwell Science 1997.

Surgical Texts

Hamilton Bailey's Demonstrations of Physical Signs in Clinical Surgery: Lumley JSP, 18th edition, Butterworth Heinemann 1997.

Lecture Notes on General Surgery: Ellis H and Calne R, 9th edition, Blackwell Science 1998.

The Washington Manual of Surgery: Doherty GM, et al., Little Brown & Co, 1997.

Bailey and Love's Short Practice of Surgery: Mann CV, Russell RCG, Williams NS, 22nd edition, Chapman and Hall 1995.

Obstetrics and Gynaecology Texts

ABC of Antenatal Care: Chamberlain G, 3rd edition, BMJ 1997.

Lecture Notes in Gynaecology: Barnes J, Chamberlain G, Malvern J, 7th edition, Blackwell Science 1995.

Lecture Notes on Obstetrics: Musgrove F and Chamberlain G, 7th edition, Blackwell Science 1996.

APPENDIX D: MOCK EXAMINATIONS

Station	1	2	3	4	5	6
1	1.1+	1.2+	1.3+	1.4+	1.5+	1.6+
2	1.7+	1.8+	1.10	1.9	1.11	1.12
3	1.13	1.14	1.15	1.16	1.17	1.18
4	1.19	1.20	1.21	1.22	1.23	1.24
5	1.25	1.26	1.27	1.28/a	1.29+	1.30+
6	1.31	1.33	1.34	1.35	1.36	2.1+
7	2.2+	2.3+	2.4+	2.5+	2.6+	2.7+
8	2.8+	2.9+	2.10+	2.11	2.12	2.13
9	2.14	2.15	2.16	2.17	2.18	2.19
10	2.20	2.21	2.22	2.23	2.24	2.25
11	2.26	2.27	2.28	2.29	2.30	3.1+
12	3.2+	3.3+	3.4+	3.5+	3.6+	3.7
13	3.8	3.9	3.10	3.11	3.12	3.13
14	3.14	3.15	3.16	3.17	3.18	3.22
15	3.20	3.21	3.19	4.1+	4.2+	4.3
16	4.4/a+	4.5/a+	4.6+	4.7+	4.8+	4.10
17	4.11	4.14+	4.15+	4.16+	4.17+	4.18+
18	4.19+	4.20+	4.21+	4.25	4.26	4.27
19	5.1+	5.5+	5.2+	5.3+	5.4+	5.6
20	5.7	5.8	5.9	5.10	5.11	5.12+
21	5.13	5.14	5.19/a	5.15	5.17+	5.16

Each examination includes 5 and 10 minute stations and takes 2 hours to complete. History stations (+) require a 'subject' to give the responses provided in the second half of the book. Questions with an '/a' include a preparatory station.

PASTEST BOOKS FOR UNDERGRADUATES

PasTest are the specialists in study guides and revision courses for professional medical qualifications. For over 25 years we have been helping doctors to achieve their potential. The PasTest range of books for medical students includes:

OSCEs for Medical Undergraduates: Volume 1
Feather, Visvanathan & Lumley
- Chapters covering history taking, examinations, investigations, practical techniques, making a diagnosis, prescribing treatment and other issues.
- Answers in a separate section so that students can assess their performance and identify areas needing further attention.
- Covers Neurology and Psychiatry, Ophthalmology and Otolaryngology, Cardiovascular diseases and Haematology, Respiratory medicine, Orthopaedics and Trauma, Ethics and Legal medicine, including Consent and IV procedures.

Surgical Finals: Passing the Clinical
Kuperberg & Lumley
- 90 examples of favourite long and short surgical cases
- Syllabus checklist for structured revision
- 18 detailed examination schemes with action tables
- 36 tables of differential diagnosis
- 134 popular viva questions for self-assessment
- Recommended reading list and revision index.

Medical Finals: Passing the Clinical
Moore & Richardson
- 101 typical long cases, short cases and spot diagnoses
- Syllabus checklist for systematic revision
- Vital tips on preparation and presentation
- Structured examination plans for all cases
- Concise teaching notes highlight areas most relevant to finals
- Revision index for easy access to specific topics

Surgical Finals: Structured Answer and Essay Questions - second edition
Visvanathan & Lumley
- Prepare for the written examination with this unique combination of essay questions and the new structured answer questions
- 138 structured answer questions with detailed teaching notes
- 52 typical essay questions with sample essay plans and model essays
- Invaluable revision checklist to help you to track your progress
- Short textbook reviews enable you to select the best textbooks

Medical Finals: Structured Answer and Essay Questions
Feather, Visvanathan & Lumley
- Prepare for the written examination with this unique combination of essay questions and the new structured answer questions
- 141 structured answer questions with detailed teaching notes
- 73 typical essay questions with sample essay plans and model essays
- Invaluable revision checklist to help you to track your progress
- Short textbook reviews enable you to select the best textbooks

150 Essential MCQs for Surgical Finals
Hassanally & Singh
150 Essential MCQs for Medical Finals
Singh & Hassanally
- The crucial material for your exam success
- Extended teaching notes, bullet points and mnemonics
- Revision indexes for easy access to specific topics

For priority mail order service, please contact PasTest on FREEPHONE

0800 980 9814

PasTest, FREEPOST, Egerton Court, Parkgate Estate,
Knutsford, Cheshire WA16 7BR
Telephone: 01565 752000 Fax: 01565 650264
E-mail: books@pastest.co.uk Web site: http//www.pastest.co.uk